MILITARY SPENDING

Facts and Figures,
Worldwide Implications
and Future Outlook

MILITARY SPENDING

Facts and Figures, Worldwide Implications and Future Outlook

Wassily Leontief
Faye Duchin

New York   Oxford
OXFORD UNIVERSITY PRESS
1983

Copyright © 1983 by Oxford University Press, Inc.

Library of Congress Cataloging in Publication Data

Leontief, Wassily, 1906-
Military spending.

Bibliography: p.
1. Disarmament—Economic aspects.   2. War—
Economic aspects.   3. Armed Forces—Appropriations
and expenditures.   I. Duchin, Faye, 1944-   II. Title
HC79.D4L46   1983   338.4'3355   82-12399
ISBN 0-19-503191-1

Printing (last digit): 9 8 7 6 5 4 3 2 1

Printed in the United States of America

Preface

The research leading to the results described in this book was carried out over a two-year period ending in late summer 1980. Since then the model of the world economy on which that analysis is based has been improved in many minor and several major respects. As an example of the latter, the detailed description of the Soviet economy has been replaced by the most recent available data, and the anticipated growth rates of most regions, including the Soviet Union, have been revised downwards.[1] While these improvements naturally modify some of the detailed numerical findings, they do not alter the general order of the magnitudes involved and the substantive conclusions presented in the following pages.

In assessing this work two and a half years after its completion, the authors consider that there are two areas, in addition to the overall upgrading of the model which continues to take place (and which we try to accelerate!), that must receive particular attention in the course of further systematic study of the economic implications of military spending.

1. Structural change will naturally continue to take place with respect to both the composition of direct military purchases and the processes by which these goods and services are produced. Available information supplemented by informed conjecture has to be organized into hypothetical scenarios about the forms that these changes may take in the future in the United States, Western Europe, the Soviet Union, and indeed in every region of the world. While prospective technological changes in all branches of civilian production and consumption have been taken into account in the present study, this could not be carried out on the same level of detail with respect to military technology in the present work.

2. The rich, industrialized nations are assumed in this volume to maintain the same aggregate levels of employment over the long term, under a wide range of hypothetical levels of military spending. This of course is not necessarily the case. Growth may be constrained not only by the limited supply of certain categories of labor but also by the availability of capital and raw materials, the amount of pollution the society is prepared to accept, and numerous other considerations. Current work by the authors and our colleagues on technological change and its impacts on different types of employment and the preliminary implementation in this same context of an empirical dynamic input-output model should make it possible to make some progress in the difficult task of refining the representation of the numerous constraints under which an actual economy must operate.

This said, the work presented in this volume will, it is hoped, reflect a significant advance in the analysis of the economic impacts of military spending in terms of substantive results, methodology, and the coordination of a large quantity of data.

1. See Wassily Leontief, Jorge Mariscal, and Ira Sohn, "The Prospects for the Soviet Economy to the Year 2000," *Journal of Policy Modeling*, Vol. 5, no. 1 (March 1983).

New York
January 1983

W. Leontief
F. Duchin

Acknowledgments

We would like to thank Daniel Szyld for designing and supervising the implementation of all computational procedures. We have also benefited greatly from his careful reading of the manuscript and the reports on which this book is based.

A major contribution was made by Dr. Stephen Dresch who provided expert advice and constructive criticism throughout all phases of the research. Daniel Berg was primarily responsible for ferreting out and piecing together the data describing world trade in military goods. Elizabeth Hall and Mary Parker helped turn a technical report into a readable manuscript. Sherry Morse produced the draft for camera-ready art.

The following graduate and undergraduate assistants participated actively in the research: Raymond Antes, Ernest Battifarano, Linda Fan, Anne George, John Kassianos, and Steven Strauss. Glenn-Marie Lange assisted in the preparation of the book. We gratefully acknowledge their assistance.

This book is based upon two reports prepared with the support of the United States Arms Control and Disarmament Agency and the United Nations Centre for Disarmament. The authors are solely responsible for the content, which does not necessarily reflect the views of the funding organizations.

Contents

List of Figures

List of Tables

List of Abbreviations

The following are abbreviations used in this volume.

ACDA   U.S. Arms Control and Disarmament Agency
BEA   U.S. Department of Commerce, Bureau of Economic Analysis
DOD   U.S. Department of Defense
FPA   U.S. Federal Preparedness Agency
GDP   Gross Domestic Product
ILO   International Labor Office
n.e.c. not elsewhere classified
SIPRI   Stockholm International Peace Research Institute

MILITARY SPENDING

Facts and Figures,
Worldwide Implications
and Future Outlook

CHAPTER 1

Introduction

1.1 The Setting of the Problem

The purpose of this study is to improve our understanding of the role military sectors play in different national economies and in the world economy as a whole. The allocation of resources to military uses clearly imposes substantial demands in terms of labor, raw materials, capital, and intermediate goods: worldwide, military uses account for about 6 percent of all goods and services produced. Put another way, military demands each year are about one-third as great as all investment in productive plant and equipment capital stocks.

The decision to allocate resources for military end use is essentially political and not economic. While some analysts claim that the civilian economy benefits from "spin-offs" from military training and infrastructure in less developed countries and from research and development in developed countries which balance the negative effects of the military burden, a well-funded program for space exploration, building or re-building a large-scale railroad network—or constructing modern pyramids—could serve a similar purpose. Few would deny the increased potential for the civilian economy from applying these resources directly to selected civilian objectives. Furthermore, even in the absence of an organized program, these resources would in the long-run be absorbed in market-determined proportions into various types of civilian consumption and investment.

A distinction must be made between a sector, in this case military end use, growing slowly and its actual contraction in real terms. It is only in the latter case, when in addition the rate of contraction exceeds the normal rates of attrition of the labor force and retirement of capital, that the redeployment of fixed capital and labor already in place in that sector must be envisaged. Since the framework of the present study makes it possible to evaluate the longer term impacts of alternative policies, this type of analysis can provide guidelines for subsequently dealing with "transition" problems even in cases more extreme than those considered in this volume.

While, short of this type of transition problem, resources could from an economic point of view be freely transferred from military to nonmilitary uses, the specific combination of goods and services required for the production of military outputs is different from the mix of inputs required for the production of civilian outputs of comparable value. Consequently, even a moderate slowdown (or speed-up) in military spending could cause bottlenecks or idle capacity in other sectors of the economy. Identifying these bottlenecks is one motivation for studying the impacts of changes in military spending.

There will doubtless be some future time of reduced international tension and renewed interest in multilateral arms limitation agreements. If it can be confirmed that systematic differences do exist in the inputs required, directly and indirectly, for military and civilian production, it may be feasible to monitor the amount of military activity in a country with an analytic approach of the type developed in this study. The consistency imposed by the structure of the model described in this book would make it difficult to conceal production for military end use. Exploring the potential for this type of verification is another objective of this study.

The economic implications of military expenditures clearly are not restricted to individual national economies. Through international trade the military goods produced in a handful of countries are distributed throughout the world. One of the direct effects of this trade is a redistribution of international purchasing power away from less developed regions where foreign exchange could alternatively be used for imports that contribute directly to development and growth. In addition, military requirements for specific raw materials affect the relative costs and prices of other goods and services and, thereby, the international economic positions of different economies. This study systematically explores some alternative arrangements for trade in military goods and aid transfers.

The study described in this book analyzes the impact of alternative scenarios on individual regional economies and on the world economy as a whole; each scenario specifies a different policy with respect to military spending. The analysis is based on an input-output, or inter-industry, model which partitions the world into fifteen regions, each of which is described in terms of the production and consumption of over fifty categories of goods and services, including eleven serving exclusively military purposes. International, in this case inter-regional, flows of goods and capital are explicitly represented. The six scenarios elaborated on the basis of this model cover the years 1970 through 2000 in three 10-year intervals.

A great quantity of data from diverse sources had to be assembled to make this study possible. The database incorporated into this model contains several hundred thousand (non-zero) figures. It was initially developed on a very limited budget and is already somewhat outdated. As is the case with all large-scale empirical work, the data must be regarded as tentative. The acknowledgment of these shortcomings should not be interpreted as invalidating the conclusions drawn from the model. While there is no doubt that this type of work would benefit from and indeed requires the continual upgrading of the quality and comprehensive coverage of the data on which it is based, all types of studies of worldwide military spending are similarly limited by the availability of information. The analytical framework developed in this book represents the most comprehensive and internally consistent quantitative description of the world economy, particularly the military economy, available at the present time.

1.2 Historical Trends

Estimated worldwide military spending doubled between 1951 and 1970 from about $100 billion to over $200 billion in constant 1970 U.S. dollars, as shown in the left-hand panel of Figure 1.[1] During this period

1. Unless otherwise noted, all variables throughout the book are reported in either constant 1970 U.S. dollars or physical units except the balance of payments, which is reported in current year relative dollar prices. If military purchases were reported in rubles instead of dollars, the ratio of Soviet to U.S. purchases would appear lower than when measured in dollars. See, for example, [Becker, 1977] on this "index number" problem.

total worldwide spending closely followed the pattern of the combined spending of the NATO and Warsaw Pact countries, with NATO consistently outspending the Warsaw Pact. Figure 1 also shows that the United States accounts for a smaller proportion of the NATO military budget (74 percent in 1970) than the Soviet Union bears of the Warsaw Pact's military budget (89 percent in the same year).

The World Model projections of military spending under the baseline scenario, shown in the right-hand panel of Figure 1, are based on the assumption that world military spending will continue its past tendency to increase, reaching $646 billion in 2000. Countries outside NATO and the Warsaw Pact account for most of the increase; their military expenditures are projected to grow from $34 billion in 1970 to $187 billion in 2000.

This projected acceleration in the military spending of countries outside NATO and the Warsaw Pact is already apparent in the historical data. As shown in Figure 2, 86 percent of world military spending in 1957 was accounted for by NATO and the Warsaw Pact. By 1978, these two groups spent only 71 percent of the (much larger) world total. The three groups of countries whose shares of world military spending increased the most over this period are the Middle East (including many OPEC countries), the Far East (including Japan and China), and Africa.

The two largest producers and exporters of military goods are North America and the Soviet Union. The region importing the largest amount of military goods from both sources is the Middle East and African oil producing countries, which imported about $9 billion in military goods from each of the Soviet Union and North America between 1974 and 1978, as shown in Figure 3. For both regions, the next largest importers of military goods were their closest allies. Over the same period, Western Europe imported $6 billion in arms from the United States; and Eastern Europe, $7 billion from the Soviet Union. Both North America and the Soviet Union also export large amounts of arms to Africa and Low income Asia: Africa imported close to $6 billion in arms from each region while Low income Asia imported $3 billion from North America and $2 billion from the Soviet Union. Thus North America and the Soviet Union have in the recent past exported nearly equivalent amounts of arms to the same strategic areas of the world.

The next largest producers and exporters of arms are High income Western Europe and Eastern Europe. High income Western Europe exports most of its arms to the Middle East and African oil producing countries, for a total of more than $5 billion from 1974 to 1978. It also exports large quantities of arms

FIGURE 1 World Military Purchases in 1951–1970 and World Model Projections under the Base Scenario for 1970–2000

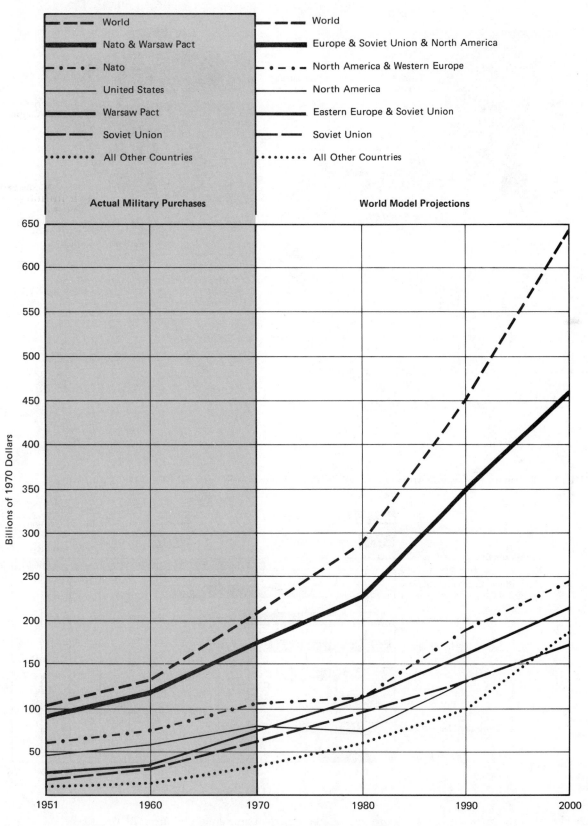

Source: Actual military purchases, (SIPRI, 1973 and 1975); projections for Base scenario, Annex C

FIGURE 2   Geographical Distribution of World Military Expenditures in 1957 and 1978

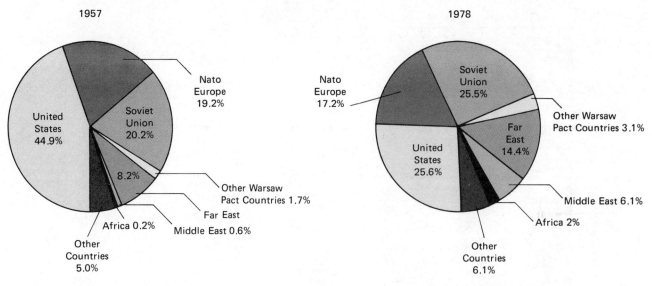

Note: The data used to calculate these percentages are in 1973 dollars. Source: (SIPRI, 1978 and 1979)

FIGURE 3   Destination of Major Arms Suppliers' Exports of Weapon Systems in 1974–1978 (Cumulative)

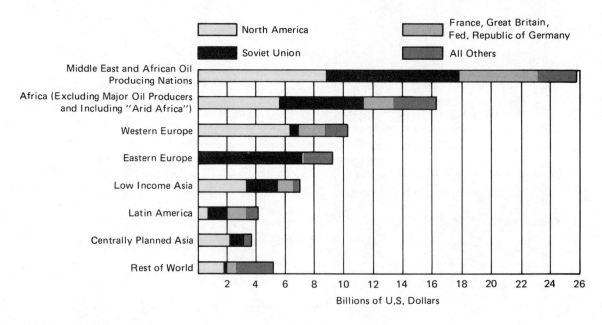

Note: These figures are reported in the source as the sum of current year dollars. Source: (ACDA, 1980)

FIGURE 4   Alternative Projections of Military Spending in North America

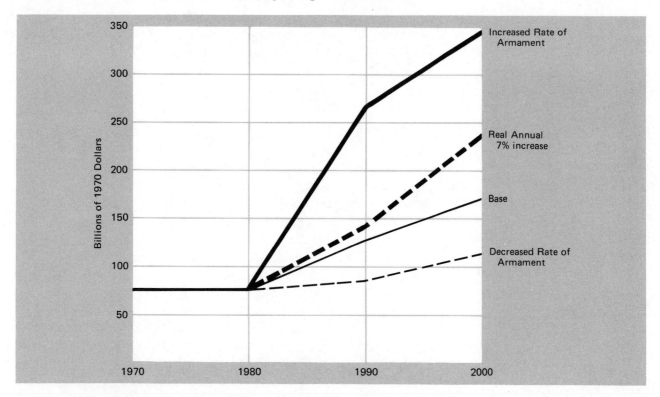

Source: Projections for Base scenario, Annex C; projections for scenarios A1 and D2, computer printouts shown for 1970 and 2000 in Annex C

to Africa ($2 billion) and Medium income Western Europe ($1 billion). During this same period, Eastern Europe sent more than 50 percent of its arms exports, about $2 billion, to the Soviet Union and most of the remainder to the Middle East and African oil producing countries.

The range of military spending alternatives that this study projects for North America between 1970 and 2000 is shown in Figure 4. Current U.S. policy[2] of a 7 percent real annual increase is also represented and is extended for purposes of comparison to the year 2000.

The text of this book is divided into two parts. Part I is devoted to the research methodology and includes three chapters describing, respectively, the

model, the sources and preparation of data, and the six scenarios investigated in this study. The results are reported in Part II, which contains six chapters, the last of which offers some concluding observations. Annexes A and B, which follow the Bibliography, show, respectively, the model's regional and the sectoral classification schemes. Annex C is a condensed version of the computer printouts and contains the baseline scenario in full sectoral detail for 1970, 1980, 1990, and 2000. The other five scenarios, which are identical with the baseline scenario in 1970 and 1980, are shown for the year 2000. To save space, the two Western European regions (High income and Medium income) have been aggregated into a single region in the printouts. The same is true of the two Latin American regions.

2. Reported in the *New York Times*, Aug. 3, 1981.

PART ONE

Methodology

CHAPTER 2

The World Model

Input-output analysis was first used to study the economic effects of reduced military spending about twenty years ago in [Leontief and Hoffenberg, 1961], which analyzed the impacts on different sectors of the U.S. economy and on national employment of a reduction in military spending compensated by increases in various categories of civilian final demand. A later study, [Leontief *et al.*, 1965], extended the analysis to distinguish the impacts on different regions within the U.S.

The international impacts of a cut in U.S. military spending were investigated in [Leontief and Petri, 1971], which examined the effects of a compensated reduction of military spending in the U.S. both on the demand for strategic materials and on the export earnings of the countries which supplied these materials.

Later work, commissioned by the United Nations, began to link the issue of reduced military spending with increased aid to developing countries. The impacts on the U.S. economy of two alternatives for reducing military spending combined with five alternative types of compensating nonmilitary expenditure were investigated in [Dresch, Goldberg, and Lin, 1972] and [Dresch, 1972]. Both papers also examined the effects of disarmament on the growth rates of developing countries. In addition, recent input-output studies of the economic impacts of reductions in military spending combined with increases in development aid have been carried out for countries other than the U.S. and include [Bernard and Truchon, 1980] for Canada, [Bjerkholt *et al.*, 1980] for Norway, and [Filip-Kohn, Krenzel, and Schumacher, 1980] for the Federal Republic of Germany.

The development in the mid-1970s of an input-output model of the world economy covering the three decades from 1970 to 2000 laid the groundwork for extension of the previous work. This World Model and the first scenarios computed with it are described in [Leontief, Carter, and Petri, 1977]. That book investigated, through the analysis of eight scenarios, various alternatives for accelerating the economic growth of less developed countries so as to narrow the discrepancies in economic well-being between them and the developed countries by the year 2000.

The work described in the present volume is the first application of the World Model to the analysis of military spending: this work was supported by the U.S. Arms Control and Disarmament Agency [Leontief and Duchin, 1980b] and by the United Nations Centre for Disarmament and Development [Leontief and Duchin, 1980a]. An exploratory version of these two reports was prepared for the United Nations and appeared as [Leontief *et al.*, 1978]. Subsequent analysis based on the present work includes [Duchin, 1983].

The World Model, including the conceptual framework, computer programs, and database, was designed as a tool for investigating the economic impacts of alternative views of the future. The model divides the world into fifteen regions, based primarily on the level of economic development as measured by per capita income levels and the share of manufacturing in GDP. The regional divisions also take continental boundaries and geo-political groupings into account. In addition, consideration of similar natural resource endowments led to formation of a single region that comprises the major oil-producing nations of the Middle East and Africa. The present classification scheme includes some revisions of the original one (e.g., Cambodia and South Vietnam have been transferred from Low income Asia to Centrally planned Asia) and is shown in Annex A.

These fifteen regions can be further grouped into three broad categories. The first group consists of eight developed regions—Eastern Europe, High income Asia, North America, Oceania, Soviet Union, South Africa, and both High and Medium income Western Europe—which are characterized by considerable industry and high per capita income. The second group consists of three regions—Resource rich Latin America, the Middle East and African oil-producing nations, and Tropical Africa—which are less developed countries with significant endowments of natural resources. The final group consists of four developing regions—Arid Africa, Centrally planned Asia, Low income Asia, and Resource poor Latin America—which have no significant natural resource endowments.

The World Model represents the technical and structural basis of the economy of each of the fifteen regions by a separate matrix of so-called input-output coefficients. In its initial version the model described forty-five producing sectors (which are listed in Annex B) for each economy. Each column of a regional matrix describes the inputs of labor, capital, and intermediate goods and services required by a given producing sector and for different categories of final demand such as personal consumption, government purchases, and investment. Thus the entries in the jth column represent the technology used (on the average) in producing the output of the jth sector, and the ith component of this column is the number of units of output of sector i required to produce one unit of output of sector j. Entries across the rows show deliveries from one sector to the rest of the economy. The rows correspond to balance equations describing the allocation of output among intermediate and end-user sectors. Each region matrix has more columns than rows, that is, more variables than equations.

The model includes global equations representing inter-regional flows of sectoral outputs and of capital. Trade among nations within a region is *included* in the regional flows. Each traded commodity[1] (or capital flow) is exchanged through a separate world "trade pool" which receives shipments from all regions exporting that commodity in a given year and from which all regions' imports in the year are taken. For each commodity, the total amount shipped into the corresponding world trade pool equals the total of all deliveries made from it.

In most cases a region's imports of a particular commodity in a given year are assumed to be equal to some proportion of the corresponding domestic output; the parameter specifying this proportion is the commodity-specific import coefficient. (If there is no corresponding domestic production, the level of imports is specified directly.) The level of each pool is then determined by an equation that sums all regions' imports. Export shares specify the fraction of the pool provided by each region: for each commodity and each year, the sum of the fifteen export shares is naturally equal to unity.

The state of each regional economy is depicted at four points in time—1970, 1980, 1990, and 2000. The representation of consecutive decades is linked by the accumulation of capital stocks and the depletion of mineral reserves. These links are represented by additional equations.

The 1970 matrices are based on historical data. Technological forecasts and, where necessary, historical trends were the basis for projections (which describe prospective changes in the structure of the world economy) to 1980, 1990, and 2000. For each year, some variables (corresponding in number to the excess of variables over equations) are treated as exogenous to the model, and their values are considered as "given" or prescribed; for example, population projections for each region and for each year were obtained from outside sources while certain other variables, such as levels of final demand, were projected by the model builders. Consistent values for all the remaining (endogenous) variables are generated by solving the model.[2]

The model as described represents one path for the world economy between 1970 and 2000, based on specific assumptions regarding the structural parameters and the values of certain exogenous variables. This description is the Base scenario. Alternative scenarios can specify values different from those of the baseline for up to seventy variables for each region in each year and can also modify any of the structural parameters.

The next two chapters describe the ways in which the original model was extended for purposes of the present study. The revised World Model now contains explicit estimates of the composition of military purchases in each region. Major armaments industries have been separately identified, and detailed specifications of their demands on other sectors of the economy were made. International trade in military goods and the corresponding financial arrangements have been represented too. Thirty-four new rows and columns were added to each input-output matrix, corresponding to eleven production sectors, eleven import and eleven export sectors, and the military final demand sector. Updating the rest of the database was limited to a few critical areas.[3] In addition, several alternative scenarios have been formulated, incorporating different assumptions concerning changes in the purchase and trade of military goods and services.

---

1. At the level of aggregation of this study, no distinction is made between a sector and the commodity it produces. In a more disaggregated framework it is necessary to account for the existence of secondary products.

2. The model and, in particular, the procedures for assembling and projecting data are described in detail in [Petri and others, 1974-1979]. A summary is given in [Duchin, forthcoming].

3. The model is extended and updated on a continuing basis. For example, the North American region has been disaggregated into separate U.S. and Canadian regions since the work described in this book was completed.

CHAPTER 3

Data

Eleven sectors of the economy that produce goods and services for military end use have been explicitly represented in the World Model for the purposes of this project.

The original World Model representation naturally accounted for the military sectors of the economy but aggregated them with roughly similar civilian counterparts within each region. Thus, for example, the single aircraft sector of the original World Model accounted for the production of all types of both military and civilian aircraft. Similarly, a single column represented the various categories of both military and nonmilitary government final demand.

This major extension to the database required detailed descriptions of the input structures for the eleven military sectors, international flows of military goods and financial aid, and the composition of military final demand. The new as well as the original World Model sectors are listed in Annex B.

The secrecy which surrounds every country's military activities obviously made the data work for this study even more difficult than for the comparable civilian sectors. Since there are considerably more publicly available data describing the production and consumption of military goods and services for the United States than for any other country, heavy reliance was placed on this information. The United Nations recently issued a standardized form for reporting military expenditures and asked all member nations to participate. However, by mid-1981 only 13 countries, including the United States, responded. Notably absent are China, the Soviet Union, and Eastern Europe, as well as Western European countries with large military budgets.

It will become clear to the reader that a great deal of subjective judgment had to be exercised and a great many simplifying assumptions made in filling the gaps in the available data. While there is a lot of room for significant improvement in the accuracy of the data, the assembly of that information which is available into a consistent, comprehensive framework nevertheless represents a substantial advance in the analysis of worldwide military spending.

In addition to these extensions regarding the military sectors, the database of the original World Model was also revised to include more recent estimates of population, labor force, and petroleum prices. The new projections of population and labor force were taken from [United Nations, 1973b] and [International Labor Office, 1977], respectively. Petroleum prices were updated and projected according to estimates in [Glassey, 1979]. The impacts of these changes in petroleum prices on the prices of other goods were then computed, using the World Model's input-output price equations, and incorporated into the database.

The remainder of this chapter is divided into three sections: Production of Military Goods and Services, World Trade in Military Goods and Services, and Government Final Demand. Each section provides a summary of the sources used, the procedures followed, and the simplifying assumptions made to arrive at the data required to describe these activities in the World Model framework. A more detailed description is given in the technical annexes of [Leontief and Duchin, 1980b].

3.1 Production of Military Goods and Services

The following sectors producing goods and services exclusively for military use were added to the description of each regional economy in the World Model: military aircraft, military ships, military communication equipment, new military construction, repair and maintenance of military facilities, missiles, ammunition not elsewhere classified, tanks, small arms, small arms ammunition, and other ordnance. For each new sector, the model requires a description of its input structure, which takes the form of a column vector showing the amount of each type of input required to produce a dollar's worth of the particular output. The corresponding row vector, which describes the deliveries of that good to the rest of the economy, is relatively simple in the case of these military sectors since most of their deliveries are made directly to military final demand.

The principal sources of data describing the production of military goods and services in the United States circa 1970 is the official 496-sector U.S. input-output table for 1972, [BEA, 1979]. This table includes eight sectors which produce goods and services exclusively for military use: new military construction, repair and maintenance of military facilities, missiles, tanks, small arms, two categories of ammunition, and other ordnance. It does not, however, distinguish the input structures for three important categories of military hardware—aircraft, ships, and communications equipment—from the input structures of their civilian counterparts.

Through efforts to locate the information necessary to disaggregate these three sectors into separate military and civilian components, it was discovered that this work had already been carried out in an engineering study [Econoscope, 1977] performed under contract to the U.S. Federal Preparedness Agency. The FPA (which has since been incorporated into the Federal Emergency Management Agency) generously made that work available for the present study.

Five sectors from the 367-sector U.S. input-output table for 1967 were disaggregated into separate military and civilian components for the FPA: shipbuilding and repairing, communication equipment, aircraft, aircraft engines and engine parts, and other aircraft equipment. These distinctions among the three aircraft sectors are important from many points of view; for example, the sectors differ in their use of critical materials and in their positions in world trade. Nonetheless, for the purposes of the present study the three sectors were combined into a single military aircraft sector since it was not feasible to disaggregate the information on worldwide imports and exports to a finer level of detail. Thus, the FPA study provided the data for 6 columns (3 military and 3 civilian) and 6 rows in the detail of a 367-order input-output table.

The entire BEA flow table for 1972 and the 6 FPA rows and columns based on the 1967 flow table were aggregated to World Model sectoral classifications. Both the BEA and FPA data were adjusted in separate computations to conform to the definitions and conventions used in the World Model. These adjustments involved in particular the treatment of imports and of margin sectors.[1]

Since the World Model measures resources in physical as well as value units, it was necessary to convert the value terms for these sectors of the BEA and FPA data to physical units using World Model base year (i.e., 1970) prices. Then, the new columns were transformed into vectors of input coefficients in the usual way by dividing each flow by the corresponding column total. No attempt was made to adjust these data for changes in relative prices between 1967 and 1972 largely because of the difficulty of establishing useful price indices over this period for the military sectors.

Because the U.S. is the dominant producer of military goods within North America, the input structure for U.S. military production circa 1970 was incorporated without adjustments into the World Model's representation of North America for 1970. The eleven columns of current input requirements (8 BEA, 3 FPA) were, for lack of more specific information, supplemented by the World Model capital and labor requirements and pollution emission characteristics for roughly corresponding sectors. The correspondence is shown in Table 1.

Each of the three original World Model sectors for aircraft, shipbuilding and other transportation equip-

TABLE 1   World Model Sectors Producing Military Goods and Services and Corresponding Civilian Sectors

Military Sectors	Corresponding Civilian Sectors
Military aircraft	Aircraft
Military ships	Shipbuilding and other transportation equipment
Military communication equipment	Electric Machinery
New military construction	Construction
Repair and maintenance of military facilities	Construction
Missiles	Aircraft
Ammunition, n.e.c.	Metal products
Tanks	Motor vehicles
Small arms	Metal products
Small arms ammunition	Metal products
Other ordnance	Metal products

Note: "Corresponding sectors" refer to original World Model sectors. Data specifically describing the military sector are supplemented where necessary with data describing the corresponding sector in the original World Model database, as described in the text.

1. Margin sectors for metals, food, and petroleum are those industries which provide the processing and refining services which bring the goods from their initial state to the state in which they are consumed.

ment,[2] and electric machinery, should in principle be replaced by two new ones governing military and civilian production, respectively. Since both military shipbuilding and military communication equipment constituted less than 20 percent of the value of output of the corresponding original World Model sectors, the input structures of these original sectors were assumed to be reasonable representations of the requirements of the residual civilian activities. In the case of aircraft, however, where military production in 1970 accounted for about one-third of aggregate output, the original aircraft sector was replaced by the FPA sector corresponding to civilian aircraft.

Finally, it was necessary to estimate the input structures in 1970 of the eleven military industries for the regions other than North America and to project changes in production technology to 1980, 1990, and 2000. Considering the significant increase in the overseas transfer of U.S. military technology since the early 1970s and given the paucity of information on military technology in other countries, it was assumed that the same input structures held for all regions. The same technologies were also assumed for future years.

3.2 World Trade in Military Goods and Services

World Model levels of imports and exports of tradable goods are governed by separate import coefficients and export shares for each traded commodity and each region for the years 1970, 1980, 1990, and 2000. The fundamental problem faced in estimating these parameters for military goods and services is simply

2. This is in fact a residual sector (BEA Sector 61) which includes all transportation equipment except motor vehicles and aircraft.

the lack of comprehensive, consistent information. Data from numerous sources had to be pieced together using large doses of subjective judgment.

A region's trade in a particular commodity is governed in the model by two parameters, the import coefficient and the export share (described in Chapter 2). Base year (1970) import coefficients for a region are computed from historical data as the quotient of that year's imports of a particular commodity divided by domestic production of the same item. (The important case where the latter is zero is discussed later in this section.) The corresponding export share is computed as that region's exports divided by total world exports. Thus, the data necessary for these calculations are the estimated values for the year 1970 (and in 1970 U.S. dollars) of production, imports, and exports of the various categories of military goods and services for each of the fifteen regions. The same calculations were performed with data (also in 1970 U.S. dollars) for 1977, the most recent year for which such information was available, as a basis for projecting the parameters to 1980. Projections for subsequent years, and for scenarios other than the baseline, are discussed later in this section.

Data were collected for five categories of traded goods, identified in Table 2. While exchanges of nuclear weapons are not accounted for in these data, their exclusion should at the present time result in a relatively small understatement of the magnitude of world military trade. It also proved impossible to track the flow of services like military training and advisers or the construction of military facilities on foreign soil. Military construction and maintenance and repair of facilities were assumed to be non-traded services, i.e., services that had to be provided from

TABLE 2   Categories of Traded Military Goods

World Model Production Sector	Description
Aircraft	Supersonic and subsonic combat planes, trainers, transport planes, helicopters, and spare parts.
Shipbuilding	Major and minor surface combatants, submarines, guided missile patrol boats, and spare parts.
Missiles	Surface-to-air, air-to-air, and air-to-surface missiles and spare parts. Strategic nuclear weapons excluded.
Tanks	Tanks and self-propelled guns, artillery, armored personnel carriers, armored cars, and spare parts.
Military communication equipment Ammunition not elsewhere classified Small arms Small arms ammunition Other ordnance	Electronics, small arms, ammunition, and spare parts.

domestic sources, and sparse data about "Other" goods were arbitrarily split in equal proportions among the five World Model sectors shown in the last row of Table 2.

One of the two principal sources for this work is the annual publication of the Stockholm International Peace Research Institute. These SIPRI Yearbooks, which rely exclusively on publicly available information, assemble valuable data on numerous transactions involving specific weapons systems but offer little in the way of comprehensive coverage.

The second principal source is the annual publication of the United States Arms Control and Disarmament Agency, which in the 1979 issue includes the value of total military imports and exports for about 150 countries for all years between 1968 and 1977 and also contains some information about the number of deliveries of several categories of weapon systems [ACDA, 1979b].

These data, and a fortiori those that were derived from them, must be considered very tentative because of both the disclosure issues surrounding the availability and accuracy of sensitive data and conceptual problems such as evaluating Soviet military purchases in U.S. dollars.

The total value of each World Model region's imports and exports of military goods was aggregated from country data given in [ACDA, 1979b] for each year from 1968 to 1977. In cases where the reported

value of a region's military trade varied a lot from year to year, due presumably to actual fluctuations and perhaps also to incomplete information, the estimates for 1970 and 1977 were "smoothed"—sometimes using simple regressions and sometimes judgmentally—with respect to adjacent years.

No data were available allocating the total value of each region's military imports and exports among specific categories of goods. The estimated percentage breakdowns developed for this study, shown in Tables 3 and 4, are based on the analysis, comparison, and reconciliation of information appearing in many sources, primarily [SIPRI, various years]. These percentages were then multiplied by the corresponding regional aggregates to yield estimated levels of imports and exports by sector of military production for each region for 1970 and 1977.

Data were also assembled on military aid, financial and in kind. The various sources are listed in the Bibliography.

A region's export share measures its exports of a particular good as a fraction of total world exports of that good in the same year. In the case of aid, the export share corresponds to the percentage of worldwide military assistance which is received by that region. The export shares for military goods computed for 1970 are shown in Table 5. The shares calculated for 1977 were assumed in the baseline scenario to hold for 1980, 1990, and 2000; they are shown

TABLE 3   Decomposition of Military Exports by Sector
(proportions of dollar value)

	Aircraft	Ships	Missiles	Tanks	Other[a]	Total[b]
Arid Africa	.17	.03	.12	.02	.67	1.00
Centrally planned Asia	.41	.06	.01	.02	.50	1.00
Low income Asia	.68	.00	.00	.00	.32	1.00
Eastern Europe	.59	.00	.00	.20	.21	1.00
High income Asia	.25	.00	.00	.00	.75	1.00
Resource rich Latin America[c]	—	—	—	—	—	—
Resource poor Latin America	.24	.00	.00	.30	.46	1.00
North America	.44	.03	.09	.16	.28	1.00
Oceania	.46	.05	.24	.00	.26	1.00
Middle East and African oil producers[c]	—	—	—	—	—	—
Soviet Union	.45	.07	.12	.16	.21	1.00
Southern Africa	.75	.00	.00	.00	.25	1.00
Tropical Africa[c]	—	—	—	—	—	—
High income Western Europe	.33	.12	.06	.19	.30	1.00
Medium income Western Europe	.39	.28	.00	.06	.27	1.00

a. Evenly divided among Military communication equipment, Ammunition n.e.c., Small arms, Small arms ammunition, and Other ordnance.

b. Totals may not add exactly due to rounding.

c. These regions are assumed to have exported no military goods over the period 1968-1977.

TABLE 4   Decomposition of Military Imports by Sector
(proportions of dollar value)

	Aircraft	Ships	Missiles	Tanks	Other[a]	Total[b]
Arid Africa	.41	.06	.07	.19	.27	1.00
Centrally planned Asia	.45	.04	.10	.14	.27	1.00
Low income Asia	.46	.06	.08	.14	.27	1.00
Eastern Europe	.41	.01	.21	.10	.27	1.00
High income Asia	.45	.04	.10	.14	.27	1.00
Resource rich Latin America	.41	.19	.03	.10	.27	1.00
Resource poor Latin America	.41	.18	.03	.10	.27	1.00
North America	.40	.10	.17	.07	.27	1.00
Oceania	.45	.04	.10	.14	.27	1.00
Middle East and African oil producers	.42	.06	.07	.18	.27	1.00
Soviet Union	.61	.02	.00	.10	.27	1.00
Southern Africa	.42	.15	.03	.13	.27	1.00
Tropical Africa	.42	.15	.03	.13	.27	1.00
High income Western Europe	.36	.02	.12	.23	.27	1.00
Medium income Western Europe	.44	.06	.04	.20	.27	1.00

a. Evenly divided among Military communications equipment, Ammunition n.e.c., Small arms, Small arms ammunition, and Other ordnance which jointly were assumed to account for about 27% of each region's imports.

b. Totals may not add exactly due to rounding.

TABLE 5   Base Scenario Export Shares for 1970

	Aircraft	Ships	Communication Equipment	Missiles	Ammunition n.e.c.	Tanks	Small Arms	Small Arms Ammunition	Other Ordnance	Grants Received
Arid Africa	0	0	0	0	0	0	0	0	0	.1497
Centrally planned Asia	.03	.04	.06	0	.06	0	.06	.06	.06	.1454
Low income Asia	0	0	0	0	0	0	0	0	0	.6570
Eastern Europe	.06	0	.04	0	.04	.06	.04	.04	.04	.0051
High income Asia	0	0	0	0	0	0	0	0	0	0
Resource rich Latin America	0	0	0	0	0	0	0	0	0	.0030
Resource poor Latin America	0	0	0	0	0	0	0	0	0	.0045
North America	.57	.39	.59	.58	.59	.57	.59	.59	.59	0
Oceania	0	0	0	0	0	0	0	0	0	0
Middle East and African oil producers	0	0	0	0	0	0	0	0	0	.0054
Soviet Union	.27	.36	.20	.35	.20	.26	.20	.20	.20	0
Southern Africa	0	0	0	0	0	0	0	0	0	0
Tropical Africa	0	0	0	0	0	0	0	0	0	.0101
High income Western Europe	.07	.21	.11	.07	.11	.11	.11	.11	.11	0
Medium income Western Europe	0	0	0	0	0	0	0	0	0	.0397
Total	1.00	1.00	1.00	1.00	1.00	1.00	1.00	1.00	1.00	1.0000

in Table 6.[3] Different assumptions for other scenarios are described in Chapter 4.

World Model import coefficients measure imports as a proportion of domestic production in the same sector. For purposes of computing import coefficients, domestic production—for which no comprehensive historic data were available—was estimated as the sum of domestic final demand[4] and net exports. In the case of military aid, the "import coefficient" measures aid given as a percentage of GDP. Import coefficients used in the baseline scenario are shown for most regions in Tables 7 and 8. The remaining regions, which are assumed to have no domestic production of one or more categories of military goods, were naturally expected to import the entire quantity purchased by the military. In these cases, the import parameters can be expressed as a proportion of total military purchases; these are shown in Table 9.

3. In 1980 actual Soviet export shares were higher and American export shares lower than those appearing in Table 6 (reflecting the temporary restraint in military exports imposed by the Carter administration). However, as of the end of 1982, the increase in military exports suggests that the export shares used in this study for the years "around" 1980 and for 1990 and 2000 remain realistic after all.

4. The data on military final demand are described in Section 3 of this chapter.

3.3 Government Final Demand

Government final demand refers to the purchases of goods and services for all purposes and by all levels of government. For this study, the World Model government final demand sector was split into a civilian and a military component. The level of each type of government final demand for a given region and year is represented as a proportion of Gross Domestic Product (GDP) while its composition is specified, as in the case of other sectors, by a vector describing its input structure.

Estimates of both military spending and Gross National Product (GNP) for each year in the period 1968 to 1977 are given in [ACDA, 1979b] for about 150 countries and are easily aggregated to World Model regions. ACDA estimates of military expenditures differ from the military final demand concept of the World Model's accounting framework in that the former includes grants in the donor region's spending while the latter accounts for them as part of the recipient region's purchases. (This probably explains why some regions' military spending is shown in the ACDA report to be less than the value of their military imports.) The ACDA estimates were adjusted to the World Model framework using data on military grants.

TABLE 6 Base Scenario Export Shares for 1980, 1990, and 2000

	Aircraft	Ships	Communication Equipment	Missiles	Ammunition n.e.c.	Tanks	Small Arms	Small Arms Ammunition	Other Ordnance	Grants Received
Arid Africa	0	0	.02	.01	.02	0	.02	.02	.02	.1178
Centrally planned Asia	.01	.01	.01	0	.01	0	.01	.01	.01	.1693
Low income Asia	.01	0	.01	0	.01	0	.01	.01	.01	.3475
Eastern Europe	.09	0	.04	0	.04	.07	.04	.04	.04	.0075
High income Asia	0	0	0	0	0	0	0	0	0	0
Resource rich Latin America	0	0	0	0	0	0	0	0	0	.0113
North America	.40	.22	.42	.42	.42	.39	.42	.42	.42	0
Oceania	0	0	0	0	0	0	0	0	0	0
Middle East and African oil producers	0	0	0	0	0	0	0	0	0	0
Soviet Union	.32	.32	.23	.41	.23	.29	.23	.23	.23	0
Southern Africa	0	0	0	0	0	0	0	0	0	0
Tropical Africa	0	0	0	0	0	0	0	0	0	0
High income Western Europe	.16	.38	.24	.16	.24	.24	.24	.24	.24	0
Medium income Western Europe	.01	.07	.02	0	.02	.01	.02	.02	.02	.0395
Total	1.00	1.00	1.00	1.00	1.00	1.00	1.00	1.00	1.00	1.0000

TABLE 7   Base Scenario Import Coefficients for 1970

	Aircraft	Ships	Communication Equipment	Missiles	Ammunition n.e.c.	Tanks	Small Arms	Small Arms Ammunition	Other Ordnance	Grants[a] Given
Arid Africa	2.333	1.778	2.030	2.448	2.030	1.623	2.030	2.030	2.030	0
Centrally planned Asia	.351	.087	.250	.667	.250	.429	.250	.250	.250	.00148
Low income Asia	2.570	1.500	.887	3.545	.887	1.632	.887	.887	.887	0
Eastern Europe	.111	.111	.087	.429	.087	.031	.087	.087	.087	0
High income Asia	.136	.031	.111	.667	.111	.389	.111	.111	.111	0
Resource poor Latin America	.538	.613	.408	.538	.408	.471	.408	.408	.408	0
North America	.010	.010	.010	.010	.010	.010	.010	.010	.010	.00139
Oceania	.220	.042	.136	1.000	.136	.613	.136	.136	.136	0
Soviet Union	.010	0	.010	0	.010	.010	.010	.010	.010	.00111
Southern Africa	.250	1.000	.163	.149	.163	.408	.163	.163	.163	0
High income Western Europe	.075	.010	.075	.087	.075	.176	.075	.075	.075	.0000576
Medium income Western Europe	1.222	.220	1.222	2.333	1.222	—	1.222	1.222	1.222	0

Note: Three regions not shown, Resource rich Latin America, Middle East and African oil producers, and Tropical Africa, are assumed to have no domestic production and give no military grants. Medium income Western Europe is assumed to have no production of tanks. (See also Table 9.)

a. The coefficients corresponding to "Grants Given" are applied to GDP.

TABLE 8   Base Scenario Import Coefficients for 1980, 1990, and 2000

	Aircraft	Ships	Communication Equipment	Missiles	Ammunition n.e.c.	Tanks	Small Arms	Small Arms Ammunition	Other Ordnance	Grants[a] Given
Arid Africa	2.846	2.030	2.030	2.571	2.030	1.857	2.030	2.030	2.030	0
Centrally planned Asia	.030	.010	.020	.053	.020	.052	.020	.020	.020	.000351
Low income Asia	.960	.818	.516	1.381	.516	.852	.516	.516	.516	0
Eastern Europe	.176	.250	.176	1.220	.176	.053	.176	.176	.176	0
High income Asia	.099	.020	.087	.538	.087	.266	.087	.087	.087	0
Resource poor Latin America	.538	.613	.408	.538	.408	.471	.408	.408	.408	0
North America	.010	.010	.010	.010	.010	.010	.010	.010	.010	.0000611
Oceania	.149	.031	.099	.538	.099	.370	.099	.099	.099	0
Soviet Union	.020	0	.010	0	.010	.010	.010	.010	.010	.000164
Southern Africa	.176	.667	.111	.149	.111	.333	.111	.111	.111	0
High income Western Europe	.075	.010	.075	.087	.075	.149	.075	.075	.075	.0000298
Medium income Western Europe	.818	.149	1.000	1.500	1.000	7.333	1.000	1.000	1.000	0

Note: Three regions not shown, Resource rich Latin America, Middle East and African oil producers, and Tropical Africa, have zero domestic production and give no military grants (See also Table 9.)

a. The coefficients corresponding to "Grants Given" are applied to GDP.

TABLE 9   Military Import Parameters for Regions with No Domestic Production

	Aircraft	Ships	Communication Equipment	Missiles	Ammunition n.e.c.	Tanks	Small Arms	Small Arms Ammunition	Other Ordnance
Base Scenario 1970									
Resource rich Latin America	.04136	.01855	.01860	.00313	.00507	.01020	.00030	.00091	.00188
Middle East and African oil producers	.04980	.00747	.02232	.00847	.00608	.02215	.00036	.00109	.00225
Tropical Africa	.04248	.01479	.01860	.00251	.00507	.01347	.00030	.00091	.00188
Medium income Western Europe	—	—	—	—	—	.02300	—	—	—
Base Scenario: 1980, 1990, and 2000									
Resource rich Latin America	.10341	.04639	.04650	.00783	.01267	.02549	.00074	.00228	.00469
Middle East and African oil producers	.10376	.01556	.04650	.01765	.01267	.04614	.00074	.00228	.00469
Tropical Africa	.16143	.05619	.07069	.00952	.01926	.05118	.00113	.00347	.00713

Note: These parameters are applied to total military purchases.

Estimates of the proportion of GDP allocated to military spending are also given in [SIPRI, 1979]. These estimates generally follow those of ACDA but are lower for the Soviet Union and somewhat higher for some developing countries in some years. The ACDA estimates are used in this study mainly to ensure consistency with the import and export control totals taken from this source. The important exception is the Soviet Union: we follow SIPRI in assuming parity between Soviet and American military spending. In future work, the other SIPRI revisions should be considered.

Significant differences between the ACDA GNP series and World Model base year GDP, which are much greater for some regions than would be anticipated on the basis of the conceptual difference between the two measures, are presumably due to different estimation techniques and assumptions in the source data (International Bank of Reconstruction and Development in the case of ACDA and the United Nations for the World Model). Parameters were calculated using the ACDA military expenditures and GNP series, but in computing scenarios they are applied to World Model GDP.

These parameters were calculated for each year between 1968 and 1977. When the proportion of a region's income devoted to military spending varied considerably from year to year, the estimates for 1970 and 1977 were smoothed with respect to adjacent years' values. The value for 1977 was used for the baseline scenario in 1980, 1990, and 2000. These parameters are shown in Table 10. Japan (High income Asia) is the only region for which it was assumed

that military spending as a fraction of GDP would increase between 1980 and 2000.

The fraction of GDP allocated to government purchases was computed from about twenty input-output tables covering sixteen different countries, and the proportion corresponding to military purchases was netted out. On the basis of these results, the rough assessment was made that most countries allocate

TABLE 10   Government Military Purchases as a Percent of Gross Domestic Product

	1970	1980	1990	2000
Arid Africa	.100	.150	.150	.150
Centrally planned Asia	.135	.094	.094	.094
Low income Asia	.040	.040	.040	.040
Eastern Europe	.073	.067	.067	.067
High income Asia	.008	.009	.020	.030
Resource rich Latin America	.018	.027	.027	.027
Resource poor Latin America	.019	.013	.013	.013
North America	.074	.050	.050	.050
Oceania	.032	.025	.025	.025
Middle East and African oil producers	.065	.119	.119	.119
Soviet Union	.140	.133	.133	.133
Southern Africa	.026	.055	.055	.055
Tropical Africa	.019	.039	.039	.039
High income Western Europe	.035	.034	.034	.034
Medium income Western Europe	.039	.039	.039	.039

about 10 percent of GDP to the types of non-military purchases typically made by central and local governments. This same 10 percent ratio is used throughout the study.

Detailed descriptions of the composition of both military and civilian government final demand for the U.S. in 1972 are available in the 496-sector input-output tables [BEA, 1979]. These column vectors, aggregated to World Model sectoral classifications and conventions, were included in the representation of the North American economy in 1970 in the World Model database.

Comparably detailed, systematic data were not available for the other fourteen regions. The total dollar value of military purchases of these regions in 1970 was decomposed into four broad categories—procurement, construction and maintenance of facilities, personnel, and operations—based on work commissioned (expressly for this study) by the U.N. Centre for Disarmament and Development [Huisken, 1976]. These four categories were further decomposed to World Model detail as indicated schematically in Figure 5.

The percentage breakdowns describing the first stage of the decomposition given in Table 11 are based on [Huisken, 1976] with adjustments for Centrally planned Asia (China) and the Soviet Union based on price data from [U.S. Central Intelligence Agency, 1978] and [U.S. Congress, 1975–1978].

The percentages corresponding to procurement were further decomposed to proportions corresponding to each of the nine categories of military hardware described in Section 1 of this Chapter and are shown in Table 12. Since Resource rich Latin America, Tropical Africa, and the oil producing nations of the Middle East and Africa are assumed to have no domestic production, their procurement goods are distributed in the same proportions as those reported earlier for imports of military goods.

The portion of military final demand corresponding to the category including both construction and maintenance costs was further decomposed into two components assuming the same relative importance as they had in the military final demand vector for North America. Likewise, the proportion corresponding to the residual category called operations was divided into 43 components, each with the same relative importance as in the military final demand vector for North America (based on [BEA, 1979]).

Finally, estimates were developed for person-years of labor (the World Model unit for labor inputs) employed directly for military end use: these were estimated directly rather than through a dollar-equivalent average wage rate applied to the military

TABLE 11   Breakdown of Military Final Demand

Region	Procurement	Construction and Maintenance	Personnel	Operations	Total
Arid Africa	.425	.025	.350	.200	1.0
Centrally planned Asia	.240	.100	.460	.200	1.0
Low income Asia	.290	.030	.048	.200	1.0
Eastern Europe	.420	.050	.330	.200	1.0
High income Asia	.278	.033	.522	.167	1.0
Resource rich Latin America[a]	.250	.030	.530	.190	1.0
Resource poor Latin America	.250	.030	.550	.170	1.0
North America	.270	.030	.390	.310	1.0
Oceania	.350	.050	.450	.150	1.0
Middle East and African oil producers[a]	.250	.080	.450	.220	1.0
Soviet Union	.380	.050	.340	.230	1.0
Southern Africa	.450	.050	.300	.200	1.0
Tropical Africa[a]	.380	.030	.400	.190	1.0
High income Western Europe	.310	.050	.440	.200	1.0
Medium income Western Europe	.230	.030	.590	.150	1.0

Source: The above figures are based in general on [Huisken, 1976].

a. Since these three regions do not produce military goods domestically, procurement is provided by imports. The percentage breakdown of military final demand for these three regions changes between 1970 and 1980 in the model: that shown is for 1980, 1990, and 2000. For all other regions the proportions given in this table are assumed for all years between 1970 and 2000.

FIGURE 5   Schema for Decomposing Military Final Demand

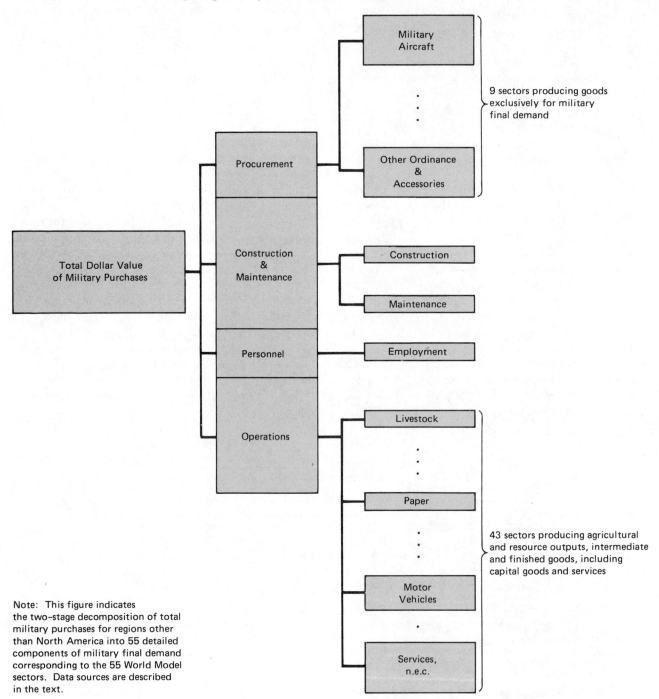

Note: This figure indicates
the two-stage decomposition of total
military purchases for regions other
than North America into 55 detailed
components of military final demand
corresponding to the 55 World Model
sectors. Data sources are described
in the text.

TABLE 12   Percentage Breakdown of Military Procurement by Region and Weapon System

	Aircraft	Ships	Missiles	Tanks	Other[a]	Total[b]
Arid Africa	.40	.06	.07	.21	.27	1.00
Centrally planned Asia	.39	.11	.06	.10	.38	1.00
Low income Asia	.39	.06	.06	.14	.35	1.00
Eastern Europe	.39	.01	.06	.27	.27	1.00
High income Asia	.46	.16	.03	.06	.29	1.00
Resource rich Latin America	.41	.19	.03	.10	.27	1.00
Resource poor Latin America	.40	.17	.03	.10	.30	1.00
North America	.35	.15	.18	.06	.26	1.00
Oceania	.40	.16	.03	.06	.35	1.00
Middle East and African oil producers	.42	.06	.07	.18	.27	1.00
Soviet Union	.35	.15	.18	.06	.26	1.00
Southern Africa	.40	.06	.03	.10	.41	1.00
Tropical Africa	.42	.15	.03	.13	.27	1.00
High income Western Europe	.40	.17	.10	.10	.23	1.00
Medium income Western Europe	.40	.17	.03	.10	.30	1.00

Sources: For North America, [BEA, 1979]. All others based on [Huisken, 1976].

a. Evenly divided among Military communication equipment, Ammunition n.e.c., Small arms, Small arms ammunition, and Other ordnance.

b. Totals may not add exactly due to rounding.

TABLE 13   Labor Coefficients for Military Final Demand

Region	(1) 1970 Military Personnel (millions)	(2) 1970 Military Purchases (billions) of 1970$)	(3) 1970 Labor Coefficient (1) ÷ (2)	(4) 1977 Military Personnel (millions)	(5) 1977 Military Purchases (billions) of 1970$)	(6) 1977 Labor Coefficient (7) ÷ (8)
Arid Africa	1.015	3.713	.273	1.904	5.981	.318
Centrally planned Asia	6.707	22.302	.301	8.145	24.087	.338
Low income Asia	5.750	4.465	1.288	6.261	7.294	.858
Eastern Europe	1.838	12.127	.152	2.133	15.110	.141
High income Asia	.328	2.295	.143	.347	3.696	.096
Resource rich Latin America	.409	.874	.468	.576	1.808	.319
Resource poor Latin America	1.144	2.247	.509	1.535	2.399	.640
North America	4.399	78.755	.056	3.205	68.042	.047
Oceania	.139	1.993	.070	.122	1.931	.063
Middle East and African oil producers	1.001	5.656	.177	1.595	19.694	.081
Soviet Union	5.977	72.864	.082	6.909	90.594	.076
Southern Africa	.056	.420	.133	.098	1.207	.081
Tropical Africa	.304	.445	.683	.509	1.207	.422
High income Western Europe	3.335	32.370	.103	3.069	38.981	.079
Medium income Western Europe	3.307	4.263	.518	2.195	6.071	.362

Note: 1. Labor coefficients expressed as millions of employee years per billion (1970) dollars of military purchases.

2. The armed forces figures from [ACDA, 1979b] were multiplied by the ratio of military personnel to armed forces in the United States for 1970 and 1977. These ratios, equal to 1.39 in 1970 and 1.42 in 1977, were derived from [U.S. Department of Commerce, 1978, Table No. 603].

3. Data on military purchases are from [ACDA, 1979b].

bill for personnel. For this purpose, figures on country armed forces for 1970 and 1977 in [ACDA, 1979b] were aggregated to World Model regions. Total personnel, military plus civilian, directly employed in the U.S. for military end use in 1970 and 1977 was obtained from [U.S. Department of Commerce, 1978]. The ratio of total military personnel to armed forces in the U.S. in these years was assumed to hold in other regions as well.

World Model labor coefficients, measured in millions of employee years per billion dollars of military final demand, are shown for 1970 and 1977 in Table 13

along with supporting information. The coefficients calculated for 1977 were used in the Model for 1980, 1990, and 2000.

The original World Model government final demand vector for North America in 1970 was replaced by the vector in [BEA, 1979] describing the composition of U.S. government civilian purchases in 1972. This same composition was assumed for 1980, 1990, and 2000. For the other regions the original vectors which registered no purchases from the military sectors were left unchanged.

CHAPTER 4

Scenarios

World Model scenarios are distinguished from one another by different assumptions about the ways in which the various economies operate. Concretely, these assumptions take the form of mathematical equations, each of which specifies particular parametric relations among a selected set of variables. Each scenario identifies those variables which it assumes to be constraining, that is, the exogenous variables, and specifies the values to be assumed by both the structural parameters and the exogenous variables. The data described in Chapter 3, which constitute a portion of the World Model database, provide the values for some of these parameters and variables for the Base scenario. Given these assumptions, the values of the endogenous variables are uniquely determined[1] and become a part of the scenario. Thus a scenario can be completely described in terms of either the assumptions, which are presented in this chapter, or by the levels of activity implied by these assumptions which are obtained by solving the model. The latter are the subject of Part II of this book.

Six different scenarios are analyzed. The Base scenario updates the A scenario described in [Leontief, Carter, and Petri, 1977], projecting into the future current economic trends. The principal differences between the Base scenario and the A scenario—as discussed in Chapter 3—consist of an explicit representation of the military sectors, revised estimates of future population growth, and changes in the size of the labor forces in the developed regions. Other differences regard the selection and values of exogenous variables, essentially reflecting the impacts of increases in the price of petroleum. These differences are indicated in Table 14 and discussed in the following paragraphs.

1. The *existence* of a solution corresponds to a "feasible" economy.

Like the A scenario, the Base scenario limits the growth of most developed regions by a labor constraint. Under Base, however, revised full-employment labor force estimates are reduced by 2 percent in 1980 and 5 percent in 1990 and 2000 to reflect present and anticipated future conditions.

Southern Africa is treated differently from the other developed regions because of its ability to maintain its standard of living despite the increased cost of imported petroleum through increasing its exports of gold. Base scenario GDP is exogenously fixed at the same level as the A scenario (i.e., before the increase in the price of petroleum), and the employment constraint is instead relaxed. A new variable corresponding to gold exports is introduced (for this region only) and allowed to assume any value necessary to balance the net outflow of capital.

The level of personal consumption in the Middle East and African oil producing nations is fixed exogenously in the Base scenario at a level considerably higher than its endogenous value in the A scenario. This increase in consumption (in constant 1970 dollars) reflects the command over additional resources resulting from the increased relative price of petroleum.

Growth in the remaining regions is constrained by the balance of payments; that is, any deficits in the balance of trade must be covered by the scheduled net inflow of capital. The increased oil wealth of Resource rich Latin America is assumed to take the form of an exogenously specified balance of payments surplus. (Neither the significant worldwide conservation of petroleum nor the rapid growth of Mexican exports of the last two years was anticipated when this scenario was formulated.)

For all regions except North America and the Soviet Union, military spending under the Base scenario is endogenously determined as a given proportion of

TABLE 14   Description of the Base Scenario

A. Developed Regions

	A Scenario	*Base Scenario*
GDP	Endogenous	Southern Africa: Exogenous, set at A Scenario level. Others: Endogenous
Consumption	Endogenous	Endogenous
Employment	ILO Estimates	Southern Africa: Endogenous. Others: Revised ILO Estimates
Capital Requirements	Endogenous	Endogenous
Balance of Payments	Medium income Western Europe: Exogenous, set at zero. Others: Endogenous	Medium income Western Europe: Exogenous, set at zero. Southern Africa: See text. Others: Endogenous
Military Purchases	Not separately identified.	North America, Soviet Union: Exogenous in 1990, 2000. Others: Endogenous

B. Resource Rich Developing Regions

	A Scenario	*Base Scenario*
GDP	Resource rich Latin America and Tropical Africa: Endogenous. Middle East and African oil producers: U.N. target	Endogenous
Consumption	Endogenous	Resource rich Latin America and Tropical Africa: Endogenous. Middle East and African oil producers: Exogenous
Employment	Endogenous	Endogenous
Capital Requirements	Resource rich Latin America and Tropical Africa: Investment constraint. Middle East and African oil producers: Endogenous.	Endogenous
Balance of Payments	Endogenous	Resource rich Latin America: Exogenous. Middle East and African oil producers: Endogenous. Tropical Africa: Endogenous, set at zero.
Military Purchases		Endogenous

C. Resource Poor Developing Regions

	A Scenario	*Base Scenario*
GDP	Endogenous	Endogenous
Consumption	Endogenous	Endogenous
Employment	Endogenous	Endogenous
Investment	Centrally planned Asia: Savings constraint. Others: Endogenous	Centrally planned Asia: Aggregate investment exogenous. Others: Endogenous
Balance Payments	Centrally planned Asia: Endogenous. Others: Exogenous, set at zero	Centrally planned Asia: Endogenous. Others: Exogenous, set at zero
Military Purchases		Endogenous

Notes: 1. The A Scenario is described in greater detail in [Leontief, Carter, and Petri, 1977]. Base is the baseline scenario of the present study.
2. For both scenarios, population, the levels of pollution abatement activities, and the values of certain historic or "lagged" variables are exogenous. The military variables added for this study are endogenous except for the levels of military spending in North America and the Soviet Union, which are described in the text.

GDP. So far as North America and the Soviet Union are concerned, the assumption that a given percentage of national income would be devoted to military spending in each region would imply that, in the case of unequal rates of growth in both regions, total military spending in the faster growing region would tend in the long run to exceed that of the slower growing region. However, any realistic projection, with or without agreements on arms limitation, must be based on the assumption that the total level of military spending in the United States and the Soviet Union will be kept approximately at par. Hence for the Base scenario, and consequently also all other scenarios formulated as deviations from it, it was assumed that the total military spending of the Soviet Union will equal that of North America in 1990 and 2000.

The absolute level of this spending assumed in the Base scenario was determined by adding the amount of military spending in the two regions, under the assumption that each will spend a given percentage of its GDP (an estimated 13 percent for the Soviet Union and 5 percent for North America as of the mid-1970s) and then dividing this sum by two.

Two scenarios, A1 and A2, both specifying higher levels of military purchases than the baseline by 1990 and 2000, are described in the left-hand portion of Table 15. For North America and the Soviet Union, parity is maintained at double the Base level. For the other regions, where military purchases are determined as a proportion of GDP, the value of this parameter under the Base scenario in the corresponding year is doubled.

Scenarios A1 and A2 differ in their assumptions about trade in military goods. Under A1, it is assumed that military purchases increase faster than most countries' abilities to increase domestic production of hardware. For all regions with some domestic production, the import coefficients (parameters which determine imports as a proportion of domestic production) corresponding to procurement goods were set at double the corresponding Base values. The three resource rich, less developed regions, assumed to have no domestic production, naturally continued to rely exclusively on imports.

Under scenario A2 current world trends toward greater reliance on domestic production of military goods, as compared with imports, were accelerated. In those regions which under Base had some domestic production in 1990 and 2000 the import coefficients were set to half their Base values. The three regions with no domestic production under Base—Resource rich Latin America, the Middle East and African oil-producing nations, and Tropical Africa—were assumed to begin production and assigned import coefficients used in the Base scenario for Resource poor Latin America which is a less-developed region with nascent military industries.

The remaining scenarios shown in Table 15, D1, D2, and D3, specify lower levels of military purchases than those assumed under the Base scenario. For North America and the Soviet Union, parity is again main-

TABLE 15   Description of Five Military Scenarios

	A1	A2	D1	D2	D3
Government Purchases, Military	North America and Soviet Union: Parity at double the Base level. Others: Proportions of GDP. Double the corresponding Base value in 1990 and 2000.		North American and Soviet Union: Parity at $^2/_3$ the Base level Others: Proportions of GDP. 75% and 60% the corresponding value of Base in 1990 and 2000, respectively.		
Military Import Coefficients	Resource rich Latin America, Middle East and African oil producers, and Tropical Africa: All procurement goods imported, as in Base. Others: Double the corresponding values in Base.	Resource rich Latin America, Middle East and African oil producers, and Tropical Africa: Set to Base values for Resource poor Latin America. Others: Half of corresponding values in Base.	As in Base.		Resource rich Latin America, Middle East and African oil producers and Tropical Africa: Set to Base values for Resource poor Latin America. Others: Reduced according to values in Table 17.
Additional Economic Aid	None		Transfer from donor to recipient regions (identified in Table 16) of 15% of "savings" on military spending in 1990, 25% in 2000.		

Note: The five scenarios are identical with Base (and with each other) for 1970 and 1980. The changes described are assumed to take place between 1981 and 2000 and thus to be effective in model years 1990 and 2000.

TABLE 16 Recipients and Donors of Additional Aid under Scenarios D2 and D3 in 1990 and 2000

a. Distribution of Additional Aid Received in 1990 and 2000 (proportions):

Arid Africa	.15
Low income Asia	.45
Resource poor Latin America	.10
Tropical Africa	.30
Total	1.00

b. Donors of Additional Aid:

Centrally planned Asia
Eastern Europe
High income Asia
North America
Oceania
Middle East and African oil producing nations
Soviet Union
High income Western Europe

Note: Amount of aid given is 15% of the difference between military purchases under these scenarios and under the Base scenario for 1990, and 25% of the difference for 2000.

tained but at two-thirds of the Base scenario level. For all other regions, the parameter determining military purchases as a proportion of GDP is reduced to 75 percent of the corresponding Base value in 1990 and 60 percent in 2000.

Furthermore, scenario D2 requires that in 1990 15 percent of the "savings" released in the developed countries through reduction of military spending be transferred in the form of some kind of developmental assistance to poor regions. This percentage is increased to 25 percent in 2000. The top part of Table 16 shows in what proportion this aid was distributed among the four recipient regions. These regions were selected because they register the lowest per capita GDPs among the fifteen World Model regions in 1990 and 2000 under the Base scenario. The donors of this aid

are shown in the second portion of the table. China (Centrally planned Asia) was for political reasons specified as a donor despite its low level of per capita GDP. The remaining portion of the savings in developed regions and all of them in less-developed regions are retained for increased domestic consumption and growth.

Finally, scenario D3, like A2, involves also a decreased dependence on military imports but at levels of military spending lower than these assumed under the Base scenario. Table 17 shows the proportion by which Base scenario import coefficients are progressively reduced in 1990 and 2000 in those regions where there is some domestic production. As in scenario A2, the three resource rich, less developed regions, which are assumed under Base to have no domestic production, are assigned the Base scenario import coefficients of Resource poor Latin America.

TABLE 17 Proportions by which Base Scenario Military Import Coefficients are Decreased under Scenario D3

	1990	2000
Aircraft	.25	.50
Ships	.25	.50
Electronic equipment	.25	.50
Missiles	0	.25
Ammunition	.50	.60
Tanks	.25	.50
Small arms	.75	.80
Small arms ammunition	.75	.80
Other ordnance	.75	.80

Note: These proportions apply to all regions except Resource rich Latin America, Middle East and African oil producers, and Tropical Africa, which are discussed in the text.

PART TWO

Results

CHAPTER 5

Base Scenario

The Base scenario assumes a continuation of current trends in military purchases and maintenance of the present pattern of international arms trade through the year 2000. In addition to the production and allocation of military goods themselves, the categories singled out for comments include per capita GDP and consumption, labor force and capital stock, the production of some important fuel and non-fuel minerals, and the availability of grain. The other five scenarios described in subsequent chapters are essentially deviations from the Base scenario.

Results reported for 1970 are based on historical data. In the original World Model the assumptions made for 1980, as well as the subsequent years, were based on information available in the mid-1970s. The attempt has been made to keep these assumptions more or less up to date. However, because of the amount of work involved in monitoring the entire world economy, a variety of recent events and trends may not yet be reflected in the assumptions.

The bar charts in Figure 6 show per capita GDP and that portion of it corresponding to per capita consumption, for each of the fifteen regions under the Base scenario in 1970 (first bar for each region) and in 2000 (second bar for each region). The projections of both of these variables are shown to increase (in constant 1970 U.S. dollars) over the period for most regions, but a decline is projected for Resource poor Latin America and Arid Africa.

The two developing regions which can be expected not only according to this but also according to all the other scenarios to have the greatest economic growth are the Middle East and African oil producing nations and Resource rich Latin America: by the year 2000, per capita consumption in each of these two regions is projected to be more than ten times and more than three times, respectively, its 1970 level. Despite this high growth rate, the per capita GDP

and consumption of the two regions will surpass by the year 2000 those of only two developed regions, South Africa and Medium income Western Europe, which means that the proverbial economic gap between developed and most developing regions will continue to exist.

North America, with the highest per capita GDP and consumption in 1970, is projected to maintain this position in 2000. While High income Asia (Japan) had the fourth highest per capita level of GDP and consumption in 1970, it advances to second position among the fifteen regions by the year 2000. The Soviet economy is also projected to have a high rate of growth, but at the end of the century its per capita GDP and consumption still are below those of North America, High income Asia, and High income Western Europe.

Military purchases increase substantially between 1970 and 2000 under the Base scenario. Figure 7 shows the level of military purchases in 1970 (first bar for each region) and in 2000 (second bar for each region), separating portions provided by domestic production from those covered by imports.

The value of military purchases in the Middle East and African oil producing countries increases from $2.4 billion in 1970 to $79.6 billion in 2000: a rate of growth (12 percent average annual real increase) exceeding that of any other region and sustained primarily by a large rise in military imports. The second largest rate of increase is projected for High income Asia, whose military purchases rise from $1.6 billion to $26.8 billion between 1970 and 2000. However, this increase, unlike that in the oil-producing nations, is accompanied not by an accelerated dependence on military imports but by increased domestic production.

The Soviet Union's military purchases are projected to almost triple in real terms between 1970 and 2000.

FIGURE 6   Per Capita Consumption and Per Capita Gross Domestic Product under the Base Scenario in 1970 and 2000

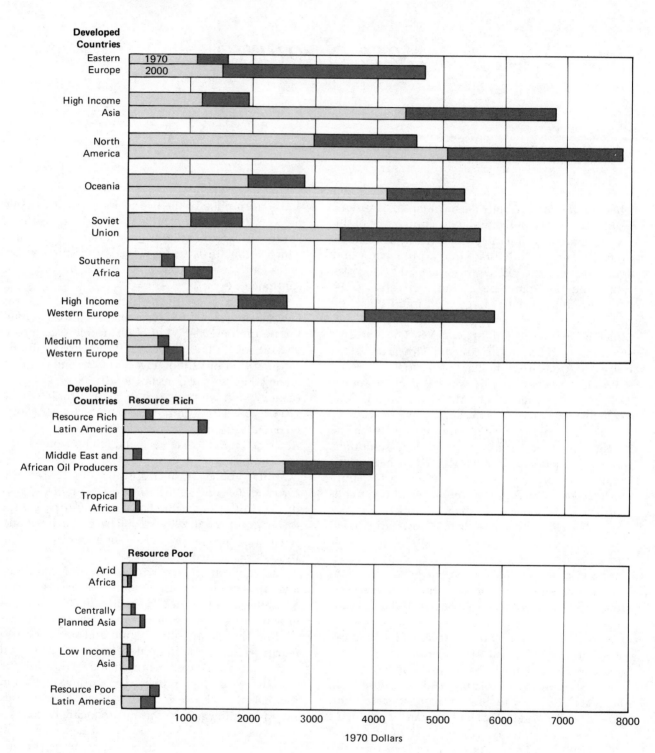

Source: Annex C

FIGURE 7 Military Purchases under the Base Scenario in 1970 and 2000

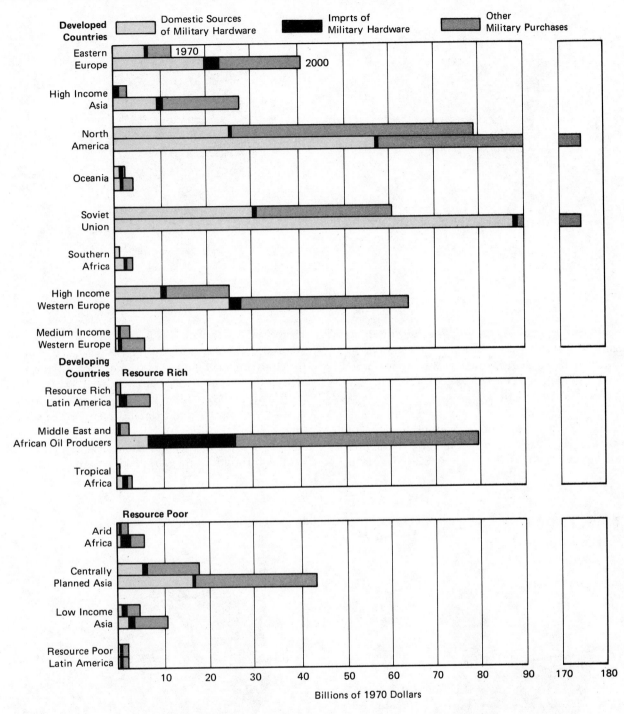

Note: Domestic procurement of military hardware equals domestic output less net exports.
Source: Annex C

33

FIGURE 8   Geographical Distribution of Military Exports under the Base Scenario in 1970 and 2000

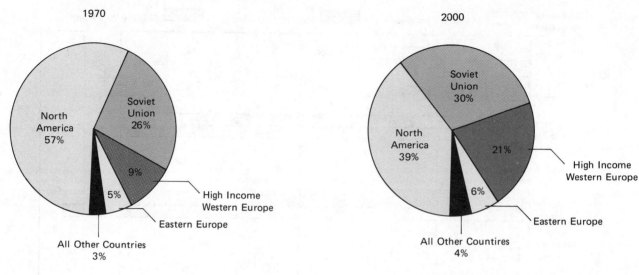

Source: Annex C

At least through the end of this century, the maintenance of military parity between the super-powers would continue to require the Soviet Union to devote a much higher proportion of its GDP to the military than does North America.

In 1970 and still by the year 2000, virtually all military exports continue to come from the same four developed regions: North America, the Soviet Union, High income Western Europe, and Eastern Europe.

However, North America is projected to lose a substantial share of its military export market, primarily to High income Western Europe. North America's share drops from 57 percent in 1970 to 39 percent in 2000 while High income Western Europe's share increases over this period from 9 percent to 21 percent. (See Figure 8.)

The developing regions remain the principal importers throughout the period. (See Figure 9.) Never-

FIGURE 9   Geographical Distribution of Military Imports under the Base Scenario in 1970 and 2000

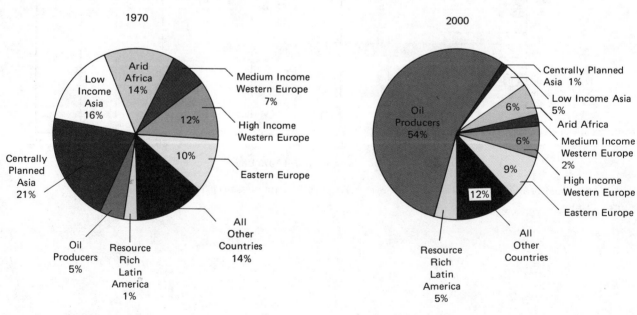

Source: Annex C

theless, the distribution of military imports changes strikingly. The large increase in military purchases by the Middle East and African oil producing nations causes their share of world military imports to rise from less than 5 percent in 1970 to over 50 percent in 2000.

Turning to the civilian part of the world economy, we see in Figure 10 that the stock of capital equipment and structures, valued in constant 1970 dollars, is projected to increase between 1970 and 2000 in all regions, with the Middle East and African oil producing countries experiencing an average annual rate of growth close to 17 percent. The lowest rates of growth are projected for Arid Africa, Resource poor Latin America, and Medium income Western Europe, where capital stock approximately doubles in thirty years.

Throughout the period from 1970 to 2000, the capital stock of the Soviet Union and Eastern European countries will, according to the Base Scenario,

grow much faster than that of North America and the Western European countries. However, while the value of the combined capital stock of North America and Western Europe was almost four times as great as that of the combined stock of the Soviet Union and Eastern Europe in 1970, it would still be more than twice as large by the year 2000.

The size of the labor force in the developed regions is fixed at values shown in Figure 11 and remains unchanged from one scenario to the next. These flat growth paths contrast with the considerable anticipated increases in capital stock.

Turning our attention now to strategic materials, the output of conventional fuel minerals is projected to increase in all parts of the world between 1970 and 2000, and, as shown in Figure 12 the three largest producers (in terms of total BTU content) are the Middle East and African oil producers, North America, and the Soviet Union. The consumption of fuel minerals is shown in Figure 13. North America's fuel

FIGURE 10   Capital Stock under the Base Scenario for 1970–2000

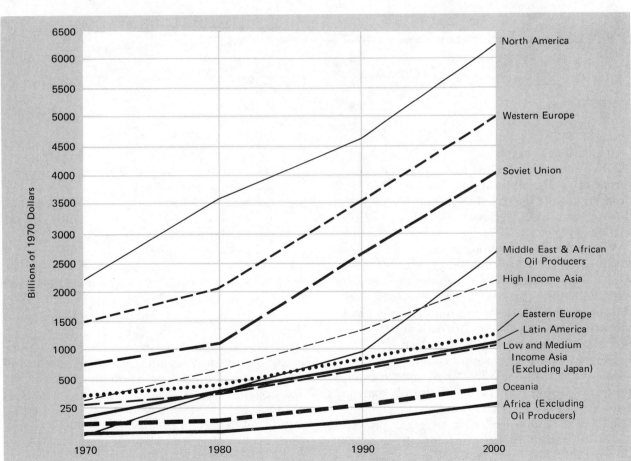

Source: Annex C

FIGURE 11 Employment in Developed Regions under All Scenarios for 1970–2000

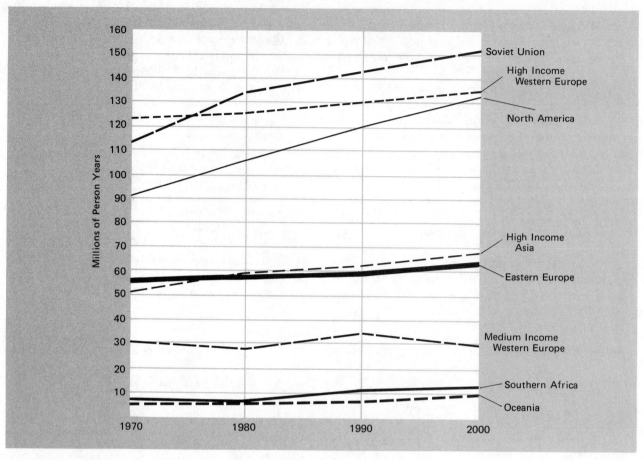

Source: (ILO, 1977)

resource output, the highest in the world in 1970, is surpassed by that of the Middle East and African oil producers before the end of the century even though these scenarios assume energy independence for North America by 2000.

North America was the dominant coal and natural gas producer in 1970. At this time, Centrally planned Asia and the Soviet Union ranked second in terms of coal and natural gas output, respectively. However, the Soviet Union turns out in our projections to be the second largest producer of coal and the largest producer of natural gas by the year 2000.

The developing areas with the highest energy resource outputs are the Middle East and African oil producers, Centrally planned Asia (mainly coal) and Latin America (mainly petroleum).

The Soviet Union has by far the largest projected output of iron in all years between 1970 and 2000, shown in Figure 14 to increase from 117 million metric tons in 1970 to 515 million metric tons in

2000. In contrast, the output of North America, the second largest iron producer in 1970, is shown to increase over the period from 79 to only 183 million metric tons. Japan has the smallest iron output among all the fifteen regions throughout the period.

Low income Asia and the Soviet Union are projected to produce the largest quantities of nickel in the year 2000: 680 thousand and 520 thousand metric tons, respectively. (See Figure 15.) The output of North America, the largest producer until 1990, falls thereafter due to depletion of its nickel reserves.

Significant differences among the fifteen regions persist over the period with respect to the production and consumption of food. Centrally planned Asia and Low income Asia have the largest total amount of grain available for domestic use (output less net exports) of the fifteen regions throughout the period from 1970 to 2000. However, because of their large populations, neither has high levels available on a per capita basis. (See Figure 16.)

FIGURE 12   Energy Output under the Base Scenario for 1970–2000

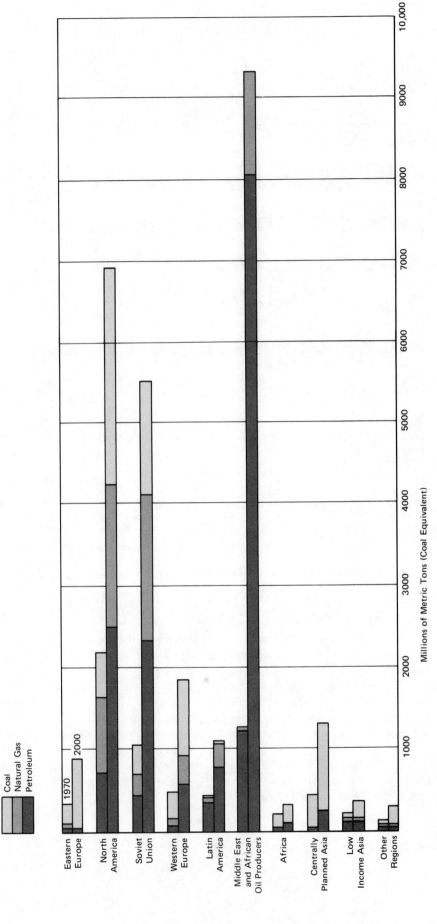

Millions of Metric Tons (Coal Equivalent)

Source: Annex C

37

FIGURE 13   Energy Consumption under the Base Scenario for 1970–2000

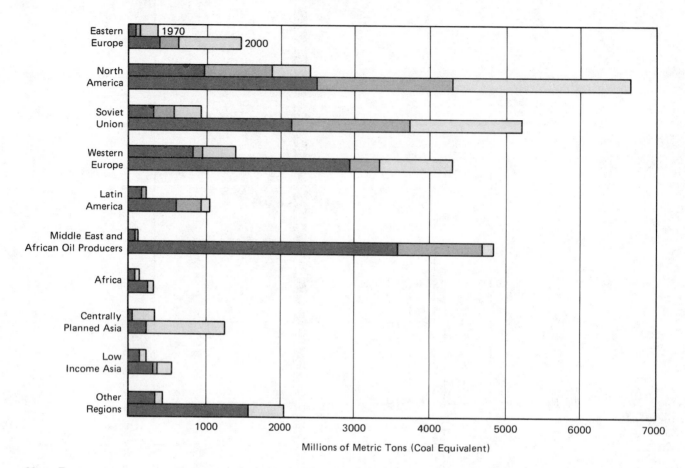

Note: Energy resource consumption equals domestic output less net exports. Source: Annex C

Three developed regions—the Soviet Union, Eastern Europe, and North America, have the highest levels of grain available on a per capita basis for direct and indirect human consumption in 2000. Even Southern Africa, with the lowest level among the developed regions, has more grain per capita than every one of the developing regions. Arid Africa on the other hand ranks last among the fifteen regions in 2000.

In summary, the Base scenario projections indicate that among the developing regions, only the Middle East and African oil producing countries and to a lesser extent Resource rich Latin America will make significant progress in approaching the economic well-being of developed regions. Being endowed with significant petroleum resources, these two regions reap now and can be expected to enjoy for a long time in the future the benefits of what might be called a self-made gigantic Marshall Plan. The other developing regions appear to be unable to "catch up" to the developed regions if current trends continue. At the same time, projected military purchases continue to grow throughout the period in all regions.

FIGURE 14   Iron Output under the Base Scenario for 1970–2000

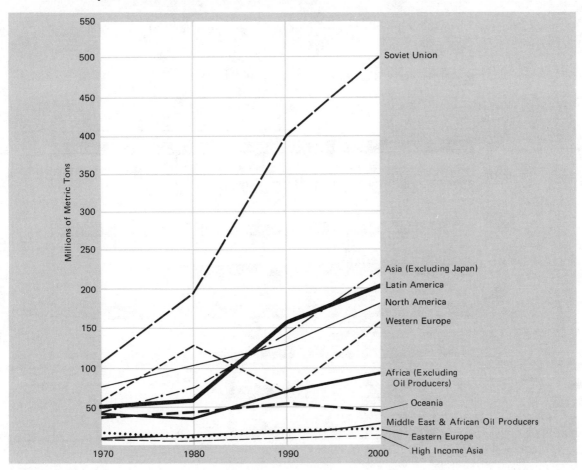

Source: Annex C

FIGURE 15   Nickel Output of Major Producers under the Base Scenario for 1970–2000

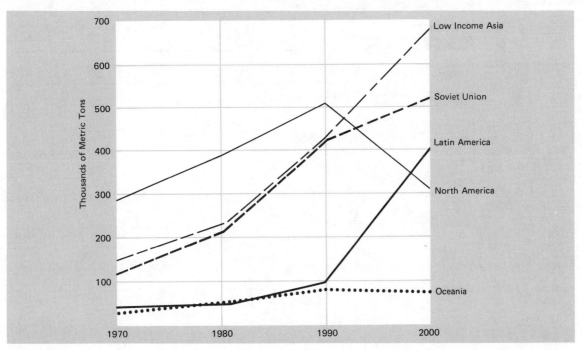

Source: Annex C

39

FIGURE 16   Per Capita Domestic Consumption (Direct plus Indirect) of Grain under the Base Scenario for 1970–2000

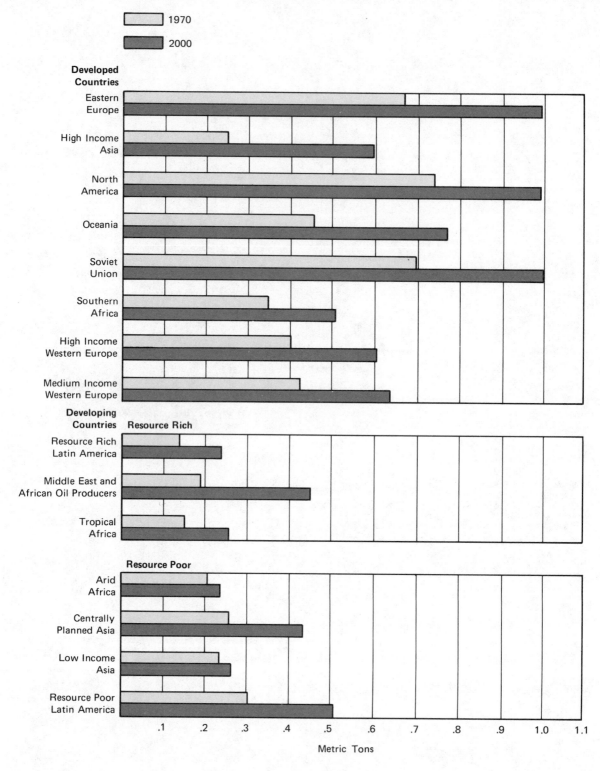

Note: Grain available for domestic consumption equals domestic output less net exports.
Source: Annex C

40

CHAPTER 6

Reduced Military Spending and Increased Aid Transfers

While even societies with very low standards of living allocate substantial resources to military activities, the bulk of military spending is incurred by wealthy nations. Both rich and poor countries in times of crisis temporarily increase their military outlays, sometimes to unsustainable proportions of the national product. For example, both Israel and Egypt in the early 1970s devoted up to 40 percent of their GDPs to military purposes according to [SIPRI, 1979]; estimates in [ACDA, 1979b] are about half as large but are still significantly higher than in other years before and since. In these cases, outlays fall once the immediate crisis is past.

The proportion of GDP allocated to military spending in different regions of the world can be expected to rise and fall periodically in response to the development of regional troublespots as well as the overall level of worldwide tensions. According to the Base scenario described in the preceding chapter, the proportion of GDP allocated to military purchases in 1980 was assumed to remain unchanged in 1990 and 2000 in all regions (except Japan). This chapter and Chapter 7 are devoted to a description of the direct and indirect economic impacts of substantial sustained decreases and increases, respectively, in the proportion of all regions' resources devoted to military purposes between 1980 and the year 2000 relative to the Base scenario.

In this chapter we examine the potential for accelerated growth and increased consumption made possible by a reallocation of resources set free by reductions in military spending in general and a transfer of some of these resources from the developed to the less developed countries. Without specific, multilateral agreements on arms control and disarmament and on massive developmental aid to be granted by the rich to the poor regions, some of the assump-

tions on which the projections described below have been based will prove to be overly optimistic.

It should be emphasized that the economic impacts discussed in this chapter are projected in the absence of specific structural changes. It is possible within this model framework to explore, for example, the effects of shifting all military savings into investment in advanced technology in the agricultural sector, or other priorities; but such experiments have not yet been carried out. Instead the alternatives are *endogenously* determined by the structures of the economies as incorporated in the Base scenario.

Three World Model scenarios called D1, D2, and D3 involve reductions in all regions' military purchases below those included in the Base scenario. While D1 allows each region to reallocate this portion of its military purchasing power for its own growth and increased consumption, D2 requires the transfer of part of these savings to the poorest, less developed regions. D3 combines this transfer with decreased reliance for all regions on foreign sources of military hardware. The three scenarios are described in more detail in Chapter 4. The analysis in this chapter focuses mainly on comparing the outcomes of the Base scenario and scenarios D1 and D2; D2 and D3 are analyzed in detail in Chapter 8, which focuses on trade in military goods.

In scenarios D1, D2, and D3, the coefficient which in the Base scenario determines the amount of military purchases as a proportion of GDP, is reduced by 25 percent in 1990 and by 40 percent in 2000. Given the constraints under which the different economies are assumed to operate, a labor constraint in the case of the developed economies and a balance of payments constraint for most of the less-developed economies, this reduction in military purchasing power turns out to be more than compensated by increases in non-military final demand. This results in some-what larger GDPs than under the Base scenario (see Figure 17) and consequently less than proportionate (e.g., less than 40 percent in 2000) reductions in the level of military purchases relative to the Base scenario (see Figure 18) for most regions under scenario D1. The real level of military spending is significantly lower in 1990 and 2000 than under Base but it is systematically higher in 2000 than in 1970. (See Figure 19.)

A few regions stand out as exceptions to these general observations. One is Southern Africa, where GDP is assumed to remain unchanged from its Base scenario level for reasons discussed in Chapter 4. In the Middle East and African oil producing nations and in Centrally planned Asia, consumption and investment levels, respectively, are assumed to remain at the Base scenario levels. Since large components of final demand are thus not allowed to rise to compensate the reduction in military outlays, there is a small decrease in GDP in these last two regions. Finally, only in Resource poor Latin America are military purchases projected to *fall* between 1970 and 2000: real GDP rises, but not enough to compensate for the simultaneous reduction in the proportion allocated to military purposes.

In addition to the generally higher growth of total domestic product, all regions register an increase in consumption relative to the Base scenario (both absolutely and on a per capita basis since the same population projections are used in all scenarios) to offset the decline in military purchases. (See Figure 20.) The region whose per capita consumption can be seen to increase the most relative to the Base scenario is Arid Africa, where it is more than 20 percent higher under scenario D1 than under the Base scenario by 2000. The Soviet Union and Eastern Europe rank next in terms of percentage increases in personal consumption made possible by reduced military spending. The same pattern holds for per capita GDP.

The three regions mentioned in the last paragraph devote among the highest proportions of GDP to military purchases of all fifteen regions; thus a given percentage reduction naturally releases a higher proportion of GDP for alternative uses than in other regions. *For each dollar* of reduced military spending, however, it is the poorest of the less-developed regions (Arid Africa, Resource poor Latin America, Low income Asia, and Tropical Africa) whose GDP and per capita consumption increase the most. These economies operate in the World Model under a balance of payments constraint, and reducing military spending allows them to replace military imports with machinery and other capital goods contributing directly to economic growth. The growth of GDP per dollar

reduction in military spending of the developed regions, resulting mainly from a reallocation of part of the labor force to civilian production, is positive but relatively small. Both North America and the Soviet Union, who are of course the major producers of military goods, register greater increases in per capita consumption (per dollar reduction in military spending) than the other developed countries. These two regions reduce not only their military spending but also their production of military goods for their own use as well as those destined for export. Oceania and Japan, with low military budgets and little military production, are as could be anticipated the least affected.

Looking at world economic activity in sectoral detail, Tables 18 and 19 show the ten industries whose output expands the most and the least, respectively, with reductions in military spending, and Table 20 shows the percentage change in mineral output. The heavy representation in Table 18 of sectors providing agricultural goods, clothing, and construction activities and materials indicates where bottlenecks can be expected to appear when military spending is reduced. In contrast, the outputs of producers' goods like electrical machinery, instruments, and primary metals processing increase the least, while production of civilian aircraft actually declines significantly. (See Table 19.) Table 20 indicates a moderate increase in the demand for and in output of most resources,

TABLE 18 Goods and Services Showing the Greatest Increase in World Output under Scenarios D1 and D2 (Percentage Change from the Base Scenario) in 2000

	Base	D1	D2	Percentage Change Between Base and D2
Furniture, fixtures	161.7	166.1	175.9	8.8
Textiles, apparel	514.3	534.7	555.2	8.0
Construction	1,537.0	1,629.1	1,652.7	7.5
High protein crops	347.9	352.5	372.6	7.1
Fertilizers	234.3	238.6	250.7	7.0
Shipbuilding and other transportation equipment	66.9	69.3	71.3	6.6
Cement	26.5	27.8	28.1	6.0
Wood and cork	121.5	126.4	128.6	5.8
Glass	226.3	236.5	239.5	5.8
Animal products	480.6	487.0	505.9	5.3

Note: All goods and services are measured in billions of 1970 U.S. dollars except for animal products, fertilizers, and high protein crops which are measured in millions of metric tons.

Source: Annex C

FIGURE 17   Gross Domestic Product under Scenarios D1 and D2 in 2000 (Percentage Change from the Base Scenario)

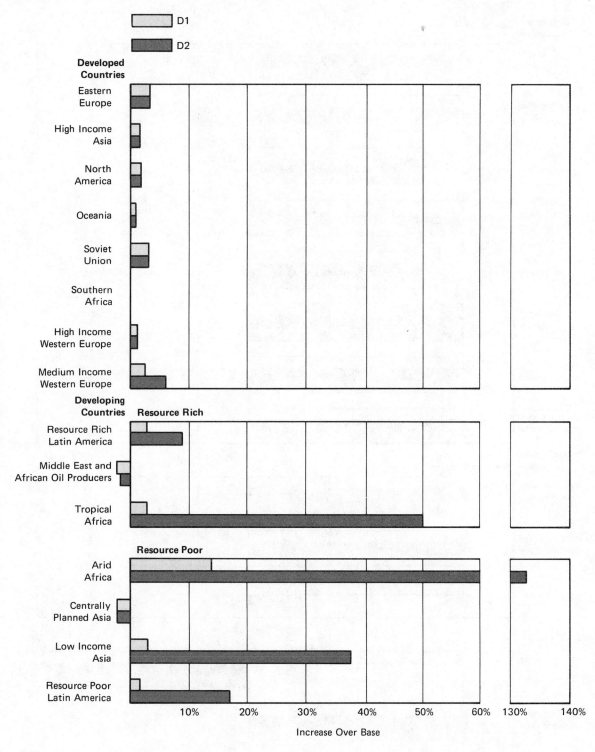

Source: Annex C

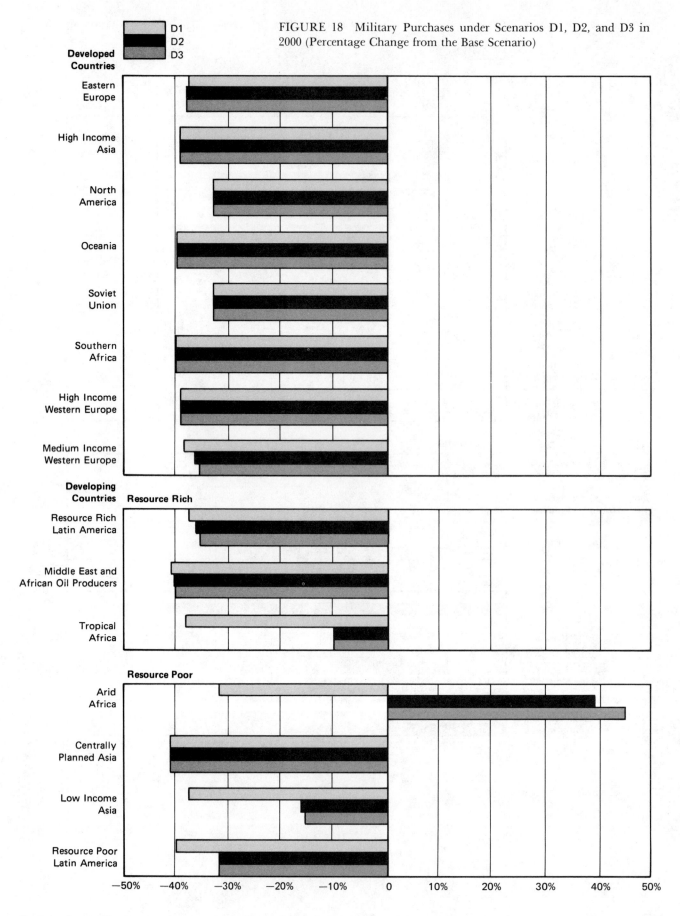

FIGURE 18 Military Purchases under Scenarios D1, D2, and D3 in 2000 (Percentage Change from the Base Scenario)

Source: Annex C

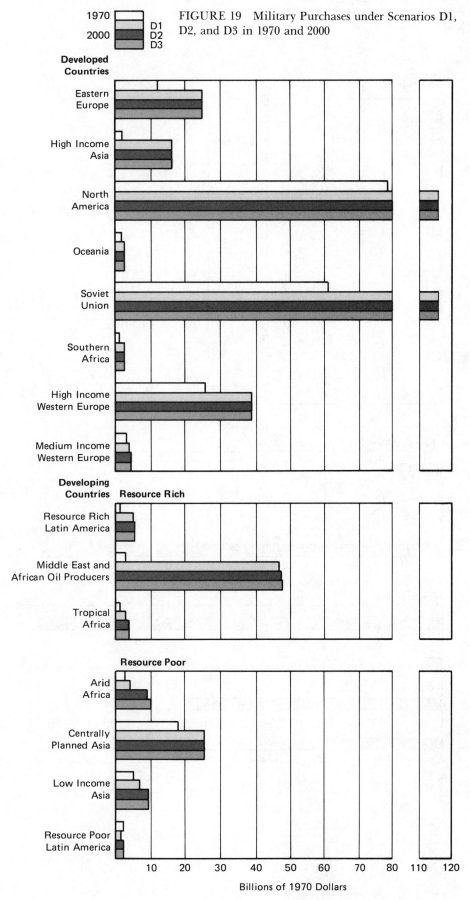

FIGURE 19 Military Purchases under Scenarios D1, D2, and D3 in 1970 and 2000

1970
2000

D1
D2
D3

Developed Countries

Eastern Europe

High Income Asia

North America

Oceania

Soviet Union

Southern Africa

High Income Western Europe

Medium Income Western Europe

Developing Countries   Resource Rich

Resource Rich Latin America

Middle East and African Oil Producers

Tropical Africa

Resource Poor

Arid Africa

Centrally Planned Asia

Low Income Asia

Resource Poor Latin America

10   20   30   40   50   60   70   80   110   120

Billions of 1970 Dollars

Source: Annex C

45

FIGURE 20 Personal Consumption under Scenarios D1 and D2 in 2000 (Percentage Change from the Base Scenario)

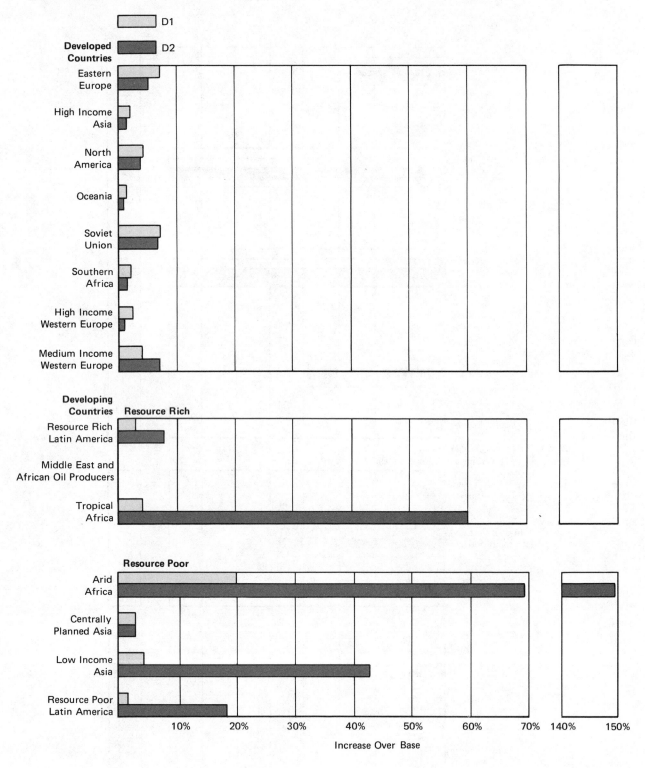

Source: Annex C

TABLE 19 Goods and Services Showing the Smallest Increase in World Output under Scenarios D1 and D2 (Percentage Change from the Base Scenario) in 2000

	Base	D1	D2	Percentage Change Between Base and D2
Aircraft	128.1	118.1	120.8	− 5.7
Electrical machinery	416.2	416.5	423.6	1.8
Instruments	94.2	94.6	96.6	2.5
Primary metal processing	434.0	437.6	445.3	2.6
Communications	233.7	236.7	240.1	2.7
Utilities	399.8	407.2	412.1	3.1
Food processing	581.5	595.6	600.3	3.2
Rubber	157.1	160.6	162.4	3.4
Petroleum refining	167.7	170.7	173.4	3.5
Motor vehicles	418.7	431.4	433.2	3.5

Note: All goods and services are measured in billions of 1970 U.S. dollars.
Source: Annex C

except petroleum and nickel, whose output changes very little.

The computation of scenario D2 results in additional aid transfers amounting to 19.3 billion 1970 U.S. dollars in 1990 and $54.8 billion in 2000. The distribution among donor regions (proportional to their savings from reduced military spending) is shown in Figure 21. (The distribution among recipient re-

TABLE 20 World Resource Output under Scenarios D1 and D2 (Percentage Change from the Base Scenario) in 2000

	Base	D1	D2	Percentage Change Between Base and D2
Other resources	61.80	64.00	65.20	5.5
Coal	7,712.90	7,864.10	8,022.20	4.0
Natural gas	5,556.40	5,681.70	5,747.06	3.4
Iron	1,475.60	1,497.46	1,525.40	3.4
Lead	13.56	13.60	13.99	3.2
Bauxite	35.79	35.90	36.87	3.0
Zinc	16.70	16.70	17.15	2.7
Copper	21.97	22.00	22.49	2.4
Nickel	1,998.80	1,975.80	2,043.55	2.2
Petroleum	14,757.40	14,551.60	14,906.92	1.0

Note: All resources are measured in millions of metric tons except Other resources (billions of 1970 U.S. dollars) and nickel (thousands of metric tons). Petroleum and natural gas are expressed in coal (BTU) equivalent.
Source: Annex C

gions was specified in Table 16 in the definition of the scenario.) The overall effect of this redistribution of international purchasing power toward the poor regions is an expansion of the world economy.

The additional capital outflow has no noticeable impact on the GDPs of the seven donor regions. Their per capita consumption is, however, slightly lower under D2 than D1.

The economies of regions not directly involved in the transfer as donors or recipients appear to benefit through increased demand for their exports. GDPs of Resource rich Latin America and of Medium income Western Europe are higher under D2 than D1, reflecting in the first case, increased petroleum exports, and in the second, across the board increases but mainly in transportation and other services.

The increase of the GDPs of the four recipient regions is, of course, a desired result of the aid transfer. However, one side effect of this increase in national wealth is the accompanying increase in military outlays amounting in the case of Arid Africa, for example, to close to 50 percent above the Base scenario level. (See again Figures 17 and 18.)

Of the four recipient regions, Arid Africa appears by all measures to be able to use this aid most effectively as shown in the comparisons of scenarios D1 and D2 in Table 21: each billion dollars of additional aid in 2000 is accompanied in that year by an increase (made possible also by the additional aid already received in 1990) of $6.8 billion in GDP and of $18.80 in per capita consumption. By contrast, Tropical Africa's GDP increases by $2.7 billion and its per capita consumption by $7.50 for each billion dollars of additional aid. On a per capita basis, Low income Asia responds least to a billion-dollar infusion with per capita consumption in 2000 increasing under scenario D2 by $1.70 over the corresponding level under scenario D1. In all four regions the proportion of increased GDP going to personal consumption is higher in 2000 than in 1990.

All four recipient regions operate in the World Model under a balance of payments constraint, and the additional aid prescribed under scenario D2 takes the form of a credit to their balance of payments. Thus the immediate effect is to enable them to increase their imports. Table 22 lists in order of decreasing importance the five import items showing the greatest percentage increase for each region from the Base scenario to D2. The furniture and fixtures industry figures prominently in this list. It can be expected that at least in this and other light manufacturing industries import substitution would eventually satisfy a significant portion of increased domestic demand.

TABLE 21 Impacts of Additional Aid on Recipient Regions in 2000

	Arid Africa	Low income Asia	Resource poor Latin America	Tropical Africa
Increase from Scenario D1 to D2 (1970 U.S. dollars)				
Aid Received (billions)	$ 8	$ 25	$ 5	$ 16
GDP (billions)	54	100	26	43
Consumption (billions)	43	86	20	40
Per Capita Consumption	$150	42	44	120
Increase from Scenario D1 to D2 per dollar of Additional Aid Received				
GDP	$ 6.8	$ 4.0	$ 5.2	$ 2.7
Consumption	5.4	3.4	4.0	2.5
Per Capita Consumption (per billion dollars)	18.8	1.7	8.8	7.5
Increase in Consumption from Scenario D1 to D2 as a Proportion of Increase in GDP				
1990	.72	.79	.73	.91
2000	.80	.86	.77	.93

TABLE 22 Import Items Showing the Greatest Increase from the Base Scenario to Scenario D2 in 2000 for those Regions Receiving Additional Aid

Arid Africa	Low income Asia	Resource poor Latin America	Tropical Africa
Coal	Furniture & fixtures	Furniture & fixtures	Electrical machinery
Furniture & fixtures	Shipbuilding and other transportation equipment	Printing	Furniture & fixtures
Shipbuilding and other transportation equipment	Machinery (except electrical)	Textiles & apparel	Shipbuilding and other transportation equipment
Machinery (except electrical)	Metal products	Glass	Machinery (except electrical)
Professional instruments	Glass	Other manufactured goods	Professional Instruments

Even after the economic benefits resulting from decreased military spending and a sizable inflow of aid from the developed countries, the four recipient regions by 2000 still remain the poorest in the world measured in terms of per capita GDP and personal consumption. Furthermore, the improvements that can be attained require significant increases in the availability of the industrial labor force (Figure 22) and in productive capital (Figure 23). Perhaps the results of experiments involving specific development objectives and detailed plans for achieving them might make the outlook for 2000 appear less gloomy.

FIGURE 21   Shares of Aid Received and Given under Scenarios D2 and D3

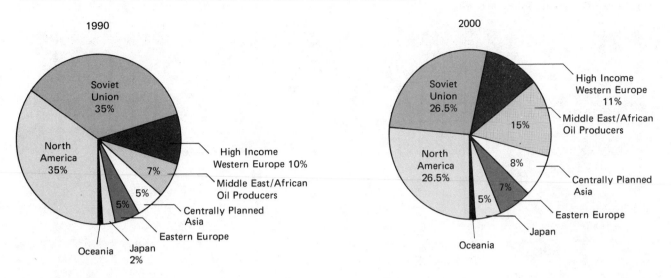

Source: Computer printouts and Annex C

FIGURE 22   Industrial Employment under the Base and D2 Scenarios for 1970–2000
in Regions Receiving Additional Aid

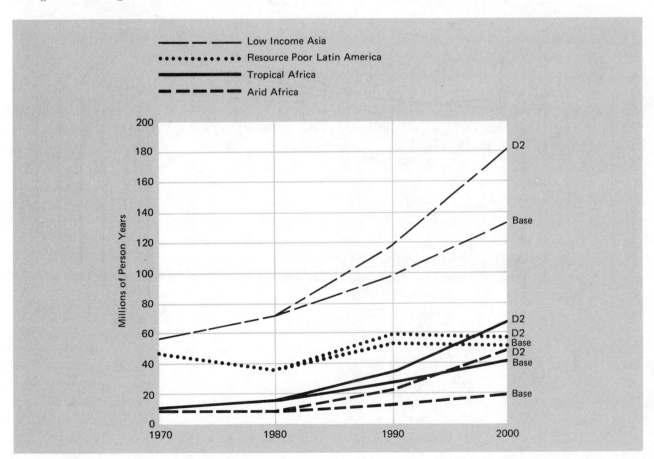

Source: Annex C

FIGURE 23   Capital Stock Requirements under the Base and D2 Scenarios for 1970–2000 in Regions Receiving Additional Aid

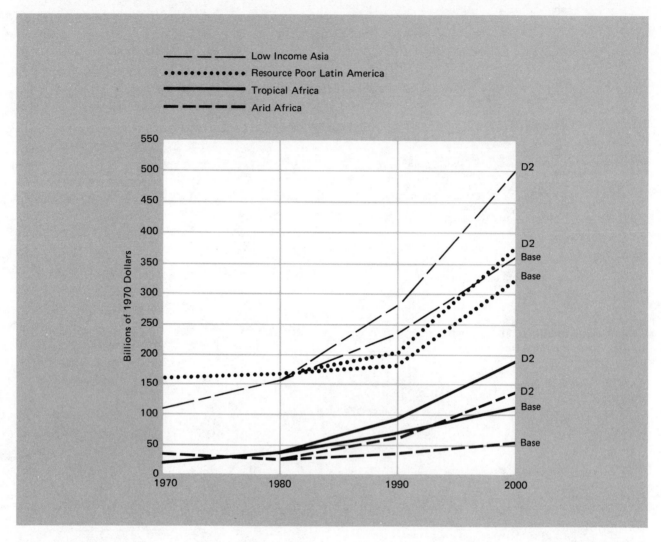

Source: Annex C

CHAPTER 7

Increased Military Spending

The preceding chapter dealt with the economic impacts of significant, sustained reduction in worldwide military spending and concluded that this would have a stimulating effect on the world economy in general, on most regional economies, and particularly on sectors producing the basic consumer goods. This chapter is devoted to a description of the impacts of the direct and indirect economic effects of increases in military spending.

Scenarios A1 and A2 specify increases in military spending above that of the Base scenario over the period 1981 to 2000; in other words they describe the consequences of an intensified worldwide armament race. Both postulate a doubling in 1990 and in 2000 of the *proportions* of GDP which under the Base scenario were allocated to military purchases in each of those years for all regions except North America and the Soviet Union, whose Base scenario *levels* of military purchases are doubled. Scenario A1 moreover increases the proportion of military procurement covered by imports, while scenario A2, on the contrary, specifies significant import substitution. Both scenarios have already been described in more detail in Chapter 4. The following discussion focuses on the comparison of scenario A1 with the Base scenario. Scenarios A1 and A2 will be compared with each other as well as with D2 and D3 in Chapter 8, which examines trade in military goods.

Changes in GDP and in the level of military purchases between the Base and A1 scenarios are shown in Figure 24. In most regions GDP falls as a consequence of increased military demand, and consequently the total volume increase in military spending is less than twice as large as it is under the Base scenario. The region most adversely affected is Arid Africa, where GDP falls about 30 percent from the Base scenario value. Both Low income Asia and the Soviet Union experience more than an 8 percent decline in

total GDP. The decline in GDP and the increase in military spending both squeeze personal consumption (see Figure 25), which falls the most (as a percent of the Base scenario level) in Arid Africa, the Soviet Union, Eastern Europe, and Low income Asia. Investment also falls in virtually all regions (see Figure 26) with increased military spending, registering a drop of about 30 percent of the Base scenario level in the Soviet Union, North America, Arid Africa, and Resource rich Latin America.

Analogous to the results reported in Chapter 6 in the case of lowered military spending, it is the poorest of the less developed regions whose GDP and personal consumption fall the most from their Base scenario levels for *each dollar* of increased military spending specified under scenario A2. These regions operate in the World Model under a balance of payments constraint, and increasing military spending requires them to replace imports of capital goods with military imports. The inter-regional differences are even more extreme when scenario A1 is compared with Base, since the same level of military spending (as under A2) is accompanied by greater reliance on imports of military goods.

The economies of Centrally planned Asia and of the Middle East and African oil producers show higher GDPs at increased levels of military spending than under the Base scenario and sustained investment levels, but neither shows an improvement in personal consumption.

Since the total global GDP is lower under scenario A1 than under the Base scenario, one would expect a decline in the output of many sectors. This is indeed the case. Tables 23 and 24 identify those industries producing goods and services whose output declines the most and least, respectively, while Table 25 shows the percentage change in mineral outputs. Food and raw materials are least affected by the

FIGURE 24   Military Purchases and Gross Domestic Product under Scenario A1 in 2000 (Percentage Change from the Base Scenario)

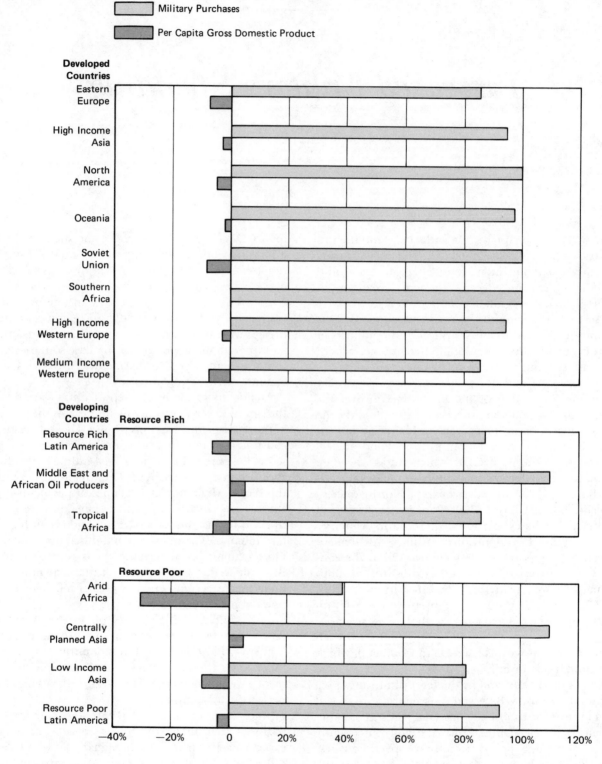

Source: Annex C

FIGURE 25 Components of Gross Domestic Product under Scenario A1 and the Base
Scenario in 2000

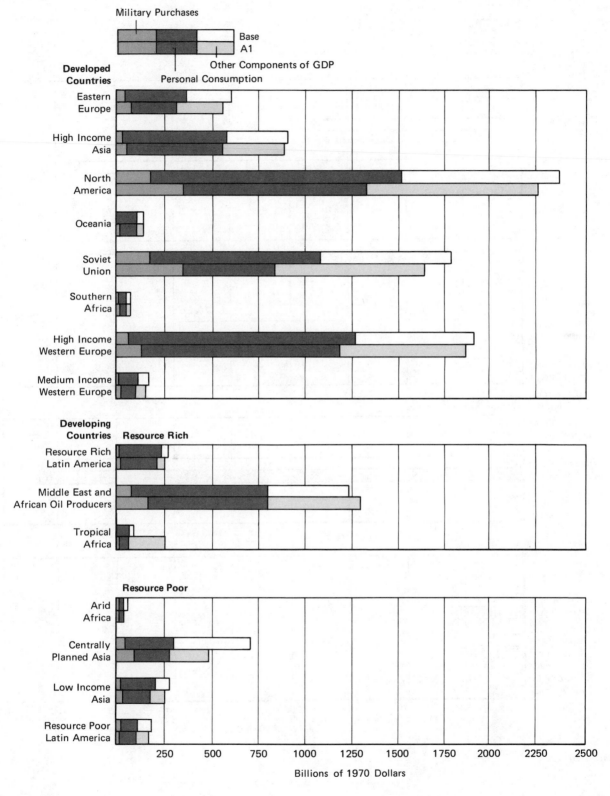

Source: Annex C

FIGURE 26 Investment under Scenario A1 and the Base Scenario in 2000

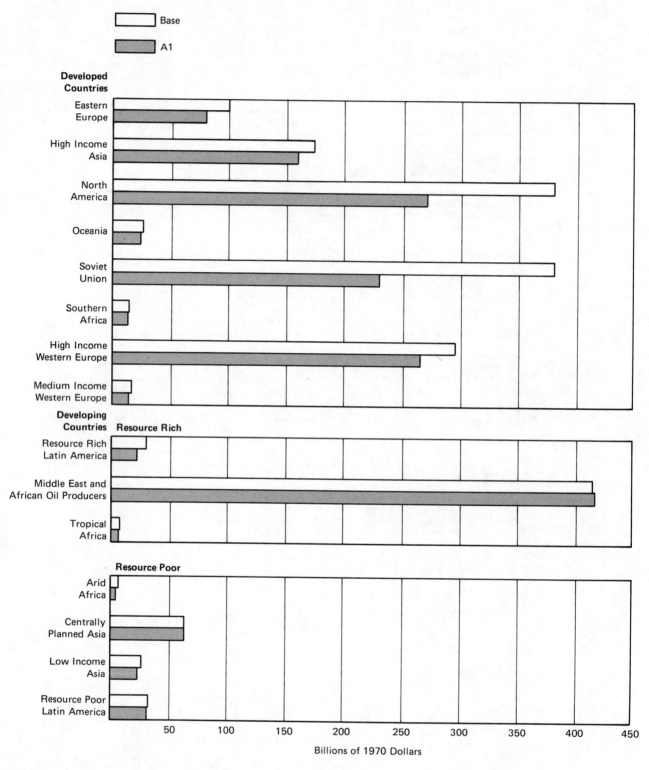

Source: Annex C

TABLE 23 Ten Goods and Services Showing the Greatest Decline in World Output from the Base Scenario to Scenario A1 in 2000

	Base	A1	Percentage Change
Construction	$1,537.0	$1,290.5	− 16.0
Cement	26.5	23.3	− 12.1
Glass	226.3	198.7	− 12.1
Textiles, apparel	514.3	457.1	− 11.1
Wood and cork	121.5	108.3	− 10.9
Shipbuilding and other transportation equipment	66.9	60.6	− 9.4
Trade	2,026.1	1,848.9	− 8.7
Motor vehicles	418.7	383.7	− 8.4
Printing	243.4	223.2	− 8.3
Services	3,535.6	3,244.8	− 8.2

Note: All goods and services are measured in billions of 1970 U.S. dollars.
Source: Annex C.

TABLE 24 Goods and Services Showing the Smallest Decline in World Output from the Base Scenario to Scenario A1 in 2000

	Base	A1	Percentage Change
Aircraft	128.1	154.1	20.3
Electrical machinery[a]	416.2	416.0	0
Instruments	94.2	93.4	− 1.0
Primary metal processing	434.0	424.7	− 2.1
Root crops	901.2	884.4	− 1.9
Machinery	554.3	539.6	− 2.7
Grains	2,871.6	2,788.8	− 2.9
High protein crops	347.9	335.8	− 3.5
Animal products	480.6	463.9	− 3.5
Communications	233.7	225.0	− 3.7

a. Includes civilian electronic components except those explicitly classified as military electronics.
Note: The agricultural products are measured in millions of metric tons. All other goods are measured in billions of 1970 U.S. dollars.
Source: Annex C.

TABLE 25 World Resource Output under Scenario A1 (Percentage Change from the Base Scenario) in 2000

	Base	A1	Percentage Change Between Base and A1
Petroleum	14757.40	15332.5	3.9
Nickel	1998.80	2061.1	3.1
Copper	21.97	21.91	− 0.3
Zinc	16.70	16.65	− 0.3
Bauxite	35.79	35.39	− 1.1
Lead	13.56	13.31	− 1.8
Iron	1475.60	1418.0	− 3.9
Coal	7712.90	7290.70	− 5.5
Natural gas	5556.40	5192.90	− 6.5
Other resources	61.80	55.80	− 9.7

Note: All resources are measured in millions of metric tons except nickel (thousands of metric tons), and the residual Other resources (billions of 1970 U.S. dollars). Petroleum and natural gas are expressed in coal (BTU) equivalent.
Source: Annex C.

shift to military spending. Requirements for construction activities and related materials like cement, glass, and wood decline the most. Demand for most raw materials at the World Model level of aggregation is only moderately affected. The great surge (increase of about 20 percent) in the production of civilian aircraft appears certain to be a bottleneck.

CHAPTER 8

Trade in Military Goods

According to the Base scenario computations, about 12 percent of the military hardware produced in 1980 entered into international trade compared with 8 percent in 1970 and a projected 16 percent by the year 2000.

The United States and the Soviet Union cover their military needs almost entirely through domestic production, but imports are as high as 12 percent of procurement in Western Europe and 16 percent in Eastern Europe. (See Table 26.) The rest of the world imports about half of the military hardware it deploys: this percentage would naturally be even higher if China were excluded.

While the Soviet Union and Eastern Europe account for more than half of the military goods (in dollar value) produced in the world in 1980 according to World Model computations, over 60 percent of the world exports originate in North America and Western Europe. The ten World Model regions comprising the rest of the world produce about 8 percent of world output and furnish 3 percent of exports, with the proportions varying by type of commodity; their procurement, however, amounts to about 16 percent of the world total. These ten regions absorb over 70 percent of world exports of military goods. (These figures are given in Table 27.)

At levels of military spending lower than those of the Base scenario, a reduced reliance on military imports in these ten regions can be accomplished by some combination of reduced procurement and increased domestic production. With steep increases in military spending above Base scenario levels, even a reduction in the proportion of procurement goods that is imported may require increases both in domestic production and in the level of imports.

Both scenarios D2 and D3 described in this chapter specify lower levels of military spending than those assumed in the Base scenario. They differ from each other in that under scenario D2 the import coefficients, which govern the ratio of imports to domestic

TABLE 26   Military Imports as a Percentage of Total Procurement under the Base Scenario in 1980

	North America	Soviet Union	Western Europe	Eastern Europe	All Other Regions
Military aircraft	1.3	2.2	11.1	1.6	51.6
Military shipbuilding	1.1	0	2.4	20.1	45.2
Military communications Equipment	1.2	1.1	13.8	15.9	44.9
Missiles	1.1	0	10.5	54.9	55.2
Tanks	3.2	1.2	23.6	5.3	63.1
Other[a]	1.2	1.1	13.3	15.8	43.6
Total	1.2	1.2	11.7	16.2	50.6

a. "Other" includes Ammunition, Small arms, and Other ordnance.
Source: Annex C.

TABLE 27 Geographical Distribution of Procurement, Production, and Trade
in Military Goods under the Base Scenario in 1980

	Soviet Union and Eastern Europe				North America and Western Europe				All Other Regions			
	Percentage of Worldwide:				Percentage of Worldwide:				Percentage of Worldwide:			
	Procure-ment	Out-put	Ex-ports	Im-ports	Procure-ment	Out-put	Ex-ports	Im-ports	Procure-ment	Out-put	Ex-ports	Im-ports
Military aircraft	48	50	41	17	34	40	57	13	18	10	2	70
Military shipbuilding	54	56	32	2	31	36	67	8	15	8	1	90
Military communications Equipment	45	47	27	14	35	42	68	14	20	11	5	72
Missiles	55	56	41	29	37	40	58	16	8	4	1	55
Tanks	55	61	36	8	18	30	64	16	27	9	0	76
Other[a]	45	46	27	14	36	43	68	15	19	11	5	71
Total	49	52	36	15	34	40	61	14	17	8	3	71

a. "Other" includes Ammunition, Small arms, and Other ordnance.
Notes: For each region, output plus imports equals procurement plus exports.
For the world as a whole, output equals procurement and imports equal exports.
Source: Annex C.

production of military goods, are assumed to be the same as under the Base scenario, while under scenario D3 these coefficients are reduced by half. The regions which under the Base scenario import all their procurement goods are assigned the import coefficient of Resource poor Latin America, a developing region with a growing defense industry, in 1990 and 2000.

Scenarios A1 and A2 both involve increases in military spending above the Base scenario. Under scenario A2 the import coefficients for military goods are reduced to half the corresponding Base scenario values; under A1, by contrast, the Base values are doubled on the assumption that domestic production cannot keep pace with the growth in military spending. The four scenarios are described in more detail in Chapter 4.

Military imports and exports computed under scenarios D3 and A2, and under the Base scenario, are shown in Figures 27 and 28. Both the imports and the exports of military goods naturally decrease under D3 relative to the Base scenario, due to the combination of reduced military spending and reduced concentration of production. With the increased military purchases specified in A2, absolute levels of trade are generally larger than under the Base scenario despite the reduction in import coefficients.

The three resource rich less-developed regions, Resource rich Latin America, the Middle East and African oil producing nations, and Tropical Africa, are all assumed under the Base scenario to produce no military goods. Production of the new domestic

industry is large enough under scenario A2 to *reduce* imports relative to the Base scenario for these regions.

Another apparent exception illustrated in Figure 27 is Arid Africa, whose military imports are greater under scenario D3 than the Base scenario. This is explained by the significant increase of GDP and thus the overall level of military activity in this region (see Chapter 6), which are higher than under the Base scenario, made possible by the inflow of additional aid.

Scenarios A1 and A2 and, respectively, scenarios D2 and D3 differ only in assumptions regarding import coefficients for military goods: the GDPs of all regions increase (or remain unchanged) with the worldwide decline in military trade (assumed under scenarios A2 and D3) accompanied by significant increases in military production in the present client regions and corresponding declines in production in the regions that currently produce these goods for export (shown in Figure 29). The impacts on GDP are among the greatest in the three Resource rich less-developed regions: these are precisely those regions that are assumed to have the highest amount of import-substitution (by domestic production) for military goods.

Changes in per capita consumption, shown in Figure 30, generally follow those of GDP. Consumption *declines* in those developed regions whose military imports under the Base scenario exceed their exports because their military production *increases* under Scenarios D3 and A2. This is the case for High income Asia, Oceania, and Southern Africa, which are

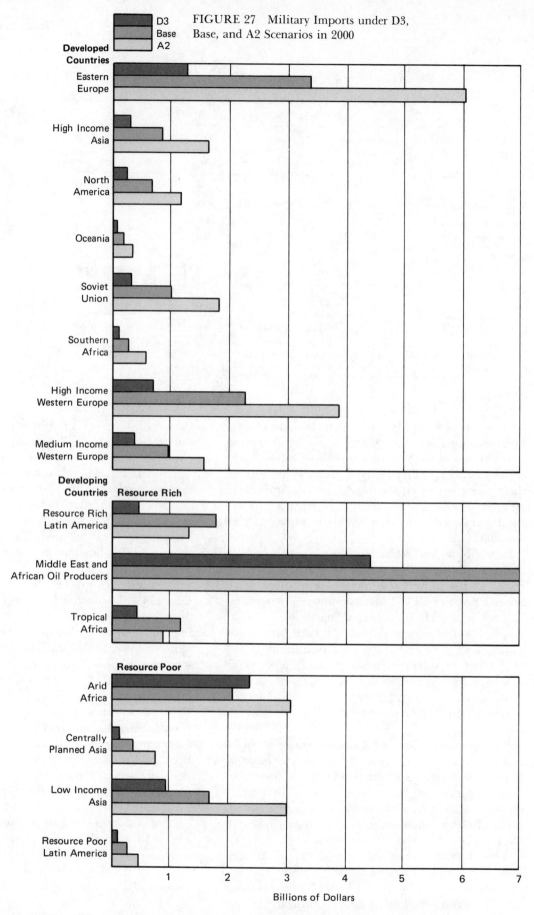

FIGURE 27 Military Imports under D3, Base, and A2 Scenarios in 2000

Note: The Gross Domestic Products of the five regions not shown were the same under A1 and A2 and under D1 and D2. Source: Computer printouts and Annex C

58

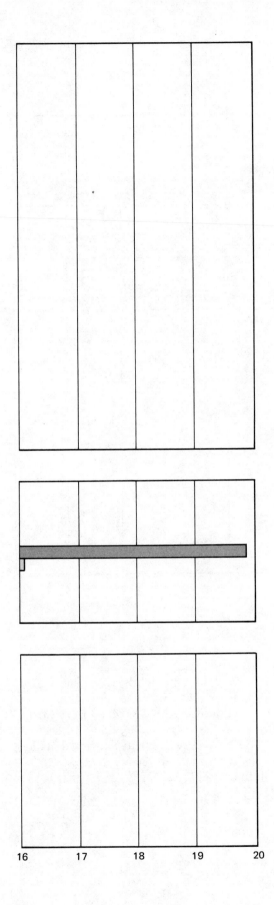

16   17   18   19   20

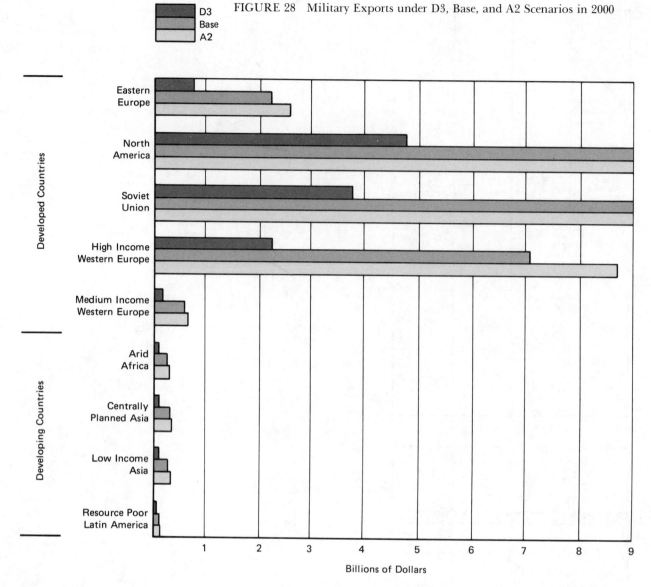

FIGURE 28   Military Exports under D3, Base, and A2 Scenarios in 2000

Source: Computer printouts and Annex C

assumed to export no military goods, as well as for Eastern Europe despite its significant level of domestic production.

The increases in GDP and in per capita consumption in those developed countries which are major arms exporters, and decreases in those which are net importers, all of which operate under a labor constraint, indicate that in all developed regions labor appears to be used more efficiently in civilian than in military production. The increases in GDP and per capita consumption in the less developed world, where growth is assumed in the model to be constrained by the balance of payments, suggest that their foreign exchange is more efficiently used for civilian than for military imports.

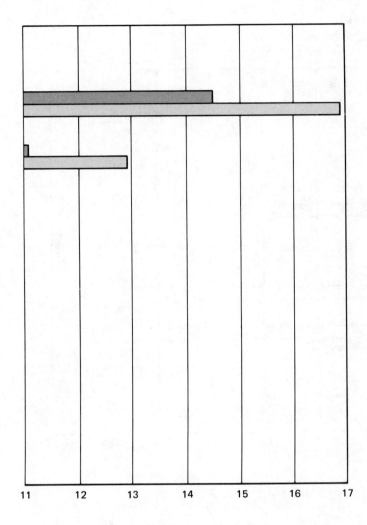

11   12   13   14   15   16   17

FIGURE 29 Gross Domestic Product under Scenarios A2 (Percentage Change from A1) and D3 (Percentage Change from D2) in 2000

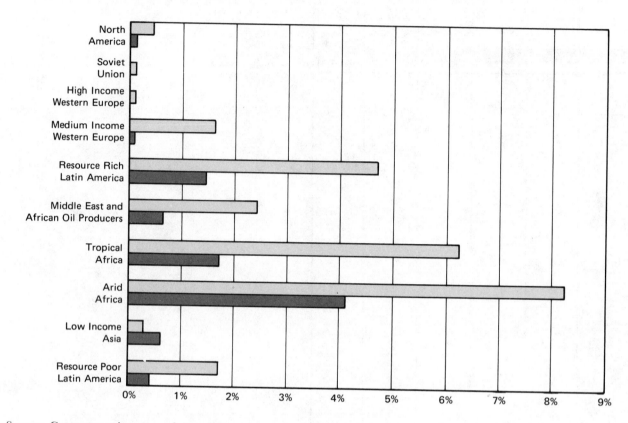

Source: Computer printouts and Annex C

FIGURE 30   Per Capita Consumption under Scenarios A2 (Percentage Change from A1) and D3 (Percentage Change from D2) in 2000

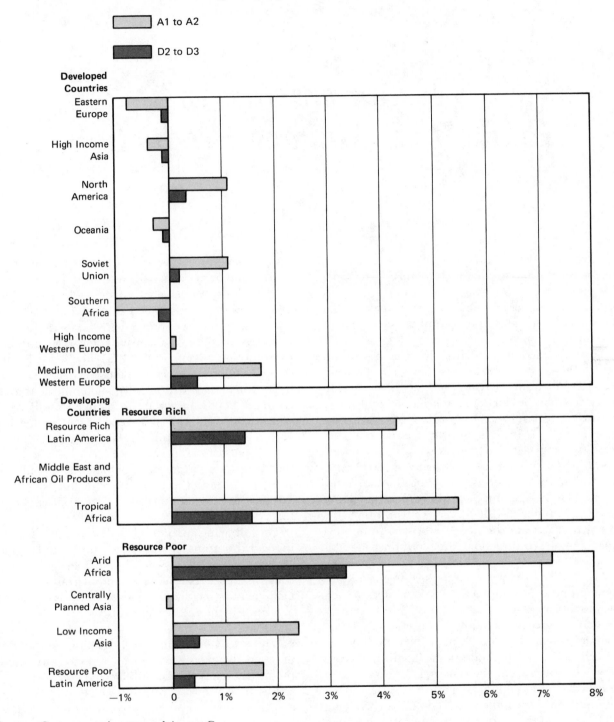

Source: Computer printouts and Annex C

CHAPTER 9

Requirements for Civilian vs. Military Production

The World Model traces the interrelationships among the producing and consuming sectors of each regional economy, making it possible to assess the direct as well as the indirect contributions of all the different industries to the satisfaction of military and civilian demand.

These distinctions are particularly useful for anticipating potential bottlenecks that might hinder a smooth shift from civilian to military or from military to civilian production. For example, contrary to the position taken by some industry spokesmen at the time, as early as 1945 the Bureau of Labor Statistics correctly predicted that the U.S. postwar economy would require even more steel than was produced at the peak of the war effort. This projection was based on the analysis of an input-output table representing the U.S. economy in 1939 that correctly identified the intensive direct and indirect use of steel in outputs like civilian construction and consumer durable goods.

The ability to make such distinctions also holds some promise, as a supplement to other techniques, for monitoring and verifying compliance with arms limitation agreements based on the analysis of fragmentary economic data. A model like the one described in this volume integrates the military economy with the rest of the economy and provides a framework for assembling data from diverse sources, for incorporating engineering data (instead of relying exclusively on the release of more sensitive information about the military economy) and for constructing scenarios based on alternative assumptions so as to make full use of all available information. In this way, the detailed flows to military final demand can possibly be deduced from the other information. The chances for success of such an endeavor are considerably enhanced if military final demand can be distinguished in terms of its direct and indirect requirements from other economic activities.

The World Model does not at the present time separately track minerals like thallium and germanium, which were apparently among the raw materials used most intensively for U.S. military consumption in 1972 [DOD, 1975]. The World Model sector "Other resources" includes these as well as nuclear materials, silicon, silver, and others. Among produced goods, important items like various types of metal fasteners with specialized uses are aggregated with many different kinds of fabricated metal products. Inputs of various types of labor are also combined into a single category. For these reasons only the economically most important raw materials and aggregate categories of other inputs can be discussed in this chapter.

The following analysis is based on a comparison of the world outputs of various resources, goods, and services under the Base scenario and under alternative scenarios specifying decreases and increases in military spending below and above the levels projected according to the Base scenario (discussed in Chapters 6 and 7).

With decreases in military spending, outputs of most goods and services increase, except for those produced exclusively for military end use. The greatest rise is registered in furniture and fixtures, textiles and apparel, construction and construction materials, fertilizer and certain food crops. (See Table 18 in Chapter 6.)

When military spending is increased, the outputs of construction and construction materials, textiles and apparel are most depressed among the civilian sectors (see Table 23 in Chapter 7), but transportation equipment other than aircraft, and services including wholesale and retail trade, decline too.

Agricultural outputs, which increase significantly with aid transfers to the poorest regions, are among those showing the smallest responses to changes in military spending; this is not surprising since military personnel have to eat in or out of uniform. (Tables 18 and 24). The mineral resources are also among the outputs which change the least from one scenario to another (Tables 20 and 25). Thus, while most minerals appear to be used less intensively in military than in the average of all other uses, nonetheless, given the constraints under which the various economies are assumed to operate, roughly the same mix and quantities of primary resources are absorbed over a relatively broad range of military spending patterns. Coal and natural gas and the residual category including all resources not specifically identified are, however, in noticeably greater demand at lower levels of military spending.

Certain goods and resources can be identified as being used more intensively, despite reduction in the overall level of economic activity, with a rise in military spending. Most notable is the case of civilian aircraft, with electrical (including electronic) machinery and measuring and other instruments registering little change. Among the minerals, demand for petroleum and nickel rises with increases in military spending. (See Tables 24 and 25.) These results naturally depend on the production technologies: if metallic alloys are progressively replaced in the aerospace industry by advanced composite materials, the use of nickel in military production can be expected to decline.

The fact that the developed regions, if they maintain their levels of aggregate employment, can raise their GDPs by reducing military spending (established in Chapter 6) and reduce their GDPs by increasing military spending (established in Chapter 7) implies that more people (including armed forces) are employed directly and indirectly to provide each additional dollar's worth of military final demand than to provide an additional dollar's worth of the presumed mix of non-military final demand. (This result cannot, of course, be expected to hold in a comparison with *selected* civilian objectives, like operating child-care centers.) Labor productivity in other words is *lower* in the "military economy" than in the overall production for non-military final demand. Capital requirements per dollar of output, on the other hand, appear in all cases to be higher at lower levels of military spending.

CHAPTER 10

Concluding Observations

The evidence presented in this volume suggests that virtually all economies are able to increase total output and per capita consumption as they progressively reduce their military spending from the very high levels assumed in some scenarios through the baseline case to levels lower than those that would be anticipated in the absence of multilateral arms control agreements. A given percentage reduction in military spending naturally releases the most resources for alternative uses, relative to the total productive capability of the economy, in regions where military spending currently absorbs the largest proportion of national income. Thus the greatest percentage increases in GDP and per capita consumption are registered in Arid Africa, the Soviet Union, and Eastern Europe. However, per dollar of reduced military purchases, it is the poorest of the less-developed regions whose output and per capita consumption improve the most: this growth is explained by sizable additions to capital stocks made possible in part by replacing military imports by shipments of machinery and other capital goods.

If all regions of the world were to reduce their military purchases and if moreover the rich regions transfer part of the resulting "savings" to the poorest of the less developed regions in the form of developmental assistance, this transfer of income would result in increased worldwide levels of production, trade, and consumption. Per billion dollars of additional aid received, consumption and growth would increase more in Arid Africa than in the other recipient regions, and least in Low income Asia. But even with a massive rise in economic aid as well as the reduction in their own military spending, the "gap" in economic well-being between the recipient regions and the others would be barely narrowed. Only if the transfers of resources just described are accompanied by changes in the *structures* of the poor economies might the economic prospects for the future of the poor less-developed regions appear less gloomy.

At the present time, production of military goods is concentrated in a handful of developed countries. All regions would appear to benefit (as measured by increases in GDP and per capita consumption) at given regional levels of military spending if client regions continued to reduce their reliance on imports of these commodities by accelerating domestic production. The labor forces of all developed regions—both those that currently specialize in military production and those that do not—seem to be used more efficiently in producing civilian than military goods and services. At the same time, the foreign exchange of less-developed regions can be spent more productively on civilian than on military imports.

Finally, our analysis suggests certain differences in the inputs required directly and indirectly to satisfy civilian vs. military final demand. The outputs of clothing and construction activities and materials increase more than those of other sectors when military spending declines, and produced consumer goods and services fall off the most when military spending increases. Aside from the goods and services produced exclusively for military final demand, only civilian aircraft, petroleum, and nickel are used more intensively in military than in civilian production. With respect to factor inputs, satisfying a billion dollars' worth of military final demand requires on the average more labor and less capital than to provide for civilian final demand of equivalent value. The demand for and output of most raw materials change only moderately under a wide range of assumptions about the level of military spending.

Bibliography

Aerospace Facts and Figures 1978/79, Economic Data Service, Aerospace Research Center, McGraw-Hill Book Co., New York, 1978.

Anderson, Marion, "The Empty Pork Barrel," Prepared for the Employment Research Associates, Lansing, Mich. (no date).

Aspin, Les, "The Three Percent Solution: NATO and the U.S. Defense Budget," *Challenge*, New York, May–June 1979.

Becker, Abraham S., *Military Expenditure Limitation, for Arms Control: Problems and Prospects*, Ballinger Publishing Co., Cambridge, Mass., 1977.

Bernard, Jean Thomas, and Michel Truchon, *L'Impact du desarmament sur l'économie canadienne*, Départment d'Économique, Université Laval, August 1980.

Binkin, Martin, *Support Costs in the Defense Budget: The Submerged One-third*, Brookings Institution, Washington, D.C., 1972.

Bischof, Henrik, "Militarbezienungen zwischen den kommunistischen Staaten und der dritten Welt," *Monats Berichte*, pp. 403–56, Bonn, June 1977.

Bjerkholt, Olav, Adne Cappelen, Nils Petter Gleditsch, and Knut Moum, *Disarmament and Development: A Study of Conversion in Norway*, International Peace Research Institute, Oslo, May 1980. Prepared for the United Nations Centre for Disarmament.

Bond, Daniel L., and Donald W. Green, *Re-analyzing the Place of National Defense in the Soviet Economy*, Strategic Studies Center of Stanford Research Institute, Washington, D.C., 1978. Prepared for the U.S. Arms Control and Disarmament Agency.

Carter, Anne P., and Peter A. Petri, "Aspects of a New World Development Strategy II: Factors Affecting the Long-Term Prospects of Developing Nations," *Journal of Policy Modeling*, Vol. 1, no. 3, September 1979, pp. 350–81.

Compagnie Française d'Assurance pour le Commerce Extérieur, *Investment and Export Financing*, Société Générale, Paris, 1977.

Dresch, Stephen P., *Disarmament: Economic Consequences and Development Potential*, United Nations, Department of Economic and Social Affairs, New York, 1972.

——, Robert D. Goldberg, and An-loh Lin, *The Economic Potential of Disarmament Alternatives*, United Nations, Department of Economic and Social Affairs, New York, 1972.

Duchin, Faye, "Economic Consequences of Military Spending," *Journal of Economic Issues*, Vol. 17, no. 2 (June 1983).

——, "The World Model: An Inter-Regional Input-Output Model of the World Economy," *Proceedings of the 8th IIASA Conference on Global Modeling*, forthcoming.

——, and Daniel Szyld, "Application of Sparse Matrix Techniques to Inter-Regional Input-Output Analysis," *Economics of Planning*, Vol. 15, no. 2–3, 1979.

Dupry, T.N., *The Almanac of World Military Power*, T.N. Dupry Associates/ Stackpole Books, Harrisburg, Pa., 1970.

The Econoscope Group, Inc., *The 1967 Structure of SIC 3741 Aircraft (Civilian and Military); SIC 3731 Shipbuilding Industry (Civilian and Military); Military Communications Equipment (560401) and Civilian Communications (560402); SIC 3729 Aircraft Equipment n.e.c. (Civilian and Military); and SIC 3722 Aircraft Engines and Parts (Civilian and Military)*. Prepared for the Federal Preparedness Administration of the U.S. General Services Administration, Washington, D.C., 1977.

Enthoven, Alain C., and K. Wayne Smith, *How Much Is Enough? Shaping the Defense Program, 1961–69*, Harper and Row, New York, 1972.

Ermarth, Fritz, *Economic Factors and Soviet Arms Control Policy: The Economic Burden of the Soviet Defense Policy*, U.S. Arms Control and Disarmament Agency, Washington, D.C., 1964.

European Parliament, *Two-Way Street. U.S.A.-Europe Arms Procurement*. The Klepsch Report by the European Parliament, Brassey's Publishers, London, 1979.

Faini, Riccardo, Patricia Annez, and Lance Taylor, "Defense Spending, Economic Structure and Growth: Evidence Among Countries and Over Time," Massachusetts Institute of Technology, Cambridge, 1980. Prepared for the United Nations Centre for Disarmament.

Fei, Edward T., "Understanding Arms Transfers and Military Expenditures: Data Problems," in *Arms Transfers in the Modern World*, Stephanie G. Neuman and Robert E. Harkavy (eds.), Praeger Publishers, New York, 1979.

Filip-Kohn, R., R. Krengel, and D. Schumacher, *Macro-Economic Effects of Disarmament Policies on Sectoral Production and Employment in the Federal Republic of Germany, with Special Emphasis on Development Policy Issues*, German Institute for Economic Research, Berlin, May 1980. Prepared for the United Nations Centre for Disarmament.

Forsberg, Randall, Martin Moore-Ede, Phillip Morrison, Phyllis Morrison, George Sommaripa, and Paul Walker (The Boston Study Group), *The Price of Defense, a New Strategy for Military Spending*, Times Books/Division of Quadrangle/The New York Times Book Co., New York, 1979.

Frank, Lewis, *The Arms Trade in International Relations*, Praeger Publishers, New York, 1969.

Freedman, Lawrence, "Britain and the Arms Trade," *International Affairs*, London, Vol. 54, no. 1, July 1978, pp. 377–93.

———, *British Foreign Policy to 1985. Arms Production in the United Kingdom: Problems and Prospects*, Royal Institute of International Affairs, Stephen Austin & Sons, Ltd., Hertford, England, 1978.

Freymond, J.F., *Some Aspects of the Arms Race Developing in Africa, South of the Sahara*, Proceedings of the 26th Pugwash Conference on Science and World Affairs, "Disarmament, Security, and Development," London, 1976.

Gansler, Jacques S., *The Defense Industry*, Massachusetts Institute of Technology Press, Cambridge, 1980.

Glassey, C. Roger, *Statement of Estimates of Prices per Barrel of Petroleum: 1970–2000*, U.S. House of Representatives, Permanent Select Committee on Intelligence, Subcommittee on Oversight, Washington, D.C., October 7, 1979.

Gillingham, Arthur, *Arms Traffic: A Selected Bibliography*, Political Issues Series, Vol. 4, no. 2, Center for the Study of Armament and Disarmament, California State University, Los Angeles, 1976.

Gilmer, Robert W., and Paul McCoy, *An Assessment of Computation Procedures to Determine Requirements of Critical and Strategic Materials*, IDA Paper P-1238, Institute for Defense Analysis, Program Analysis Division, U.S. Department of Defense, Washington, D.C., August 1977.

Haftendorn, Helga, *Militarhilfe und Rustungsexporte de BRD*, Bertelsmann Universitatsverlag, Dusseldorf, West Germany, 1971.

Hamer, John, "World Arms Sales," *Editorial Research Reports*, Congressional Quarterly, Inc., Washington, D.C., Vol. 1, no. 17, May 1976.

Harkavy, Robert, *The Arms Trade and International Systems*, Ballinger Publishing Co., Cambridge, Mass., 1975.

Hoagland, John H., *World Combat Aircraft Inventories and Production: 1970–1975, Implications for Arms Transfer Policies*, Arms Control Project, U.S. Arms Control and Disarmament Agency, Washington, D.C., 1970.

Hughes, Mark D., Sanford Baum, Evan Just, Mark D. Levine, and Steve W. Woodcock, *Strategic Resources and National Security: An Initial Assessment*. U.S. Department of Defense, Washington, D.C., April 1975. Prepared for the Rome Air Development Center, Griffith Air Force Base, New York.

Huisken, Ron, *Background Notes: Disarmament and Development*. Prepared for the United Nations Centre for Disarmament, 1976.

Information Clearing House, Inc., *The Directory of Defense Electronic Products and Services, United States Suppliers 1979*, Fifth Revised Edition by the Electronics Industries Association, Washington, D.C., 1979.

International Labor Office, *Labor Force Estimates and Projections*, ILO Publications, Geneva, 1977.

Isnard, Jacques, "Les Exportations d'armes pour la France," *Le Monde*, Paris, January 1971.

Janes Yearbook, *All the World's Fighting Ships*, Franklin Watts, New York, 1979.

———, *All the World's Military Aircraft*, Franklin Watts, New York, 1979.

———, *All the World's Weapon Systems*, Franklin Watts, New York, 1979.

Joshua, Wynfred, and Stephen Gilbert, *Arms for the Third World*, The Johns Hopkins Press, Baltimore, 1969.

Kemp, Geoffrey, *Classification of Weapons Systems and Force Designs in Less Developed Country Environments: Implications for Arms Transfer Policies*, U.S. Arms Control and Disarmament Agency, Washington, D.C., 1970.

Kends, I., *War, the Process of Armaments and Arms Trade in the Countries of Asia, Africa and Latin America*, Proceedings of the 25th Pugwash Conference in Science and World Affairs, London, 1975.

Kennedy, Gavin, *The Military in the Third World*, Duckworth and Co., London, 1974.

Klein, Jean, "Commerce des armes et politique: Le cas français," *Politique Etrangère*, Paris, Vol. 41, no. 5, 1976, pp. 563–86.

Kokat, Robert G., "Some Implications of the Economic Impact of Disarmament on the Structure of the American Industry," *International Review for Social Sciences* (Switzerland), Vol. XIX, no. 3, 1966, pp. 481–503.

Kolodziej, Edward, "Measuring French Arms Transfers," *Journal of Conflict Resolution*, Vol. 23, no. 2, 1979, pp. 195–227.

Krueger, Paul K., *Modeling Future Requirements for Metals and Minerals*, Federal Preparedness Agency of the U.S. General Services Administration, Washington, D.C., 1979. Presented at 14th International APCOM Symposium, October 1976, Penn State Univ.

La Marche, René, "France: The Hard Sell," *Agenor*, pp. 22–26, Paris, 1974.

Leontief, Wassily, S. Dresch, F. Duchin, D. Fischer, and I. Sohn, *Preliminary Study of Worldwide Economic and Social Implications of a Limitation on Military Spending (An Input-Output Approach)*, Institute for Economic Analysis, New York, 1978. Prepared for the United Nations Centre for Disarmament.

———, Anne P. Carter, and Peter A. Petri, *The Future of the World Economy*, A United Nations Study, Oxford University Press, New York, 1977.

——— and Faye Duchin, *Worldwide Economic Implica-*

tions of a Limitation on Military Spending, Institute for Economic Analysis, New York, June 1980a. Prepared for United Nations Centre for Disarmament.

—— and Faye Duchin, *Worldwide Implications of Hypothetical Changes in Military Spending (An Input-Output Approach).* Institute for Economic Analysis, New York, August 1980b. Prepared for U.S. Arms Control and Disarmament Agency.

—— and Marvin Hoffenberg, "The Economic Effects of Disarmament," *Scientific American,* April 1961.

——, Alison Morgan, Karen Polenske, David Simpson, and Edward Turner, "The Economic Impact—Industrial and Regional—of an Arms Cut," *Review of Economics and Statistics,* Vol. 47, no. 3, 1965, pp. 217–41.

——, and Peter A. Petri, *Impact of Disarmament on Strategic Raw Materials Demand: Effects of General Compensated Reductions in Worldwide Military Expenditures and Impacts on Certain Developing Countries,* United Nations, Department of Political and Security Council Affairs, New York, 1971.

Levine, Mark D., and Irving W. Yabroff, *Department of Defense Materials Consumption and the Impact of Material and Energy Resource Shortages, Final Report,* Stanford Research Institute, Arlington, Va., 1975. Prepared for U.S. Army Missile Command, Technology Assessment Office.

Maspero, François, *La France trafiquant d'armes,* Centre Locale d'Information et de Coordination pour l'Action Nonviolent, Paris, 1974.

Moodie, Michael, *Sovereignty, Security and Arms,* Center for Strategic and International Studies, Sage Publications, Beverly Hills, Calif., 1979.

Morrison, Phillip, and Paul F. Walker, "A New Strategy for Military Spending," *Scientific American,* Vol. 239, no. 4, 1978, pp. 48–61.

Petri, Peter, and others, *United Nations World Model Data Documentation* (4 Technical Reports and 11 volumes of documentation), Brandeis University, Unpublished, 1974–79.

Russett, Bruce M., *What Price Viligance?* Yale University Press, New Haven, 1970.

Ra'anan, Uri, *The USSR Arms the Third World,* Massachusetts Institute of Technology Press, Cambridge, 1969.

Sellers, Robert C., *Armed Forces of the World: A Reference Handbook,* Fourth Edition, Praeger Special Studies in International Politics and Government, New York, 1977.

Shipbuilders Council of America, *Annual Report 1977,* Washington, D.C., 1978.

Sivard, Ruth, *World Military and Social Expenditures,* Institute for World Order, WMSE Publications, Leesburg, Va., 1974.

Sreedhar, and S.K. Ghosh, "China's Foreign Aid Programme," *The Institute for Foreign Studies and Analysis Journal,* Vol. 5, no. 1, pp. 21–44, New Delhi, July 1972.

Stanley, John, and Maurice Pearton, *The International Trade in Arms,* Institute of Strategic Studies, Praeger Publishers, New York, 1972.

Stockholm International Peace Research Institute [SIPRI], *The Arms Trade with the Third World,* Humanities Press, New York, 1971.

——, *World Armaments and Disarmament, SIPRI Yearbook,* Crane, Russak and Co., New York, 1973, 1978, 1979.

——, *The Arms Trade Registers, SIPRI Monograph,* Stockholm, 1974.

Uhlig, Christian, *Entwicklungshilfe politik,* Institute für Wirtschaftsforschung, Verlag Weltarchiv, Hamburg, West Germany, 1971.

United Nations, *Disarmament: A Select Bibliography, 1967–1972.* New York, 1973a. *1973–1977,* 1978. Prepared by the Dag Hammarskjold Library.

——, *World Population Prospects as Assessed in 1973,* Population #60, XIII, New York, 1973b.

——, *Reduction of the Military Budgets of States Permanent Members of the Security Council by 10 Percent and Utilization of Part of the Funds Thus Saved To Provide Assistance to Developing Countries,* Department of Political and Security Council Affairs, New York, 1975.

——, *Reduction of Military Budgets: Measurement and International Reporting of Military Expenditures.* Prepared by the Group of Experts on the Reduction of Military Budgets, Department of Political and Security Council Affairs, New York, 1977.

——, *Statistical Yearbook 1977,* 29th Edition, New York, 1978a.

——, General Assembly (10th Special Session, Item 11), *Adoption of a Programme of Action on Disarmament,* A/S-10/9. Report of the Ad Hoc Group on the Relationship Between Disarmament and Development, with a note by the Secretary-General, New York, April 1978b.

——, *Appendix to Swedish Working Paper on Available Literature in the Field of Disarmament and Development,* Includes: *Swedish Working Paper on Available Literature in the Field of Disarmament and Development,* comp. Inga Thorson, New York, January 1979.

——, General Assembly (36th Session), *Reduction of Military Budgets,* Report of the Secretary General, New York, August 1981.

U.S. Arms Control and Disarmament Agency [ACDA], *World Military Expenditures, 1971,* Washington, D.C., 1972a.

——, *The Economic Impact of Reductions in Defense Spending: Summary of Research Prepared for the United States Arms Control and Disarmament Agency,* Washington, D.C., 1972b.

——, *The International Transfer of Conventional Arms,* Report to the U.S. Senate Committee on Foreign Affairs, Washington, D.C., 1974.

——, *Arms Control 1978,* Eighteenth Annual Report, Washington, D.C., 1979a.

——, *World Military Expenditures and Arms Transfers,* Washington, D.C., 1979b and 1980.

U.S. Central Intelligence Agency, *USSR: Hard Currency Trade and Payments, 1977–1978,* National Foreign Assessment Center, Washington, D.C., 1977.

——, *Arms Flows to LDC's: U.S.-Soviet Comparisons 1974–1978,* National Foreign Assessment Center, Washington, D.C., Novermber 1978a.

——, *Changing Patterns in Soviet-LDC Trade, 1976–1977,* National Foreign Assessment Center, Washington, D.C., 1978b.

———, *Communist Aid to Less Developed Countries of the Free World, 1977*, National Foreign Assessment Center, Washington, D.C., 1978c.

———, *Estimated Soviet Defense Spending: Trends and Prospects*, National Foreign Assessment Center, Washington, D.C., 1978d.

———, *Soviet Civil Defense*, National Foreign Assessment Center, July 1978e.

———, *A Dollar Cost Comparison of Soviet and U.S. Defense Activities, 1968–1978*, National Foreign Assessment Center, Washington, D.C., 1979.

U.S. Congress, *Foreign Military Sales and Assistance Act*, Hearings Before the Committee on Foreign Relations, 93rd Congress, Washington, D.C., May 2–4, 1973.

———, *Allocation of Resources in the Soviet Union and China*, Hearings Before the Subcommittee on Priorities and Economy in Government of the Joint Economic Committee, 94th and 95th Congress, Washington, D.C., Parts 1 through 4, 1975–78.

———, *Soviet Economy in a New Perspective: A Compendium of Papers*, Submitted to the Joint Economic Committee, 92nd Congress, 2nd Session, Washington, D.C., October 14, 1976.

———, *Report on the Activities of the Subcommittee on Defense Cooperation*, presented by A. Hamilton McDonald, Washington, D.C., 1977a.

———, Hearings before the Subcommittee on International Security, House of Representatives, March 30–31, 1977, Washington, D.C., 1977b.

———, *Security Assistance to Asia for Fiscal Year 1978*, Report of a Special Mission to Asia, April 8–21, 1977, by Members of the Subcommittee on Asian and Pacific Affairs of the House Committee on International Relations, Washington, D.C., June 19, 1977c.

———, *Issues Concerning the Transfer of United States Defense Manufacturing Technology. Co-production Manufacturing Licenses, and Technical Assistance Agreements*, Report prepared for the House Committee on International Relations, 95th Congress, 1st Session, by the Foreign Affairs and National Defense Division, Congressional Research Service, June 30, 1977, Washington, D.C., 1977d.

———, *Arms Transfer Policy*, Report to the 95th Congress, 1st Session, for the use of Committee on Foreign Relations of the U.S. Senate, Washington, D.C., July 1977e.

———, *Conventional Arms Transfer Policy. Background Information*, compilation prepared by the Subcommittee on International Security and Scientific Affairs of the House Committee on International Relations, 95th Congress, 2nd Session, Washington, D.C., February 1, 1978a.

———, *The U.S. Balance of International Payments and the U.S. Economy*, Background Paper by the Congressional Budget Office of the U.S. Congress, Washington, D.C., February 1978b.

———, *United States Arms Transfer and Security Assistance Programs*, prepared for the Subcommittee on Europe and the Middle East, House Committee on International Relations, by the Foreign Affairs and National Defense Division of the Congressional Research Service, March 21, 1978, Washington, D.C., February 1978c.

———, *U.S. Special Session on Disarmament*, Hearings before the Subcommittee on International Security and Scientific Affairs and on International Organization of the House Committee on International Relations, 95th Congress, 2nd Session, May 3, 1978, Washington, D.C., 1978d.

———, *Export Stimulation Programs in the Major Industrial Countries: The United States and Eight Major Competitors*, prepared for the Committee on International Relations of the U.S. House of Representatives, 95th Congress, 2nd Session, Washington, D.C., October 6, 1978e.

———, *Arms Trade in the Western Hemisphere*, Hearings before the Subcommittee on Inter-American Affairs of the House Committee on International Relations, 95th Congress, 2nd Session, Washington, D.C., February 1979a.

———, *Foreign Assistance Legislation for Fiscal Years 1980–1981* (part 2), Hearings before the Subcommittee on International Security and Scientific Affairs of the House Committee on Foreign Affairs, 96th Congress, 1st Session, Overview of Security Supporting Assistance Programs, Washington, D.C., February–March 1979b.

———, *Fiscal Year 1980 Arms Control Impact Statements*, submitted to the Congress by the President pursuant to Section 36 of the Arms Control and Disarmament Act, for use by the Committee on Foreign Relations and Foreign Affairs of the Senate and House, Washington, D.C., March 1979c.

———, *U.S. Export Control Policy and Extension of the Export Administration Act*, Hearings before the Senate Committee on Banking, Housing and Urban Affairs, 96th Congress, 1st Session, *Part 1: Oversight To Review U.S. Export Control Policy and Proposals To Extend and Revise the Export Administration Act of 1979, as Amended*, March 5, 6, 1979d.

———, *Department of Defense Appropriations for 1980*, Hearings before a Subcommittee of the House Committee on Appropriations, 96th Congress, 1st Session, Parts 3 through 10, Washington, D.C., 1979e.

———, *Prospects for Multilateral Arms Export Restraint*, A Staff Report prepared for the use of the Senate Committee on Foreign Relations, April, 1979, 96th Congress, 1st Session, Washington, D.C., 1979f.

———, *Department of Defense Authorizations for Appropriations for Fiscal Year 1980*, Hearings before the Senate Armed Services Committee, 96th Congress, 1st Session, on S. 428, Parts 1,2,3, and 4, January, February, March, April, and May, 1979, Washington, D.C., 1979g.

———, *The U.S. Role in a Changing World Political Economy: Major Issues for the 96th Congress: A Compendium of Papers*, Submitted to the Joint Economic Committee of the 96th Congress, 1st Session, Washington, D.C., June 25, 1979h.

———, *United States Arms Sale Policy and Recent Sales to Europe and the Middle East*, Hearings before the Subcommittee on Europe and the Middle East of the House Committee on International Relations, 95th Congress, 2nd Session, October 5, 1978, Washington, D.C., 1979i.

———, *Soviet Economy in a Time of Change: A Com-*

pendium of Papers, Submitted to the Joint Economic Committee, 96th Congress, 1st Session, Volumes 1 and 2, Washington, D.C., October 10, 1979j.

U.S. Department of Commerce, Bureau of the Census, *Statistical Abstract of the United States*, 99th edition, Washington, D.C., 1978.

U.S. Department of Commerce, Bureau of Economic Analysis [BEA], *Input-Output Structure of the U.S. Economy: 1967*, Washington, D.C., 1974.

——, *The Detailed Input-Output Structure of the U.S. Economy: 1972*, Washington, D.C., 1979.

U.S. Department of Defense, *Dictionary of Military and Associated Terms*, Joint Chiefs of Staff, Washington, D.C., 1974.

——, *Proceedings of the Department of Defense Materials Shortages Workshop*, January 14–16, 1975, Metals and Ceramics Information Center, Battelle Memorial Laboratories, Columbus, Ohio, 1975.

——, *Foreign Military Sales and Military Assistance Facts*, Security Assistance Agency, Washington, D.C., 1977.

——, *Department of Defense, Annual Report Fiscal Year 1979*, Harold Brown, Secretary of Defense, Washington, D.C., 1978.

——, *Manpower Requirements Report and Base Structure Annex to Manpower Requirements Report for FY 1980*, Prepared by the U.S. Department of Defense, Office of the Assistant Secretary of Defense (Manpower, Reserve Affairs, and Logistics), Washington, D.C., January-February 1979.

U.S. Department of Labor, Bureau of Labor Statistics, *Foreign Defense Sales and Grants, Fiscal Years 1973-1975; Labor and Materials Requirements*, Washington, D.C., July 1977.

U.S. General Services Administration, *Identifying Potential Occupational Labor Shortages in Future Mobilization Contingencies*, Federal Preparedness Agency, Washington, D.C., 1979.

Vayrynev, R., *Transnational Corporations and International Transfer of Arms*, Proceedings of the 27th Pugwash Conference on Science and World Affairs, "Peace and Security in a Changing World," London, 1977.

Walter, Robert, *American and Soviet Aid*, University of Pittsburgh Press, Pittsburgh, 1970.

Western European Union (Assembly of), *A European Armaments Policy Symposium*, by the Committee on Defense Questions and Armaments, Official Record, Paris, March 3–4, 1977.

Zurcher, Louis A., and Gwyn Harries-Jenkins (eds.), *Supplementary Military Forces. Reserves, Militias, Auxiliaries*, Sage Research Progress Series on War, Revolution, and Peacekeeping, Vol. 8, Sage Publications, Beverly Hills, Calif./London, 1978.

Note: This Bibliography does not attempt a comprehensive coverage of the enormous literature on the many aspects of worldwide military spending considered in this volume. Instead it contains references to related studies, the principal data sources for this study, and items (particularly those dealing with the international trade in military goods) from which some quantitative information could be extracted for the present work. Also included is some background material which the authors found useful.

ANNEX A

Regional Classifications

TABLE A.1   Regional Classification for the World Model

Region	Country or Territory	Region	Country or Territory
Arid Africa	Chad		Nepal
	Comoro Islands		New Hebrides
	Egypt		Pacific Territories and islands,
	Ethiopia		n.e.c.
	Djibouti		Pakistan
	Israel		Papua New Guinea
	Jordan		Philippines
	Lebanon		Sikkim
	Mali		Singapore
	Mauritania		Sri Lanka
	Morocco		Taiwan
	Niger		Thailand
	Somalia		
	Sudan	Eastern Europe	Albania
	Syrian Arab Republic		Bulgaria
	Tunisia		Czechoslovakia
	Upper Volta		German Democratic Republic
			Hungary
Centrally	China		Poland
planned Asia	Democratic Kampuchea		Romania
	Democratic People's Republic		
	of Korea	High income Asia	Japan
	Democratic Republic of		Ryukyu Islands
	Viet-Nam		
	Mongolia	Resource rich Latin American	Barbados
	Republic of South Viet-Nam		Belize
			Bolivia
Low income Asia	Afghanistan		Colombia
	Bangladesh		Costa Rica
	British Solomon Islands		Dominican Republic
	Brunei		Ecuador
	Bhutan		El Salvador
	Burma		French Guiana
	Fiji Islands		Guadeloupe
	Hong Kong		Guatemala
	India		Guyana
	Indonesia		Haiti
	Republic of Korea		Honduras
	Laos		Jamaica
	Malaysia		Martinique
	Maldive Islands		Nicaragua
	Macao		Panama

73

TABLE A.1 (*Continued*)

Region	Country or Territory	Region	Country or Territory
	Paraguay		Central African Republic
	Peru		Congo
	Surinam		Equatorial Guinea
	Trinidad and Tobago		Gambia
	Venezuela		Ghana
			Guinea
Resource poor Latin America	Argentina		Guinea-Bissau
	Bahamas		Ivory Coast
	Bermuda		Kenya
	Brazil		Lesotho
	Chile		Liberia
	Cuba		Madagascar
	Mexico		Malawi
	St. Lucia/Grenada/		Mauritius
	St. Vincent/Domenica/		Mozambique
	St. Kitts/Nevis/Anguilla/		Rwanda
	Netherlands Antilles/		Sao Tome and Principe
	Turks and Caicos Islands/		Senegal
	Montserrat		Seychelles Islands
	Uruguay		Sierra Leone
			Swaziland
North America	Canada		Togo
	Canal Zone		United Republic of Tanzania
	Greenland		Uganda
	Puerto Rico		Zaire
	United States of America		Zambia
	Virgin Islands		Zimbabwe
Oceania	Australia	High income Western Europe	Andora
	New Zealand		Austria
			Belgium
Middle East and African oil producers	Algeria		Denmark
	Bahrain		Faeroe Islands
	Democratic Yemen		Finland
	Gabon		France
	Iran		Germany, Federal Republic of
	Iraq		Iceland
	Kuwait		Ireland
	Libyan Arab Republic		Italy
	Muscat/Trucial/Oman		Luxembourg
	Nigeria		Netherlands
	Qatar		Norway
	Saudi Arabia		Sweden
	United Arab Emirates		Switzerland
	Yemen		United Kingdom of Great Britain and Northern Ireland (including the Channel Islands and Isle of Man)
Soviet Union	Union of Soviet Socialist Republics		
Southern Africa	South Africa	Medium income Western Europe	Cyprus
	Namibia		Gibraltar
Tropical Africa	Angola		Greece
	Benin		Malta
	Botswana		Portugal
	Burundi		Spain
	Cameroon		Turkey
	Cape Verde		Yugoslavia

TABLE A.2   Regional Groupings

Grouping	Region
Developed Countries	Eastern Europe
	High income Asia
	North America
	Oceania
	Soviet Union
	Southern Africa
	High income Western Europe
	Medium income Western Europe
Resource rich Less Developed Countries	Resource rich Latin America
	Middle east and African oil producing nations
	Tropical Africa
Resource poor Less Developed Countries	Arid Africa
	Centrally planned Asia
	Low income Asia
	Resource poor Latin America

ANNEX B

Sectoral Classifications

Sectors and Activities in the World Model[a]

AB Abatement Activities	FS Fishing	MM Sectoral Imports
CU Cumulative Resource Use	IN Investment and Capital	SE Selected Agriculture and Resource Outputs
EE Sectoral Exports	MA Macroeconomic variables	XX Sectoral Outputs
EM Emissions	MI Outputs of Military Goods and Services	

Sector or Activity | **Unit of Measurement**

Macro-economic variables (MA)

Gross domestic product
Personal consumption
Excess savings
Investment
Government expenditures, military and
   non-military   Billions of 1970 U.S. dollars

Balance of payments   Billions of U.S. dollars in current relative prices

Imports   Billions of 1970 dollars
Exports

Population   Millions
Urban population

Employment   Millions of person years

Nutrition (MA)

Calories   Thousands of calories per day per capita
Proteins   Grams per day per capita

Capital stocks and flows (IN)

Equipment investment, stock
Plant investment, stock
Inventory (change) investment, stock   Billions of 1970 dollars
Foreign investments income (inflow, outflow)

Irrigation investment
Land development   Millions of hectares
Cultivated land area

Selected agriculture (SE, EE, MM)
Livestock
Oil-crops   Millions of metric tons
Grains
Roots

a. The two-letter acronyms correspond to the sectoral classification scheme developed in [Leontief, Carter, and Petri, 1977].

Sector or Activity	**Unit of Measurement**
Selected resources (SE, CU, EE, MM)	
Copper	Millions of metric tons
Bauxite	
Nickel	Thousands of metric tons
Zinc	
Lead	Millions of metric tons
Iron	
Petroleum	
Natural gas	Millions of metric tons Coal (BTU) equivalent
Coal	
Other agriculture and resource variables and margin industries (XX, EE, MM)	
Residual agriculture	
Residual resource activities	Billions of 1970 dollars
Agricultural margins (food)	
Petroleum refining	
Primary metal processing	
Traded goods and services except military (XX, EE, MM)	
Textiles, apparel	
Wood and cork	
Furniture, fixtures	Billions of 1970 dollars
Paper	
Printing	
Rubber	
Industrial chemicals	
Fertilizer	Millions of metric tons
Miscellaneous chemical products	
Cement	
Glass	
Motor vehicles	
Shipbuilding and other transportation equipment	
Aircraft	
Metal products	Billions of 1970 dollars
Machinery	
Electric machinery	
Professional instruments	
Watches, clocks	
Services	
Transport	
Military goods and services (MI, EE, MM)	
Aircraft	
Ships	
Communications equipment	
New construction	
Maintenance	
Missiles	Billions of 1970 dollars
Ammunition, n.e.c.	
Tanks	
Small arms	
Small arms ammunition	
Other ordnance	
Non-traded goods and services (XX)	
Electricity, water	
Construction	Billions of 1970 dollars
Trade	
Communication	

Sector or Activity	**Unit of Measurement**
Fishing variables (FS)	
Fish catch	
Non-human consumption of fish	Millions of metric tons
Fish imports, exports	
Foreign aid and investment (EE, MM)	
Aid	Billions of 1970 dollars
Foreign capital	
Abatement activities (AB)	
Air pollution control	
Primary water treatment	
Secondary water treatment	Millions of metric tons
Tertiary water treatment	
Solid waste disposal	
Emissions of abatable and	
non-abatable pollutants (EM)	
Pesticides	
Particulates	
Biological oxygen demand	
Nitrogen water pollution	Millions of metric tons
Phosphates	
Suspended solids	
Dissolved solids	
Solid waste	

ANNEX C

Scenario Printouts

This annex is a condensed version of the computer printouts generated for this study. All scenarios are listed here in full sectoral detail. The Base scenario is shown for all four decades, 1970, 1980, 1990, and 2000. The other five scenarios are shown only for the year 2000: the results are identical to those of the Base scenario in 1970 and 1980. While the scenarios were computed in fifteen region detail, High and Medium income Western Europe have been aggregated in this Annex into a single region, Western Europe, to reduce the volume of printout. Resource rich and Resource poor Latin America have been similarly aggregated into a single region, Latin America. The region code names are explained in Table C.1, and the countries belonging to each region are listed in Annex A. The units of measurement for all sectors are given in Annex B.

TABLE C.1   Region Code

AAF	Arid Africa
ASC	Centrally planned Asia
ASL	Low income Asia
EEM	Eastern Europe
JAP	High income Asia
LAT	Latin America (Resource rich and Resource poor)
NAH	North America
OCH	Oceania
OIL	Middle East and African oil producers
RUH	Soviet Union
SAF	Southern Africa
TAF	Tropical Africa
WEU	Western Europe (High income and Medium income)

BASE SCENARIO IN 1970

	AAF	ASC	ASL	EEM	JAP	LAT	NAH	OCH	OIL	RUH	SAF	TAF	WEU
CONSUMPTION AND POPULATION													
GDP	26.9	134.8	122.6	164.4	199.8	153.6	1059.5	43.1	36.2	434.9	16.9	23.7	804.4
PERSONAL CONSUMP	20.2	91.3	97.5	106.5	123.7	115.5	684.8	29.7	20.9	242.9	12.7	18.1	564.5
GOVT.(CIVILIAN)	2.7	13.5	12.3	16.4	20.0	15.4	106.0	4.3	3.6	43.5	1.7	2.4	80.4
GOVT.(MILITARY)	2.7	18.2	4.9	12.0	1.6	2.9	78.4	1.4	2.4	60.9	0.4	0.5	28.5
POPULATION	131.2	808.4	1023.2	105.1	104.3	281.4	229.1	15.4	126.5	242.8	21.5	141.4	390.1
URBAN POPULATION	34.5	175.1	207.1	55.5	55.5	158.0	169.5	12.9	34.9	137.3	10.3	17.8	254.2
EMPLOYMENT	10.3	61.8	58.2	56.1	51.9	75.6	92.1	5.7	12.8	112.9	8.9	10.8	153.8
GDP/HEAD	205.0	166.7	119.8	1564.2	1915.6	545.8	4624.6	2798.7	286.2	1791.6	786.0	167.6	2062.0
CONSUMPTION/HEAD	153.8	112.9	95.3	1013.7	1185.6	410.4	2989.0	1926.8	165.3	1000.3	590.1	128.1	1446.9
CALORIES/HEAD	2467.5	2045.3	2047.0	3132.2	2429.0	2346.1	3225.7	3170.7	2006.8	3143.4	2796.7	2261.8	2966.6
PROTEINS/HEAD	72.7	58.8	52.6	93.7	73.2	58.1	96.5	92.4	54.2	90.4	80.4	63.5	88.6
INVESTMENT AND CAPITAL													
INVESTMENT	2.3	11.1	10.8	27.5	47.5	17.8	175.1	7.1	3.3	76.2	2.6	1.9	124.9
EQUIPMENT	1.1	6.2	5.0	13.9	21.6	8.4	70.3	3.3	1.5	38.4	1.3	0.9	57.3
PLANT	1.0	4.6	4.1	13.5	25.8	8.8	104.2	3.7	1.6	37.4	1.3	0.8	67.2
IRRIGATION	0.1	0.2	1.7	0.1	0.0	0.2	0.4	0.0*	0.1	0.1	0.0*	0.0*	0.3
LAND (AREA)	1.0	1.2	2.9	0.0	0.0	2.3	0.0	0.5	0.8	1.1	0.0	1.8	0.1
INVENTORY CHANGE	0.4	1.8	2.0	2.4	4.4	2.2	8.5	0.5	1.0	7.5	0.3	0.4	8.6
CAPITAL STOCK	26.4	144.5	110.7	292.8	334.2	210.4	2262.8	83.3	26.6	707.1	28.0	21.5	1529.0
EQUIPMENT	12.3	72.5	53.3	116.9	129.1	89.5	659.2	29.5	11.6	291.2	11.6	10.3	532.5
PLANT	14.0	72.0	57.4	176.0	205.1	120.9	1603.2	53.8	15.0	415.3	16.4	11.2	996.5
INVENTORY STOCK	7.4	40.9	39.1	42.9	41.2	41.6	189.9	11.1	12.0	107.3	4.4	8.7	177.1
CULTIVATED LAND	35.6	154.9	235.6	36.4	6.0	75.4	101.4	11.5	38.5	160.8	8.6	45.7	89.7
SURPLUS SAVINGS	0.6	-1.4	1.5	-2.5	1.6	0.0*	-17.7	-0.3	0.8	5.8	-0.3	0.0*	25.7
INTERNATIONAL TRANSACTIONS													
IMPORTS	3.8	3.2	20.3	19.1	19.0	18.3	65.0	6.7	8.6	11.7	4.3	5.9	165.6
EXPORTS	2.5	2.0	15.8	18.0	21.1	17.9	69.2	6.6	13.6	14.2	3.5	6.3	160.6
PAYMENTS SURPLUS	-0.2	-1.2	1.6	-1.1	2.6	2.3	-2.6	-0.7	8.9	1.4	-0.6	1.1	-12.2
FOR.INVEST.INFLO	0.0	0.0	0.0	0.0	0.0	0.0	0.0	0.0	0.0	0.0	0.0	0.0	0.0
FOR. INC. OUTFLO	-0.2	0.0	-0.8	0.0	-0.4	-2.6	4.9	-0.9	-3.9	0.0	-0.5	-0.4	4.8
LEVEL OF ABATEMENT ACTIVITIES													
AIR	0.0	0.0	0.0	1.10	2.41	0.0	35.55	0.49	0.0	3.04	0.09	0.0	11.60
PRIMARY WATER	0.0	0.0	0.0	0.31	0.80	0.0	5.61	0.15	0.0	0.86	0.02	0.0	3.27
SECONDARY WATER	0.0	0.0	0.0	0.02	0.05	0.0	0.32	0.01	0.0	0.06	0.0	0.0	0.19
TERTIARY WATER	0.0	0.0	0.0	0.0	0.01	0.0	0.07	0.01	0.0	0.01	0.0	0.0	0.04
SOLID WASTE	0.0	0.0	0.0	20.98	45.54	0.0	197.13	12.33	0.0	54.20	2.96	0.0	201.80
NET TOTAL EMISSIONS													
PESTICIDES	0.05	0.00*	0.17	0.25	0.13	0.16	1.00	0.02	0.05	0.15	0.01	0.02	0.60
PARTICULATES	0.18	0.96	0.62	1.42	0.27	1.43	4.09	0.06	0.14	3.57	0.12	0.12	1.83
BIOLOG. OXYGEN	0.31	1.69	1.40	2.14	1.24	1.83	9.23	0.31	0.21	4.63	0.19	0.14	7.58
NITROGEN (WATER)	0.00*	0.01	0.01	0.07	0.02	0.01	0.19	0.00*	0.00*	0.13	0.01	0.00*	0.26
PHOSPHATES	0.00*	0.01	0.01	0.04	0.01	0.01	0.11	0.00*	0.00*	0.07	0.00*	0.00*	0.14
SUSPENDED SOLIDS	0.12	0.60	0.35	1.14	0.99	0.97	6.70	0.19	0.05	3.00	0.09	0.08	4.34
DISSOLVED SOLIDS	0.95	5.28	3.75	9.38	5.84	4.61	41.15	1.19	0.41	18.72	0.69	0.39	36.85
SOLID WASTE	11.66	54.51	56.72	20.97	0.00*	78.97	0.00*	0.00*	13.44	54.20	2.96	5.19	13.79

RESOURCE OUTPUTS

	AAF	ASC	ASL	EEM	JAP	LAT	NAH	OCH	OIL	RUH	SAF	TAF	WEU
COPPER	0.0*	0.1	0.2	0.1	0.1	1.0	2.2	0.1	0.0*	0.9	0.1	1.1	0.2
BAUXITE	0.0	0.1	0.7	0.5	0.0	4.7	0.4	1.9	0.0	0.9	0.0	0.7	1.5
NICKEL	0.1	0.0	156.1	4.7	0.0	39.5	291.6	29.8	0.0	110.0	11.6	10.9	13.7
ZINC	0.0*	0.2	0.0*	0.3	0.3	0.7	1.7	0.4	0.1	0.6	0.0	0.2	0.8
LEAD	0.1	0.2	0.0*	0.2	0.1	0.4	0.9	0.4	0.1	0.5	0.0	0.1	0.5
IRON	7.0	26.0	22.9	4.3	0.9	49.2	78.5	32.8	1.5	117.0	5.5	23.2	55.8
PETROLEUM	38.2	26.1	75.4	24.1	1.0	354.4	737.3	11.1	1241.2	458.3	0.0	6.6	29.9
NATURAL GAS	0.3	0.0	13.3	45.0	0.0	53.9	912.7	2.0	30.9	263.7	0.0	0.0*	105.1
COAL	0.4	393.7	87.4	264.3	39.7	9.1	554.6	50.4	0.4	350.7	54.7	4.2	355.5

CUMULATIVE RESOURCE OUTPUT AT END OF PERIOD

	AAF	ASC	ASL	EEM	JAP	LAT	NAH	OCH	OIL	RUH	SAF	TAF	WEU
COPPER	0.	0.	0.	0.	0.	0.	0.	0.	0.	0.	0.	0.	0.
BAUXITE	0.	0.	0.	0.	0.	0.	0.	0.	0.	0.	0.	0.	0.
NICKEL	0.	0.	0.	0.	0.	0.	0.	0.	0.	0.	0.	0.	0.
ZINC	0.	0.	0.	0.	0.	0.	0.	0.	0.	0.	0.	0.	0.
LEAD	0.	0.	0.	0.	0.	0.	0.	0.	0.	0.	0.	0.	0.
IRON	0.	0.	0.	0.	0.	0.	0.	0.	0.	0.	0.	0.	0.
PETROLEUM	0.	0.	0.	0.	0.	0.	0.	0.	0.	0.	0.	0.	0.
NATURAL GAS	0.	0.	0.	0.	0.	0.	0.	0.	0.	0.	0.	0.	0.
COAL	0.	0.	0.	0.	0.	0.	0.	0.	0.	0.	0.	0.	0.

NET EXPORTS OF RESOURCES

	AAF	ASC	ASL	EEM	JAP	LAT	NAH	OCH	OIL	RUH	SAF	TAF	WEU
COPPER	-0.0*	-0.0*	0.2	-0.1	-0.7	0.6	0.4	0.1	-0.0*	0.1	-0.1	1.1	-1.8
BAUXITE	-0.0*	-0.0*	0.2	0.2	-1.1	4.6	-3.5	1.5	-0.0*	-0.2	-0.1	0.2	-1.9
NICKEL	0.0*	-0.3	94.2	-0.0*	-103.1	-1.6	109.2	-1.0	0.0	-0.0*	3.6	10.9	-111.8
ZINC	-0.0*	-0.0*	-0.2	-0.0*	-0.5	0.6	0.5	0.4	0.1	0.0*	-0.0*	0.2	-0.9
LEAD	0.1	-0.0*	-0.0*	-0.0*	-0.1	0.3	-0.0*	0.4	0.0*	-0.1	-0.0*	0.0*	-0.7
IRON	6.0	-0.2	16.4	-22.4	-57.6	32.5	3.7	-20.4	1.2	27.1	2.2	18.8	-48.1
PETROLEUM	7.9	-0.2	-38.1	-48.9	-264.3	195.2	-274.8	-27.2	1187.0	121.9	-15.5	-9.7	-833.2
NATURAL GAS	0.0	0.0	4.0	-3.2	0.0	1.1	-2.1	0.0	3.1	-0.7	0.0	0.0	-2.2
COAL	-0.7	1.0	-0.7	9.0	-50.5	-4.2	53.0	18.5	-0.3	20.2	1.9	-0.3	-46.9
OTHER RESOURCES	0.1	0.1	0.1	-0.4	-0.4	0.2	0.6	0.1	0.4	0.1	0.0*	-0.1	-1.0
PETROL. REFINING	0.1	0.0*	-0.0*	-0.2	-0.1	-0.0*	0.5	-0.0*	0.2	0.1	-0.0*	-0.1	-0.6
PRIMARY METALS	-0.2	-0.7	-1.0	-1.3	3.0	-0.2	-0.7	-0.0*	-0.8	0.7	0.1	0.1	1.2

BASE SCENARIO IN 1970

OUTPUT LEVELS

	AAF	ASC	ASL	EEM	JAP	LAT	NAH	OCH	OIL	RUH	SAF	TAF	WEU
ANIMAL PRODUCTS	3.9	17.9	13.6	13.3	3.7	19.3	46.6	5.2	3.0	26.0	2.0	3.7	52.1
HIGH PROT. CROPS	3.3	16.0	29.6	3.1	1.0	9.1	30.4	0.1	3.0	25.0	0.5	7.1	9.3
GRAINS	25.9	215.4	229.0	55.9	18.4	72.4	219.0	13.7	21.8	174.3	8.3	20.2	146.8
ROOTS	3.0	85.6	45.3	44.1	12.9	42.8	21.4	1.1	10.9	88.8	0.8	42.7	63.3
OTHER AGRICULT.	2.6	0.6	12.2	14.7	15.0	19.0	29.0	4.3	2.5	36.8	2.1	4.2	58.5
OTHER RESOURCES	0.2	2.1	0.5	0.5	0.7	0.8	6.3	3.8	0.2	2.3	0.7	0.1	2.8
FOOD PROCESSING	0.4	1.2	1.6	7.8	9.1	5.3	71.6	0.7	0.4	18.2	0.2	0.4	53.2
PETROL. REFINING	0.3	2.3	0.9	2.1	2.6	1.6	18.7	1.1	-0.0*	6.5	0.4	0.1	10.3
PRIMARY METALS	0.2	11.1	0.4	4.8	10.6	2.1	38.7	2.4	1.9	16.8	1.0	0.2	26.8
TEXT., APPAREL	2.3	1.0	12.4	11.3	14.3	12.3	36.9	0.6	0.1	22.6	0.2	1.5	53.6
WOOD AND CORK	0.2	2.5	1.2	2.4	3.0	1.7	14.4	1.7	0.6	14.4	0.7	0.2	11.1
FURNITURE, FIXT.	0.6	1.1	2.3	6.7	7.6	5.4	8.7	0.7	0.0*	6.3	0.2	0.5	32.3
PAPER	0.2	0.5	0.5	2.4	3.2	1.2	24.1	0.5	0.1	5.5	0.1	0.1	14.2
PRINTING	0.1	0.6	0.4	2.0	2.7	1.0	26.4	0.8	0.1	4.2	0.2	0.1	14.0
RUBBER	0.1	3.1	0.4	1.6	2.2	0.6	16.4	0.8	0.0*	10.5	0.1	-0.0*	9.1
INDUSTRIAL CHEM.	0.5	4.4	2.0	3.9	5.8	2.7	24.8	0.7	0.3	9.7	0.2	0.3	21.3
FERTILIZERS	0.8	1.6	3.2	6.9	2.3	3.4	17.5	0.6	0.3	7.4	0.6	0.2	17.5
OTHER CHEMICALS	0.0*	0.1	0.9	3.0	3.6	2.1	24.1	0.8	0.0*	0.7	0.3	0.0*	16.3
CEMENT	0.2	1.1	0.1	0.3	0.5	0.2	2.3	0.1	0.0*	6.9	0.0*	-0.0*	1.4
GLASS	0.0*	0.5	0.7	2.7	4.2	1.5	21.3	0.6	0.1	11.3	0.2	0.1	13.6
MOTOR VEHICLES	0.1	0.7	-0.0*	4.7	7.4	0.7	44.8	0.9	0.0*	2.4	0.1	-0.0*	27.0
SHIPBUILDING	0.2	1.6	0.3	1.6	2.9	0.0*	15.5	0.1	0.2	9.4	-0.0*	-0.0*	5.5
AIRCRAFT	0.6	3.5	0.4	1.8	0.9	0.0*	15.5	0.1	0.4	9.4	0.4	-0.0*	4.5
METAL PRODUCTS	0.6	5.1	2.1	6.5	9.3	3.4	52.3	1.7	-0.0*	19.1	0.3	0.2	33.3
MACHINERY	0.3	2.5	1.6	12.0	14.7	3.4	53.0	1.4	-0.0*	27.0	0.1	-0.0*	43.6
ELECTRICAL MACH.	0.1	0.6	0.6	6.1	8.9	1.3	43.2	0.2	0.2	15.3	0.5	-0.0*	26.1
INSTRUMENTS	0.4	1.5	0.2	1.5	2.3	0.4	10.3	0.5	0.3	4.1	0.3	0.4	6.6
OTHER MANUFACT.	0.2	1.3	1.7	2.3	3.2	2.1	10.3	0.5	0.0*	5.5	0.5	0.2	12.1
UTILITIES	1.4	6.8	0.9	3.4	4.1	1.9	35.2	0.5	0.3	8.6	1.8	1.4	20.1
CONSTRUCTION	2.3	10.7	6.9	17.5	31.0	13.1	143.6	4.9	2.2	47.9	2.8	2.1	88.7
TRADE	1.1	7.1	9.4	28.8	35.3	21.3	223.6	8.5	2.4	68.7	1.1	0.9	155.5
TRANSPORTATION	0.3	5.1	5.1	11.2	12.0	8.7	54.8	2.3	1.1	27.7	0.3	0.2	54.2
COMMUNICATIONS	0.3	1.4	1.1	2.5	3.2	2.1	26.9	0.9	0.3	7.3	0.3	0.2	12.8
SERVICES	4.1	18.8	17.2	39.7	45.7	33.5	341.8	10.9	4.6	97.8	5.2	3.6	206.0

MILITARY OUTPUT LEVELS

	AAF	ASC	ASL	EEM	JAP	LAT	NAH	OCH	OIL	RUH	SAF	TAF	WEU
AIRCRAFT	0.1458	1.5442	0.1650	2.3489	0.2203	0.1170	10.5077	0.1909	0.0000*	10.9674	0.0760	0.0000*	3.9932
SHIPS	0.0247	0.4524	0.0343	0.0458	0.0697	0.0413	1.5773	0.0750	0.0000*	3.6052	0.0060	0.0000*	1.5020
ELECTRONIC EQUIP	0.0730	1.0393	0.1905	1.0119	0.0890	0.0618	5.8714	0.1120	0.0002	4.9812	0.0522	0.0000*	1.5251
NEW CONSTRUCTION	0.0387	1.0416	0.0850	0.3467	0.0308	0.0499	1.1372	0.0398	0.1088	1.7591	0.0127	0.0078	0.7881
MAINTENANCE	0.0283	0.7616	0.0622	0.2535	0.0225	0.0365	0.8315	0.0291	0.0795	1.2863	0.0093	0.0057	0.5763
MISSILES	0.0252	0.2065	0.0211	0.2885	0.0143	0.0115	4.7124	0.0123	0.0000*	4.9805	0.0087	0.0000*	0.9546
AMMUNITION, NEC	0.0208	0.2998	0.0542	0.3180	0.0274	0.0178	1.6803	0.0325	0.0000*	1.9119	0.0151	-0.0000*	0.4506
TANKS	0.0970	0.3432	0.0808	1.6348	0.0225	0.0298	0.7922	0.0202	-0.0000*	1.4200	0.0160	-0.0000*	0.8805
SMALL ARMS	0.0012	0.0186	0.0033	0.0192	0.0034	0.0011	0.1224	0.0024	-0.0000*	0.0920	0.0010	-0.0000*	0.0355
SM. ARMS AMMUN.	0.0035	0.0483	0.0091	0.0462	0.0058	0.0029	0.2760	0.0055	0.0000*	0.2203	0.0025	-0.0000*	0.0750
OTHER ORDNANCE	0.0073	0.1028	0.0189	0.1013	0.0107	0.0062	0.5872	0.0115	0.0000*	0.4880	0.0052	-0.0000*	0.1586
TOTAL OUTPUT	0.4655	5.8583	0.7244	6.4149	0.5165	0.3757	28.0955	0.5311	0.1886	31.7119	0.2045	0.0135	10.9395

	AAF	ASC	ASL	EEM	JAP	LAT	NAH	OCH	OIL	RUH	SAF	TAF	WEU
FISH													
FISH CATCH	0.6	7.9	9.3	0.8	8.2	14.4	3.8	0.2	0.4	6.7	2.2	1.9	9.6
NON-HUMAN USE	0.3	0.1	1.0	0.1	2.0	12.5	1.2	-0.0*	-0.1	0.6	2.0	0.6	1.7
FISH IMPORTS	0.1	0.0	0.3	0.2	0.2	0.1	1.3	0.0*	0.0*	0.1	0.0*	0.1	1.6
FISH EXPORTS	0.1	0.1	0.3	0.0*	0.5	0.1	0.4	0.0*	0.1	0.4	0.0*	0.1	2.0
EXPORTS													
LIVESTOCK	0.0*	0.0*	0.0*	1.2	0.0*	1.0	0.7	1.7	0.0*	0.1	0.0*	0.0*	5.0
HIGH PROT. CROPS	0.7	0.0*	2.1	0.4	0.0*	1.1	14.7	0.0*	1.5	0.8	0.2	1.2	3.0
GRAINS	0.9	0.0	5.5	4.5	2.4	8.0	48.5	6.7	0.2	6.0	1.2	0.3	20.4
ROOTS	0.4	0.6	0.8	1.9	0.0*	0.5	2.5	0.2	0.3	0.2	0.3	0.3	6.3
OTHER AGRICULT.	0.9	0.2	4.6	1.5	0.0	4.3	3.1	1.2	0.9	1.0	0.2	2.4	7.4
FOOD PROCESSING	0.1	0.4	1.0	0.7	0.3	1.8	2.1	0.8	0.1	0.3	0.2	0.4	5.3
TEXT., APPAREL	0.2	0.0*	3.1	1.6	2.7	0.4	1.4	0.0*	0.2	0.1	0.0*	0.1	13.6
WOOD AND CORK	0.0*	0.0*	0.4	0.5	0.2	0.2	1.2	0.0*	0.0*	0.6	0.0*	0.0*	1.9
FURNITURE, FIXT.	0.0*	0.0*	0.0*	0.1	0.0*	0.0*	0.1	0.1	0.0*	0.0*	0.1	0.0*	0.8
PAPER	0.0*	0.0*	0.0*	0.1	0.1	0.1	3.4	0.0*	0.0*	0.0*	0.0*	0.0*	1.2
PRINTING	0.0*	0.0*	0.0*	0.0*	0.1	0.0*	0.4	0.0*	0.0*	0.1	0.0*	0.0*	1.4
RUBBER	0.0*	0.0*	0.1	0.1	0.2	0.0*	0.3	0.2	0.0*	0.2	0.1	0.0*	9.3
INDUSTRIAL CHEM.	0.0*	0.1	0.1	0.2	1.3	0.1	3.4	0.1	0.0*	0.7	0.0*	0.0*	2.8
FERTILIZERS	0.2	0.2	0.2	0.3	0.3	0.1	2.0	0.1	0.1	0.7	0.0*	0.0*	4.7
OTHER CHEMICALS	0.0*	0.0*	0.1	0.1	0.2	0.0*	1.3	0.0*	0.0*	0.0*	0.0*	0.0*	0.1
CEMENT	0.0*	0.0*	0.0*	0.2	0.0*	0.0*	0.0*	0.0*	0.0*	0.0*	0.0*	0.0*	2.5
GLASS	0.0*	0.0*	0.0*	0.2	0.3	0.0*	0.5	0.0*	0.0*	0.0*	0.0*	0.0*	13.5
MOTOR VEHICLES	0.0*	0.0*	0.1	1.8	2.1	0.1	8.2	0.0*	0.0*	1.1	0.0*	0.0*	2.0
SHIPBUILDING	0.0*	0.0*	0.0*	0.6	1.2	0.0*	0.2	0.0*	0.0*	0.5	0.0*	0.0*	1.4
AIRCRAFT	0.0*	0.0*	0.0*	0.0*	0.0*	0.0*	3.4	0.0*	0.0*	1.2	0.0*	0.0*	3.8
METAL PRODUCTS	0.0*	0.0*	0.2	0.2	0.6	0.0*	1.5	0.1	0.0*	0.5	0.1	0.0*	19.5
MACHINERY	0.0*	0.0*	0.4	4.4	1.9	0.1	8.2	0.1	0.0*	1.6	0.1	0.1	8.8
ELECTRICAL MACH.	0.0*	0.0*	0.0*	1.4	2.7	0.1	3.1	0.1	0.0*	0.0*	0.0*	0.0*	3.3
INSTRUMENTS	0.0*	0.0*	0.0*	0.2	0.7	0.0*	1.9	0.0*	0.0*	0.1	0.0*	0.0*	4.7
OTHER MANUFACT.	0.2	0.1	1.1	0.1	0.8	0.1	0.9	0.1	0.0*	0.2	0.3	0.3	11.7
SERVICES	0.1	0.0	0.5	0.1	0.1	2.0	3.5	0.1	0.3	0.0	1.2	0.4	17.3
TRANSPORT	0.1	0.0	1.0	0.0	1.8	0.9	4.5	0.6	0.3	0.0	0.3	0.8	8.9
AID INFLOW	1.1	0.0	6.0	0.0	0.2	2.9	5.1	0.4	1.1	0.0	0.4	0.8	11.1
CAPITAL INFLOW	0.0*	0.0	0.8	0.0	2.7	1.3	10.0	0.1	0.2	0.0	0.0*	0.2	
MILITARY EXPORTS													
AIRCRAFT	0.0	0.0767	0.0	0.1535	0.0	0.0	1.4578	0.0	0.0	0.6905	0.0	0.0	0.1790
SHIPS	0.0	0.0106	0.0	0.0	0.0	0.0	0.1011	0.0	0.0	0.0931	0.0	0.0	0.0612
ELECTRONIC EQUIP	0.0	0.0659	0.0	0.0439	0.0	0.0	0.6480	0.0	0.0	0.2197	0.0	0.0	0.1208
MISSILES	0.0	0.0190	0.0	0.0127	0.0	0.0	0.3480	0.0	0.0	0.2100	0.0	0.0	0.0420
AMMUNITION, NEC	0.0	0.0	0.0	0.0507	0.0	0.0	0.1868	0.0	0.0	0.0633	0.0	0.0	0.0348
TANKS	0.0	0.0	0.0	0.0008	0.0	0.0	0.4818	0.0	0.0	0.2198	0.0	0.0	0.0930
SMALL ARMS	0.0	0.0012	0.0	0.0021	0.0	0.0	0.0121	0.0	0.0	0.0041	0.0	0.0	0.0022
SM. ARMS AMMUN.	0.0	0.0031	0.0	0.0044	0.0	0.0	0.0308	0.0	0.0	0.0104	0.0	0.0	0.0057
OTHER ORDNANCE	0.0	0.0066	0.0	0.0	0.0	0.0	0.0650	0.0	0.0	0.0220	0.0	0.0	0.0121
TOTAL EXPORTS	0.0	0.1832	0.0	0.2681	0.0	0.0	3.3314	0.0	0.0	1.5330	0.0	0.0	0.5509
MIL. GRANTS INF.	0.3289	0.2755	1.4435	0.0112	0.0	0.0165	0.0	0.0	0.0119	0.0	0.0	0.0222	0.0872

BASE SCENARIO IN 1970

IMPORTS

	AAF	ASC	ASL	EEM	JAP	LAT	NAH	OCH	OIL	RUH	SAF	TAF	WEU
LIVESTOCK	0.1	0.0*	0.4	0.9	0.3	0.4	1.8	0.0*	0.2	0.2	0.1	0.2	5.6
HIGH PROT. CROPS	0.5	0.0*	1.1	2.0	4.4	0.6	1.4	0.1	0.6	0.1	0.0*	0.2	14.5
GRAINS	2.3	0.0*	16.1	20.2	11.3	7.4	1.4	0.1	2.7	3.1	0.5	2.5	37.0
ROOTS	0.2	0.0*	0.8	2.3	0.6	1.1	0.5	0.1	0.2	0.0	0.0	0.2	7.3
OTHER AGRICULT.	0.2	0.3	1.5	2.9	2.6	0.6	4.6	0.2	0.4	1.8	0.1	0.3	12.7
FOOD PROCESSING	0.1	0.0*	1.2	1.1	0.5	0.5	2.2	0.1	0.4	0.8	0.1	0.7	5.9
TEXT., APPAREL	0.2	0.0	1.9	0.6	0.5	0.7	4.5	0.5	0.7	1.2	0.4	0.0*	12.0
WOOD AND CORK	0.1	0.0	0.1	0.1	0.3	0.2	1.2	0.1	0.1	0.0*	0.1	0.0*	2.5
FURNITURE, FIXT.	0.0*	0.0	0.0*	0.1	0.0*	0.0*	0.3	0.0*	0.0*	0.2	0.0*	0.1	0.8
PAPER	0.0*	0.0*	0.5	0.2	0.2	0.6	1.9	0.2	0.2	0.1	0.0*	0.1	4.4
PRINTING	0.0*	0.0*	0.1	0.0*	0.0*	0.1	0.4	0.1	0.0*	0.0	0.0*	0.2	0.8
RUBBER	0.0*	0.0*	0.1	0.1	0.0*	0.1	0.4	0.1	0.1	0.0*	0.0*	0.3	1.1
INDUSTRIAL CHEM.	0.1	0.3	1.0	0.7	0.5	1.1	1.7	0.4	0.3	0.5	0.2	0.0*	8.1
FERTILIZERS	0.1	0.0*	1.2	1.0	0.2	0.9	0.6	0.1	0.3	0.1	0.0*	0.6	1.9
OTHER CHEMICALS	0.1	0.0*	0.7	0.2	0.4	0.6	0.6	0.2	0.3	0.0*	0.0*	0.1	3.4
CEMENT	0.0*	0.0*	0.0*	0.0	0.0*	0.0*	0.0*	0.0*	0.1	0.0*	0.0*	0.0*	0.1
GLASS	0.2	0.1	0.2	0.1	0.1	0.2	0.8	0.7	0.8	0.0*	0.8	0.6	2.0
MOTOR VEHICLES	0.2	0.1	1.2	0.7	0.1	1.4	11.0	0.1	0.8	1.5	0.0*	0.1	9.2
SHIPBUILDING	0.1	0.0*	0.2	0.3	0.1	0.2	0.1	0.3	0.0*	0.0	0.0*	0.2	1.9
AIRCRAFT	0.1	0.0*	0.2	0.0	0.5	0.3	1.1	0.3	0.1	0.0	0.1	0.7	3.4
METAL PRODUCTS	0.1	0.2	0.5	0.0	0.1	0.5	1.3	0.9	0.3	0.0	0.7	0.3	3.3
MACHINERY	0.3	0.2	2.4	2.6	1.1	2.7	5.0	0.9	1.2	2.6	0.7	0.1	16.0
ELECTRICAL MACH.	0.2	0.0*	1.2	0.4	0.4	1.1	3.6	0.3	0.7	0.3	0.2	0.1	7.9
INSTRUMENTS	0.0*	0.0*	0.3	0.1	0.2	0.3	1.2	0.2	0.1	0.2	0.1	0.6	3.2
OTHER MANUFACT.	0.1	0.0	0.7	0.1	0.3	0.3	2.3	0.4	0.1	0.3	0.1	0.5	4.1
SERVICES	0.0	0.0	0.0*	0.0	0.6	1.5	6.4	0.9	0.1	0.0	0.2	0.0*	10.6
TRANSPORT	0.4	0.0	1.6	0.0	2.6	1.8	4.2	0.5	0.6	0.0	0.4	0.6	14.0
AID OUTFLOW	0.4	0.1	1.1	0.0	0.9	1.3	9.0	1.5	0.8	0.6	0.2	0.5	11.5
CAPITAL OUTFLOW	0.1	0.0	1.4	0.0	1.9	2.9	6.5		0.5	0.0	0.6	0.3	11.0

MILITARY IMPORTS

	AAF	ASC	ASL	EEM	JAP	LAT	NAH	OCH	OIL	RUH	SAF	TAF	WEU
AIRCRAFT	0.3400	0.5420	0.4241	0.2607	0.0300	0.0927	0.1061	0.0420	0.1172	0.1108	0.0190	0.0191	0.4538
SHIPS	0.0439	0.0394	0.0514	0.0051	0.0022	0.0386	0.0159	0.0031	0.0176	0.0	0.0060	0.0067	0.0361
ELECTRONIC EQUIP	0.1482	0.2598	0.1690	0.0880	0.0099	0.0386	0.0593	0.0152	0.0525	0.0503	0.0085	0.0084	0.1905
MISSILES	0.0618	0.1377	0.0748	0.1238	0.0096	0.0084	0.0476	0.0123	0.0199	0.0	0.0013	0.0011	0.1016
AMMUNITION, NEC	0.0421	0.0750	0.0481	0.0277	0.0030	0.0109	0.0170	0.0044	0.0143	0.0143	0.0025	0.0023	0.0551
TANKS	0.1583	0.1472	0.1319	0.0507	0.0088	0.0214	0.0080	0.0124	0.0521	0.0193	0.0065	0.0061	0.2227
SMALL ARMS	0.0025	0.0046	0.0029	0.0017	0.0004	0.0007	0.0012	0.0003	0.0008	0.0009	0.0002	0.0001	0.0041
SM. ARMS AMMUN.	0.0071	0.0121	0.0081	0.0040	0.0006	0.0018	0.0028	0.0007	0.0026	0.0022	0.0004	0.0004	0.0094
OTHER ORDNANCE	0.0148	0.0257	0.0168	0.0088	0.0012	0.0039	0.0059	0.0016	0.0053	0.0049	0.0008	0.0008	0.0196
TOTAL IMPORTS	0.8188	1.2435	0.9270	0.5705	0.0656	0.2169	0.2639	0.0921	0.2823	0.2028	0.0452	0.0450	1.0929
MIL. GRANTS OUTF	0.0	0.1995	0.0	0.0	0.0	0.0	1.4727	0.0	0.0	0.4827	0.0	0.0	0.0420

BASE SCENARIO IN 1980

	AAF	ASC	ASL	EEM	JAP	LAT	NAH	OCH	OIL	RUH	SAF	TAF	WEU
CONSUMPTION AND POPULATION													
GDP	27.6	201.0	166.4	268.7	372.7	200.0	1509.4	64.1	187.0	735.3	22.4	37.5	1073.9
PERSONAL CONSUMP	21.3	138.7	135.9	174.0	243.4	153.7	985.0	44.5	91.5	425.5	16.8	29.0	757.4
GOVT.(CIVILIAN)	2.8	20.1	16.6	26.9	37.3	20.0	150.9	6.4	18.7	73.5	2.2	3.8	107.4
GOVT.(MILITARY)	4.1	18.9	6.7	18.0	3.4	3.6	75.5	1.6	22.3	97.8	1.2	1.5	37.0
POPULATION	169.6	954.1	1306.6	112.5	117.5	368.3	252.0	18.4	170.3	268.1	28.5	184.5	420.1
URBAN POPULATION	77.2	267.5	309.7	67.0	72.0	236.8	198.1	16.0	59.0	172.4	15.0	38.8	294.8
EMPLOYMENT	10.7	95.0	704.2	58.2	59.2	87.0	111.3	7.6	57.5	135.3	8.8	15.5	154.9
GDP/HEAD	162.5	210.7	127.3	2388.2	3172.1	543.0	5989.6	3483.7	1098.2	2742.6	786.0	203.4	2556.3
CONSUMPTION/HEAD	125.5	145.4	104.0	1546.8	2071.4	417.4	3908.9	2418.3	537.3	1586.9	587.8	157.0	1802.9
CALORIES/HEAD	2340.8	2087.5	2076.4	3119.3	2700.8	2352.3	3222.9	3251.5	2215.8	3129.2	2678.5	2336.7	3009.2
PROTEINS/HEAD	68.3	61.1	53.6	97.9	89.6	58.5	98.4	96.8	65.8	95.4	77.1	66.9	92.3
INVESTMENT AND CAPITAL													
INVESTMENT	1.1	19.9	11.4	44.6	80.0	22.2	283.8	11.7	63.4	124.0	2.2	2.7	155.3
EQUIPMENT	0.5	10.8	5.5	19.8	28.7	10.9	91.5	4.5	28.5	54.2	1.1	1.4	61.2
PLANT	0.4	8.6	5.3	24.7	51.2	10.8	192.0	7.1	34.8	69.5	1.1	1.2	93.9
IRRIGATION	0.1	0.5	0.4	0.1	0.0*	0.1	0.1	0.0*	0.5	0.4	0.0*	0.0*	0.1
LAND (AREA)	0.1	0.8	1.1	0.1	0.0	2.1	0.8	0.4	0.5	0.0	0.1	1.4	0.1
INVENTORY CHANGE	0.0*	3.6	1.3	2.2	4.3	1.9	8.3	0.3	6.4	7.1	0.1	0.3	3.1
CAPITAL STOCK	27.9	238.4	160.4	496.9	710.0	307.6	3614.6	137.3	246.6	1280.6	36.8	35.4	2206.7
EQUIPMENT	12.6	118.8	74.2	183.6	234.0	128.4	939.2	44.1	109.5	481.5	14.7	16.4	697.0
PLANT	15.3	119.6	86.2	313.2	476.1	179.2	2675.3	93.2	137.1	799.2	22.2	19.0	1509.0
INVENTORY STOCK	7.7	68.2	51.6	61.5	73.2	59.3	260.3	13.8	45.2	165.0	5.3	11.4	210.6
CULTIVATED LAND	39.7	217.6	305.9	41.8	8.7	101.9	122.8	14.5	96.9	198.7	9.8	58.3	91.2
SURPLUS SAVINGS	3.0	-1.2	9.0	3.5	8.8	4.9	-42.8	-1.1	-44.7	27.4	2.1	1.0	66.2
INTERNATIONAL TRANSACTIONS													
IMPORTS	4.8	3.3	28.4	30.0	38.9	28.8	103.5	10.7	48.1	20.1	4.8	9.0	241.2
EXPORTS	3.0	3.0	22.9	32.2	42.4	26.9	106.2	10.0	32.7	25.2	4.7	9.3	252.1
PAYMENTS SURPLUS	0.0	-0.0*	0.0	-2.1	-13.4	10.0	-15.2	-1.9	42.2	8.3	0.0	0.0	-31.0
FOR.INVEST.INFLO	-1.0	-5.9	5.2	-15.8	-37.8	44.9	-41.6	-32.1	214.5	48.6	-7.5	4.0	-190.9
FOR.INC.OUTFLOW	-0.2	-0.5	-0.4	-1.3	-3.4	1.0	1.6	-3.5	13.3	3.9	-1.1	-0.1	-10.5
LEVEL OF ABATEMENT ACTIVITIES													
AIR	0.0	0.0	0.0	3.87	5.05	0.64	56.44	0.83	0.76	11.93	0.11	0.0	17.21
PRIMARY WATER	0.0	0.0	0.0	1.07	2.57	0.23	7.97	0.42	0.11	3.25	0.03	0.0	6.12
SECONDARY WATER	0.0	0.0	0.0	0.06	0.15	0.01	0.45	0.02	0.01	0.19	0.00*	0.0	0.35
TERTIARY WATER	0.0	0.0	0.0	0.03	0.06	0.01	0.20	0.01	0.00*	0.08	0.00*	0.0	0.15
SOLID WASTE	0.0	0.0	0.0	60.84	72.19	48.07	257.35	16.61	17.13	165.20	4.81	0.0	259.86
NET TOTAL EMISSIONS													
PESTICIDES	0.15	0.02	0.37	0.44	0.29	0.40	2.05	0.05	0.46	0.37	0.01	0.04	0.85
PARTICULATES	0.18	1.78	0.83	0.30	0.23	1.60	4.21	0.26	1.60	-0.08	0.14	0.22	1.66
BIOLOG. OXYGEN	0.46	3.94	1.95	2.20	1.43	2.80	10.01	1.11	1.11	5.89	0.23	0.18	7.87
NITROGEN (WATER)	0.00*	0.03	0.01	0.07	0.03	0.03	0.20	0.01	0.01	0.22	0.01	0.00*	0.30
PHOSPHATES	0.00*	0.02	0.01	0.04	0.02	0.02	0.15	0.00*	0.01	0.11	0.00*	0.00*	0.17
SUSPENDED SOLIDS	0.13	1.17	0.50	1.37	0.95	1.32	6.82	0.18	0.69	3.56	0.11	0.19	4.27
DISSOLVED SOLIDS	1.22	15.21	4.90	10.37	9.62	10.38	49.20	1.23	3.69	30.80	0.78	0.28	43.35
SOLID WASTE	26.26	96.62	92.86	0.0	0.0	82.42	0.0	0.0	17.13	0.0	4.81	11.41	21.92

RESOURCE OUTPUTS

	AAF	ASC	ASL	EEM	JAP	LAT	NAH	OCH	OIL	RUH	SAF	TAF	WEU
COPPER	0.0*	0.2	0.2	0.2	0.2	1.7	2.8	0.2	0.0*	1.5	0.1	2.0	0.3
BAUXITE	0.0	0.2	0.9	0.9	0.0	8.2	0.2	3.1	0.0	1.0	0.0	0.7	1.6
NICKEL	0.0*	0.0	232.3	6.0	0.0	49.4	394.9	44.8	0.0	219.8	12.4	9.0	14.0
ZINC	0.0*	0.3	0.0*	0.4	0.4	1.1	2.5	0.8	0.2	0.6	0.0	0.3	0.8
LEAD	0.2	0.3	0.0*	0.3	0.1	0.8	1.4	0.9	0.2	0.6	0.0	0.0*	0.6
IRON	3.8	40.8	30.5	7.6	0.9	56.5	106.4	35.7	9.8	196.0	5.5	23.2	132.1
PETROLEUM	33.8	77.0	75.0	24.1	1.0	439.7	1264.4	11.0	2694.6	924.1	0.0	0.0	21.0
NATURAL GAS	0.0	0.0	13.0	45.0	0.0	54.0	1227.7	2.0	376.6	577.8	0.0	0.0	105.0
COAL	0.7	481.1	131.0	438.1	59.2	15.0	839.2	87.6	0.7	615.1	49.6	9.4	513.6

CUMULATIVE RESOURCE OUTPUT AT END OF PERIOD

	AAF	ASC	ASL	EEM	JAP	LAT	NAH	OCH	OIL	RUH	SAF	TAF	WEU
COPPER	0.*	2.	2.	2.	1.	14.	25.	2.	0.*	12.	1.	15.	3.
BAUXITE	0.	2.	8.	7.	0.	64.	3.	25.	0.	9.	0.	7.	16.
NICKEL	1.	0.	1942.	54.	0.	445.	3433.	373.	0.	1649.	120.	100.	139.
ZINC	0.*	3.	0.*	4.	3.	9.	21.	6.	1.	6.	0.	2.	8.
LEAD	1.	3.	0.*	3.	1.	6.	11.	7.	1.	6.	0.	1.	5.
IRON	54.	334.	267.	59.	9.	528.	925.	343.	57.	1565.	55.	232.	940.
PETROLEUM	360.	516.	752.	241.	10.	3970.	10008.	111.	19679.	6912.	0.	33.	1050.
NATURAL GAS	1.	0.	132.	450.	0.	539.	10702.	20.	2038.	4208.	0.	0.*	255.
COAL	5.	4374.	1092.	3512.	495.	121.	6969.	690.	5.	4829.	522.	68.	4346.

NET EXPORTS OF RESOURCES

	AAF	ASC	ASL	EEM	JAP	LAT	NAH	OCH	OIL	RUH	SAF	TAF	WEU
COPPER	0.0	-0.0*	0.2	-0.2	-1.4	1.3	0.5	0.1	-0.1	0.0	0.1	1.9	-2.4
BAUXITE	-0.0*	-0.0*	0.2	0.2	-2.2	7.8	-5.1	2.7	-0.2	-1.2	-0.1	0.7	-3.0
NICKEL	-0.6	-5.4	171.7	-9.9	-185.3	7.0	161.2	3.5	-2.2	3.5	3.5	9.0	-156.0
ZINC	0.0	-0.0*	-0.2	-0.2	-1.1	1.0	0.3	0.7	-0.1	-0.3	-0.0*	0.3	-1.3
LEAD	0.1	0.0	-0.0*	-0.1	-0.3	0.6	0.3	0.8	0.1	-0.3	-0.0*	0.0*	-1.1
IRON	3.0	0.0	22.4	-39.7	-115.1	41.9	6.0	19.4	0.0	35.9	1.5	22.4	-2.2
PETROLEUM	0.0	0.0	-77.9	-120.9	-484.3	202.3	-347.3	-57.4	2128.2	186.2	-20.8	-25.3	-1382.7
NATURAL GAS	-0.3	0.0	-1.4	-44.6	0.0	-35.3	0.0	-1.7	78.9	78.9	0.0	-0.0*	-74.5
COAL	-0.8	3.9	1.9	9.7	-137.4	-6.8	116.3	36.8	-6.7	23.3	1.9	0.0	-42.0
OTHER RESOURCES	0.1	0.1	0.2	-0.6	-0.8	0.3	-0.9	-0.1	0.5	0.2	0.2	0.1	-1.3
PETROL. REFINING	0.0*	0.0*	-0.4	-0.8	-2.1	0.2	-0.6	-0.2	9.1	0.8	-0.0*	-0.2	-5.6
PRIMARY METALS	-0.2	-0.7	-0.9	-1.8	1.2	1.2	0.5	0.8	-0.8	-0.0*	-0.4	1.1	-0.4

OUTPUT LEVELS

	AAF	ASC	ASL	EEM	JAP	LAT	NAH	OCH	OIL	RUH	SAF	TAF	WEU
ANIMAL PRODUCTS	4.3	27.5	20.4	16.2	8.8	25.8	54.2	7.0	9.8	34.6	2.5	6.0	60.0
HIGH PROT. CROPS	3.6	22.3	37.8	3.7	1.9	13.2	39.2	0.1	5.9	33.5	0.7	9.8	10.3
GRAINS	29.6	298.9	301.2	63.8	25.7	94.9	258.2	17.5	43.5	210.8	9.2	26.1	152.2
ROOTS	3.1	93.8	58.8	48.0	21.3	51.1	24.1	1.1	33.8	100.2	0.7	51.6	64.2
OTHER AGRICULT.	2.5	19.2	14.7	17.4	18.5	28.0	38.6	3.8	12.9	45.9	2.5	5.1	49.5
OTHER RESOURCES	0.2	1.2	0.7	0.7	1.4	1.3	9.8	0.4	1.4	4.1	0.3	0.2	4.0
FOOD PROCESSING	0.4	3.7	2.1	16.9	29.7	8.4	93.4	6.9	2.7	42.0	0.9	0.6	94.4
PETROL. REFINING	0.2	1.9	0.9	2.9	2.8	2.4	25.2	2.6	11.0	11.5	0.2	0.0*	10.4
PRIMARY METALS	0.2	4.2	1.1	9.3	16.6	4.4	61.7	2.6	3.0	30.0	0.4	1.3	36.7
TEXT. APPAREL	2.3	16.6	17.7	17.9	26.3	14.9	56.7	2.6	8.3	35.9	1.2	1.7	58.2
WOOD AND CORK	0.1	1.7	1.7	3.9	5.7	2.2	21.6	0.8	1.1	11.6	0.8	0.3	13.4
FURNITURE, FIXT.	0.5	4.3	3.3	10.8	14.6	7.4	13.0	1.6	6.0	25.0	0.8	0.8	27.5
PAPER	0.1	1.9	0.6	4.4	7.2	1.7	35.7	1.1	0.4	12.5	0.2	0.1	21.9
PRINTING	0.1	0.8	0.6	4.3	7.0	1.5	39.3	1.3	1.1	12.5	0.2	0.0*	23.3
RUBBER	0.1	0.9	0.6	3.3	5.5	0.9	23.8	0.7	0.4	9.0	0.1	0.3	14.8
INDUSTRIAL CHEM.	0.5	5.5	2.8	6.1	11.2	3.8	35.3	1.0	2.1	17.9	0.3	-0.0*	28.0
FERTILIZERS	1.3	17.4	4.4	5.8	3.0	11.9	21.9	0.7	3.3	18.3	0.7	0.1	19.4
OTHER CHEMICALS	0.2	2.7	1.2	4.9	6.9	2.8	34.0	1.2	0.4	12.7	0.4	0.1	26.1
CEMENT	0.0*	0.2	0.1	0.5	1.0	0.2	3.8	0.1	0.2	1.4	0.0*	0.0*	2.2
GLASS	0.1	1.9	1.0	5.0	9.1	2.0	34.5	1.1	2.2	13.2	0.3	0.1	20.6
MOTOR VEHICLES	0.0*	0.6	0.1	9.7	17.3	0.5	62.2	1.4	0.8	23.5	0.1	0.0*	41.2
SHIPBUILDING	0.1	1.1	0.4	2.4	4.4	0.9	8.6	0.3	1.9	3.5	0.0*	0.0*	5.4
AIRCRAFT	0.1	2.1	0.5	3.3	1.8	0.1	19.5	0.1	1.7	16.2	0.0*	0.0*	5.9
METAL PRODUCTS	0.5	5.5	2.8	12.0	19.9	4.3	78.8	2.8	5.2	36.4	0.5	0.3	48.9
MACHINERY	0.4	8.4	1.9	19.7	23.3	3.9	72.7	1.9	5.2	41.2	0.3	0.1	53.5
ELECTRICAL MACH.	0.2	3.7	0.8	11.5	18.4	1.5	58.8	1.7	1.6	27.7	0.2	0.1	39.5
INSTRUMENTS	0.1	1.0	0.2	2.4	4.3	0.6	14.2	0.3	0.7	6.7	0.1	0.0*	9.0
OTHER MANUFACT.	0.3	2.4	2.4	3.8	5.8	2.7	15.7	0.6	1.8	8.9	0.7	0.6	14.6
UTILITIES	0.3	2.5	1.7	7.7	11.9	3.5	55.5	2.5	2.9	20.6	0.5	0.4	39.3
CONSTRUCTION	0.9	12.0	9.1	31.4	61.4	16.8	246.6	8.9	36.6	88.5	1.8	2.2	125.7
TRADE	2.2	17.4	13.5	50.1	74.0	30.2	317.0	14.0	24.3	127.0	3.6	3.3	228.5
TRANSPORTATION	1.1	11.8	7.4	16.9	20.1	12.1	80.2	3.3	10.6	44.2	1.4	1.5	70.6
COMMUNICATIONS	0.3	2.2	1.7	4.4	6.0	2.9	37.3	1.3	2.1	12.5	0.4	0.4	22.3
SERVICES	4.4	32.9	26.7	68.3	94.0	49.2	509.8	19.1	35.6	180.3	7.1	6.3	319.8

MILITARY OUTPUT LEVELS

	AAF	ASC	ASL	EEM	JAP	LAT	NAH	OCH	OIL	RUH	SAF	TAF	WEU
AIRCRAFT	0.1925	2.2029	0.4626	3.5824	0.4815	0.1273	11.2270	0.2386	-0.0000*	18.2967	0.2293	0.0000*	6.0759
SHIPS	0.0348	0.5025	0.0641	0.0610	0.1478	0.0449	1.5902	0.0880	0.0001	5.8883	0.0201	0.0000*	2.2244
ELECTRONIC EQUIP	0.1286	1.3073	0.3447	1.4237	0.1915	0.0853	6.1100	0.1352	0.0022	8.2441	0.1539	0.0000*	2.4671
NEW CONSTRUCTION	0.0595	1.0814	0.1154	0.5201	0.0646	0.0620	1.0946	0.0463	0.0288	2.8255	0.0356	0.0254	1.0263
MAINTENANCE	0.0435	0.7908	0.0844	0.3803	0.0472	0.0453	0.8004	0.0339	0.7523	2.0660	0.0260	0.0186	0.7505
MISSILES	0.0406	0.3667	0.0593	0.2775	0.0332	0.0128	4.7550	0.0191	-0.0000*	8.1863	0.0249	0.0000*	1.4164
AMMUNITION, NEC	0.0366	0.3813	0.0992	0.4477	0.0612	0.0251	1.7650	0.0399	0.0003	2.3605	0.0447	-0.0000*	0.7400
TANKS	0.1366	0.5083	0.1605	2.4744	0.0530	0.0327	1.2035	0.0283	0.0002	3.3876	0.0476	-0.0000*	1.5933
SMALL ARMS	0.0022	0.0238	0.0060	0.0282	0.0094	0.0020	0.1343	0.0034	0.0004	0.1573	0.0028	0.0000*	0.0599
SM. ARMS AMMUN.	0.0238	0.0596	0.0162	0.0668	0.0144	0.0044	0.2940	0.0071	0.0004	0.3695	0.0072	0.0000*	0.1238
OTHER ORDNANCE	0.0129	0.1289	0.0342	0.1446	0.0248	0.0089	0.6187	0.0143	0.0003	0.8128	0.0153	-0.0000*	0.2584
TOTAL OUTPUT	0.6938	7.3537	1.4467	9.4067	1.1288	0.4507	29.5926	0.6542	1.7850	52.5948	0.6075	0.0440	16.7360

BASE SCENARIO IN 1980

	AAF	ASC	ASL	EEM	JAP	LAT	NAH	OCH	OIL	RUH	SAF	TAF	WEU
FISH													
FISH CATCH	0.6	7.9	9.3	0.8	8.2	14.4	3.8	0.2	0.4	6.7	2.2	1.9	9.6
NON-HUMAN USE	0.3	0.1	1.0	0.1	2.0	12.5	1.2	-0.0*	-0.1	0.1	2.0	0.1	1.7
FISH IMPORTS	0.1	0.0	0.3	0.2	0.2	0.1	1.3	0.0*	0.0*	0.1	0.0*	0.6	1.6
FISH EXPORTS	0.1	0.1	0.3	0.0*	0.5	0.1	0.4	0.0*	0.1	0.4	0.0*	0.1	2.0
EXPORTS													
LIVESTOCK	0.0*	0.0	0.0*	1.4	0.0*	1.5	1.1	2.4	0.0*	0.2	0.1	0.0*	5.9
HIGH PROT. CROPS	0.7	0.0	2.1	0.4	0.1	1.5	22.4	0.0*	1.5	0.8	0.2	1.2	3.1
GRAINS	0.8	0.0	5.1	4.3	2.2	10.9	67.2	9.3	0.2	5.6	1.1	0.4	19.1
ROOTS	0.5	0.0	0.9	2.1	0.0*	0.5	2.8	0.2	0.3	0.3	0.0	0.4	7.2
OTHER AGRICULT.	1.0	0.6	5.1	1.6	0.0*	4.8	3.4	1.3	1.0	1.1	0.4	2.7	8.3
FOOD PROCESSING	0.2	0.3	1.2	0.9	0.3	2.2	2.7	1.0	0.1	0.4	0.2	0.1	6.3
TEXT., APPAREL	0.3	1.0	6.0	3.9	6.8	0.7	2.7	0.4	0.1	0.4	0.1	0.1	28.6
WOOD AND CORK	0.0*	0.0*	0.7	1.0	0.4	0.3	2.2	0.0*	0.5	1.3	0.0*	0.1	3.5
FURNITURE, FIXT.	0.0*	0.1	0.0*	0.2	0.1	0.0*	0.1	0.0*	0.1	0.3	0.1	0.0*	1.4
PAPER	0.0*	0.0*	0.1	0.1	0.5	0.1	7.0	0.1	0.0*	0.0*	0.0*	0.0*	9.2
PRINTING	0.0*	0.0*	0.1	0.1	0.2	0.0*	0.4	0.0*	0.0*	0.3	0.1	0.0*	2.7
RUBBER	0.0*	0.1	0.1	0.4	0.6	0.1	0.9	0.1	0.0*	0.0*	0.0*	0.0*	2.5
INDUSTRIAL CHEM.	0.2	0.4	0.1	0.6	3.0	0.3	5.1	0.2	0.2	0.4	0.1	0.0*	14.5
FERTILIZERS	0.0*	0.1	0.1	0.3	0.5	0.2	3.3	0.0*	0.1	1.4	0.0*	0.0*	4.7
OTHER CHEMICALS	0.0*	0.1	0.3	0.3	0.5	0.3	2.5	0.2	0.1	0.1	0.0*	0.0*	9.6
CEMENT	0.0*	0.1	0.1	0.0*	0.0*	0.0*	0.1	0.0*	0.0*	0.0*	0.0*	0.0*	0.3
GLASS	0.1	0.1	0.1	0.6	0.9	0.1	1.0	0.0*	0.0*	0.1	0.0*	0.0*	5.6
MOTOR VEHICLES	0.0*	0.0*	0.2	3.6	5.0	0.1	11.6	0.0*	0.1	2.2	0.0*	0.0*	19.8
SHIPBUILDING	0.0*	0.0	0.1	0.9	2.1	0.0*	0.2	0.0*	0.0*	0.8	0.0*	0.0*	2.2
AIRCRAFT	0.0*	0.0	0.1	0.0*	2.1	0.0*	5.0	0.0*	0.0*	2.2	0.0*	0.0*	2.1
METAL PRODUCTS	0.0*	0.0*	0.2	0.1	1.3	0.1	2.2	0.1	0.0*	0.9	0.1	0.0*	5.9
MACHINERY	0.0*	0.0*	0.3	9.5	4.7	0.2	12.4	0.2	0.0*	3.6	0.1	0.0*	30.6
ELECTRICAL MACH.	0.0*	0.0*	0.7	3.1	6.2	0.2	5.6	0.1	0.0*	0.1	0.0*	0.0*	16.7
INSTRUMENTS	0.0*	0.0*	0.1	0.4	1.7	0.0*	3.0	0.0*	0.0*	0.2	0.0*	0.0*	5.5
OTHER MANUFACT.	0.2	0.1	1.6	0.1	1.6	0.1	1.4	0.1	0.0*	0.4	0.4	0.3	7.5
SERVICES	0.3	0.0	0.7	0.0	0.2	2.9	5.0	0.2	0.4	0.0	1.8	0.1	16.5
TRANSPORT	0.2	0.0	1.6	0.0	2.8	1.3	6.9	1.0	0.5	0.0	0.4	0.5	26.6
AID INFLOW	1.8	0.0	9.5	0.0	0.3	4.6	4.1	0.7	1.7	0.0	0.7	1.3	16.3
CAPITAL INFLOW	0.0*	0.0	1.4	0.0	5.7	2.5	16.5	0.2	0.9	0.0	0.1	0.3	18.5
MILITARY EXPORTS													
AIRCRAFT	0.0	0.0574	0.0574	0.5163	0.0	0.0	2.2948	0.0	0.0	1.8359	0.0	0.0	0.9753
SHIPS	0.0	0.0077	0.0	0.0	0.0	0.0	0.1691	0.0	0.0	0.2459	0.0	0.0	0.3458
ELECTRONIC EQUIP	0.0492	0.0246	0.0246	0.0985	0.0	0.0246	1.0341	0.0	0.0	0.5663	0.0	0.0	0.6402
MISSILES	0.0120	0.0	0.0	0.0	0.0	0.0	0.5029	0.0	0.0	0.4909	0.0	0.0	0.1916
AMMUNITION, NEC	0.0140	0.0070	0.0070	0.0279	0.0	0.0070	0.2933	0.0	0.0	0.1606	0.0	0.0	0.1816
TANKS	0.0	0.0	0.0	0.1491	0.0	0.0	0.8307	0.0	0.0	0.6177	0.0	0.0	0.5325
SMALL ARMS	0.0009	0.0004	0.0004	0.0018	0.0	0.0004	0.0186	0.0	0.0	0.0102	0.0	0.0	0.0115
SM. ARMS AMMUN.	0.0024	0.0012	0.0012	0.0048	0.0	0.0012	0.0503	0.0	0.0	0.0275	0.0	0.0	0.0311
OTHER ORDNANCE	0.0050	0.0025	0.0025	0.0100	0.0	0.0025	0.1047	0.0	0.0	0.0573	0.0	0.0	0.0648
TOTAL EXPORTS	0.0835	0.1008	0.0931	0.8084	0.0	0.0357	5.2986	0.0	0.0	4.0124	0.0	0.0	2.9744
MIL. GRANTS INF.	0.0368	0.0529	0.1086	0.0023	0.0	0.0203	0.0	0.0	0.0	0.0	0.0	0.0792	0.0123

IMPORTS	AAF	ASC	ASL	EEM	JAP	LAT	NAH	OCH	OIL	RUH	SAF	TAF	WEU
LIVESTOCK	0.1	0.0*	0.6	1.1	0.6	0.6	2.1	0.0*	0.6	0.2	0.1	0.3	6.5
HIGH PROT. CROPS	0.5	0.0*	1.5	2.4	8.7	1.0	1.8	0.2	1.3	0.2	0.0*	0.2	16.2
GRAINS	2.7	0.1	21.2	23.1	15.9	9.9	1.6	0.2	5.4	3.7	0.6	3.2	38.7
ROOTS	0.2	0.0*	1.1	2.5	1.0	1.4	0.6	0.2	0.8	0.0	0.0	0.2	7.4
OTHER AGRICULT.	0.2	0.8	1.8	3.4	3.2	0.9	6.1	0.1	2.1	2.2	0.1	0.4	10.0
FOOD PROCESSING	0.2	0.0*	1.5	1.4	0.8	0.8	2.8	0.7	1.7	1.0	0.6	1.7	5.4
TEXT., APPAREL	0.5	0.1	3.9	1.8	1.8	1.3	11.2	0.1	1.9	3.8	0.1	0.1	22.2
WOOD AND CORK	0.1	0.0	0.1	0.3	0.8	0.1	2.2	0.1	0.9	0.5	0.0*	0.2	4.1
FURNITURE, FIXT.	0.0*	0.0*	0.0*	0.3	0.0*	0.0*	0.5	0.0*	0.1	0.1	0.2	0.1	0.8
PAPER	0.1	0.0*	0.7	0.4	0.7	0.9	3.4	0.3	1.3	0.4	0.0*	0.2	9.1
PRINTING	0.0*	0.0*	0.1	0.1	0.3	0.2	0.8	0.2	0.2	0.1	0.0*	0.1	1.8
RUBBER	0.0*	0.0*	0.2	0.1	0.0*	0.1	0.6	0.1	0.5	0.8	0.1	0.1	2.0
INDUSTRIAL CHEM.	0.2	0.5	1.5	1.2	0.9	1.8	2.8	0.5	1.3	0.8	0.3	0.3	12.2
FERTILIZERS	0.1	0.8	1.8	0.9	0.3	3.3	1.3	0.3	0.7	0.2	0.1	-0.4	2.4
OTHER CHEMICALS	0.1	0.0*	1.0	0.3	0.8	1.0	0.9	0.3	2.5	0.2	0.1	0.0*	6.2
CEMENT	0.0*	0.0*	0.1	0.0	0.0*	0.0*	0.1	0.0*	0.2	0.0*	0.0	0.0*	0.1
GLASS	0.0*	0.0*	0.3	0.3	0.2	0.3	1.6	0.2	1.3	0.1	0.0	0.2	4.1
MOTOR VEHICLES	0.1	0.1	0.6	1.5	0.2	1.5	18.3	1.2	2.1	0.5	0.3	0.1	16.4
SHIPBUILDING	0.0*	0.1	0.3	0.4	0.1	0.3	0.2	0.4	0.4	2.2	0.0*	0.1	2.3
AIRCRAFT	0.1	0.0*	0.3	0.1	0.9	0.3	1.7	0.4	0.4	0.0	0.1	0.4	5.3
METAL PRODUCTS	0.1	0.3	0.6	0.1	0.1	0.7	1.8	0.2	2.0	0.3	0.7	1.0	4.4
MACHINERY	0.2	0.0*	3.0	4.1	1.6	4.2	8.0	1.4	11.4	3.7	0.3	0.3	22.1
ELECTRICAL MACH.	0.2	0.0*	1.7	0.9	0.8	1.9	6.1	1.6	4.9	0.6	0.3	0.1	14.5
INSTRUMENTS	0.0*	0.0*	0.4	0.2	0.4	0.6	1.9	0.3	1.3	0.3	0.1	0.1	5.0
OTHER MANUFACT.	0.2	0.1	1.1	0.2	0.6	0.5	4.2	0.2	0.5	0.5	0.2	0.1	5.7
SERVICES	0.0	0.0	0.0*	0.0	1.2	2.0	9.1	0.6	0.7	0.0	0.5	0.1	14.2
TRANSPORT	0.4	0.0	2.2	0.0	5.0	2.7	6.3	1.4	2.5	0.0	0.5	0.9	19.8
AID OUTFLOW	0.4	0.2	1.5	0.0	1.6	1.8	12.8	0.8	4.4	1.0	0.3	0.8	15.5
CAPITAL OUTFLOW	0.0*	0.0	1.4	0.0	3.4	4.3	10.5	2.7	9.0	0.0	0.5	0.4	13.9

MILITARY IMPORTS	AAF	ASC	ASL	EEM	JAP	LAT	NAH	OCH	OIL	RUH	SAF	TAF	WEU
AIRCRAFT	0.5477	0.0661	0.4441	0.6305	0.0477	0.2634	0.1134	0.0356	2.3092	0.3659	0.0404	0.2363	0.6369
SHIPS	0.0706	0.0050	0.0524	0.0153	0.0030	0.1150	0.0161	0.0027	0.3463	0.0	0.0134	0.0822	0.0464
ELECTRONIC EQUIP	0.2610	0.0261	0.1779	0.2506	0.0167	0.1224	0.0617	0.0134	1.0349	0.0833	0.0171	0.1035	0.2938
MISSILES	0.1044	0.0194	0.0819	0.3386	0.0179	0.0216	0.0480	0.0103	0.3928	0.0	0.0037	0.0139	0.1448
AMMUNITION, NEC	0.0742	0.0076	0.0512	0.0788	0.0053	0.0341	0.0178	0.0040	0.2820	0.0238	0.0050	0.0282	0.0863
TANKS	0.2537	0.0264	0.1367	0.1311	0.0141	0.0634	0.0122	0.0105	1.0269	0.0342	0.0159	0.0749	0.3301
SMALL ARMS	0.0044	0.0005	0.0031	0.0050	0.0008	0.0022	0.0014	0.0003	0.0165	0.0016	0.0003	0.0017	0.0066
SM. ARMS AMMUN.	0.0125	0.0012	0.0084	0.0118	0.0013	0.0061	0.0030	0.0007	0.0507	0.0037	0.0008	0.0051	0.0146
OTHER ORDNANCE	0.0261	0.0026	0.0177	0.0255	0.0022	0.0125	0.0062	0.0014	0.1044	0.0082	0.0017	0.0104	0.0305
TOTAL IMPORTS	1.3547	0.1550	0.9734	1.4870	0.1088	0.6408	0.2797	0.0788	5.5636	0.5208	0.0982	0.5562	1.5899
MIL. GRANTS OUTF	0.0*	0.0706	0.0	0.0	C.0	0.0	0.0922	0.0	0.0	0.1206	0.0	0.0	0.0292

BASE SCENARIO IN 1990

	AAF	ASC	ASL	EEM	JAP	LAT	NAH	OCH	OIL	RUH	SAF	TAF	WEU
CONSUMPTION AND POPULATION													
GDP	32.5	294.6	210.6	425.9	638.5	285.0	1832.7	107.1	515.3	1329.6	29.4	61.9	1649.3
PERSONAL CONSUMP	24.2	198.3	162.5	263.4	411.4	211.8	1204.3	73.2	316.6	746.2	21.5	43.7	1092.9
GOVT.(CIVILIAN)	3.2	29.5	21.1	42.6	63.9	28.5	183.3	10.7	51.5	133.0	2.9	6.2	164.9
GOVT.(MILITARY)	4.9	27.7	8.4	28.5	12.8	5.8	133.4	2.7	33.5	133.4	1.6	2.4	56.7
POPULATION	221.8	1090.3	1670.9	119.2	126.2	481.7	278.6	21.5	233.1	293.7	37.9	247.6	453.8
URBAN POPULATION	115.3	380.0	472.3	78.5	86.2	330.7	230.6	19.2	95.5	210.4	21.9	67.2	338.1
EMPLOYMENT	14.7	140.7	104.1	60.3	63.2	128.5	120.3	8.6	117.7	144.2	11.0	27.3	167.5
GDP/HEAD	146.5	270.2	126.0	3572.9	5059.7	591.6	6578.3	4983.1	2210.7	4526.9	775.7	250.1	3634.4
CONSUMPTION/HEAD	109.1	181.8	97.2	2209.4	3260.2	439.7	4322.6	3404.5	1358.2	2540.4	566.3	176.7	2408.3
CALORIES/HEAD	2213.1	2136.8	2057.1	3179.3	3247.2	2381.4	3194.8	3232.5	2765.8	3180.4	2580.0	2359.7	3019.8
PROTEINS/HEAD	64.3	63.9	53.0	104.2	116.6	60.0	98.7	99.0	90.5	103.1	75.1	68.2	95.8
INVESTMENT AND CAPITAL													
INVESTMENT	2.6	35.6	18.5	72.7	145.7	41.8	271.4	25.6	147.3	292.9	3.0	6.8	314.9
EQUIPMENT	1.3	18.4	9.7	31.0	46.2	19.2	103.9	8.8	58.8	113.9	1.9	3.7	115.1
PLANT	1.2	16.6	7.9	41.6	99.5	21.9	167.3	16.6	88.3	178.4	1.1	2.9	199.6
IRRIGATION	0.1	0.6	1.0	0.1	0.0*	0.2	0.1	0.0*	0.1	0.6	0.0*	0.0*	0.2
LAND (AREA)	0.9	0.9	1.3	0.0	0.0	2.8	0.8	0.6	0.5	0.0	0.1	1.7	0.1
INVENTORY CHANGE	0.5	3.3	2.5	3.5	4.9	3.1	5.4	0.8	12.1	11.9	0.3	0.8	11.3
CAPITAL STOCK	38.9	409.4	243.2	833.3	1410.9	486.4	4715.7	259.3	866.1	2655.6	52.7	67.8	3697.2
EQUIPMENT	17.5	197.7	114.0	289.3	397.7	199.8	1200.9	75.5	332.5	901.3	21.5	32.6	1087.1
PLANT	21.4	211.6	129.2	544.0	1013.2	286.5	3514.8	183.8	533.6	1754.2	31.2	35.2	2610.2
INVENTORY STOCK	11.4	95.7	72.8	89.8	112.2	84.0	309.5	20.4	117.1	259.4	17.5	17.5	303.8
CULTIVATED LAND	59.9	285.3	408.6	53.1	12.7	152.9	158.3	22.2	179.2	280.7	15.0	97.2	120.7
SURPLUS SAVINGS	2.7	-1.2	11.3	12.0	2.9	-2.3	45.0	-9.2	-79.8	-31.5	3.0	-1.1	25.6
INTERNATIONAL TRANSACTIONS													
IMPORTS	7.0	5.2	41.5	48.8	78.7	48.6	138.5	21.0	116.4	37.8	7.5	16.8	442.5
EXPORTS	4.0	5.3	39.0	63.0	77.6	41.9	170.3	15.0	70.6	47.0	7.4	18.8	448.2
PAYMENTS SURPLUS	0.0	0.1	0.0	-7.3	-63.1	12.0	5.6	-8.3	163.7	13.5	0.0	0.0	-115.0
FOR.INVEST.INFLO	-1.0	-5.8	10.1	-62.7	-384.7	128.6	20.1	-121.3	1120.4	159.2	-11.9	0.4	-861.0
FOR.INC.OUTFLOW	-0.2	-0.5	-0.0*	-5.0	-31.2	7.7	6.5	-10.6	85.7	12.7	-1.4	-0.4	-64.1
LEVEL OF ABATEMENT ACTIVITIES													
AIR	0.0	0.0	0.0	5.73	8.14	0.83	58.42	1.26	0.0	20.11	0.14	0.0	23.01
PRIMARY WATER	0.0	0.0	0.0	2.62	3.52	0.30	8.97	0.69	0.0	8.87	0.04	0.0	11.20
SECONDARY WATER	0.0	0.0	0.0	0.15	1.29	0.02	0.51	0.12	0.0	0.51	0.00*	0.0	0.64
TERTIARY WATER	0.0	0.0	0.0	0.03	0.28	0.00*	0.11	0.03	0.0	0.11	0.00*	0.0	0.14
SOLID WASTE	0.0	0.0	0.0	86.47	100.94	78.64	324.04	23.32	0.0	244.60	8.48	0.0	342.04
NET TOTAL EMISSIONS													
PESTICIDES	0.35	0.17	1.28	0.48	0.78	0.79	2.29	0.03	1.95	0.67	3.56	0.09	1.24
PARTICULATES	0.30	2.51	1.31	0.53	0.23	2.52	4.21	0.05	7.79	1.17	0.20	0.48	1.85
BIOLOG. OXYGEN	1.00	5.47	4.09	2.36	1.52	3.81	10.64	0.26	4.52	6.66	0.44	0.31	8.78
NITROGEN (WATER)	0.01	0.05	0.03	0.10	0.06	0.04	0.21	0.01	0.05	0.35	0.01	0.00*	0.45
PHOSPHATES	0.01	0.03	0.02	0.05	0.03	0.03	0.16	0.00*	0.04	0.18	0.01	0.00*	0.24
SUSPENDED SOLIDS	0.22	1.65	0.86	1.52	0.95	1.83	6.82	0.18	3.13	3.99	0.18	0.55	4.50
DISSOLVED SOLIDS	4.09	20.73	13.40	13.44	15.26	12.51	51.08	1.73	15.94	48.09	1.70	0.54	62.22
SOLID WASTE	41.18	165.29	167.19	0.0	0.0	138.73	0.0	0.0	75.32	0.0	8.49	20.81	36.00

RESOURCE OUTPUTS

	AAF	ASC	ASL	EEM	JAP	LAT	NAH	OCH	OIL	RUH	SAF	TAF	WEU
COPPER	0.0*	0.3	0.3	0.3	0.2	3.8	3.6	0.5	0.0	1.7	0.0*	4.8	0.5
BAUXITE	0.0	0.1	0.9	1.2	0.0	13.3	0.5	5.8	0.0	1.3	0.0	1.8	1.8
NICKEL	0.7	0.0	437.8	0.0	0.0	103.5	514.5	82.0	0.0	435.2	0.0	0.0	0.0
ZINC	0.0*	0.2	0.1	0.6	0.1	0.4	5.4	1.8	0.0	1.0	0.0	1.1	1.3
LEAD	0.0	0.3	0.0*	0.0	0.1	0.0*	8.6	0.0	0.0	0.0	0.0	0.0*	0.0
IRON	5.3	64.7	77.2	12.3	1.5	149.0	136.0	52.5	9.4	398.4	5.9	58.8	70.2
PETROLEUM	53.9	118.1	75.0	24.1	1.0	683.5	1681.3	11.0	5479.2	1841.9	0.0	0.0	21.0
NATURAL GAS	0.0	0.0	13.0	45.0	0.0	143.0	1473.3	2.0	1007.8	1291.9	0.0	0.0	285.1
COAL	1.1	723.6	188.5	715.9	87.7	24.4	1182.5	140.2	1.1	1043.8	44.4	20.8	756.2

CUMULATIVE RESOURCE OUTPUT AT END OF PERIOD

	AAF	ASC	ASL	EEM	JAP	LAT	NAH	OCH	OIL	RUH	SAF	TAF	WEU
COPPER	0.*	4.	4.	4.	3.	41.	57.	5.	0.*	28.	2.	49.	7.
BAUXITE	0.	3.	18.	17.	0.	172.	6.	70.	0.	21.	0.	20.	33.
NICKEL	4.	0.	5292.	84.	0.	1209.	7980.	1007.	0.	4924.	182.	145.	209.
ZINC	0.*	5.	1.	9.	5.	17.	61.	20.	2.	14.	0.	9.	19.
LEAD	2.	5.	1.	4.	2.	10.	62.	11.		9.		1.	8.
IRON	100.	862.	654.	159.	21.	1556.	2137.	784.	153.	2973.	112.	641.	1951.
PETROLEUM	799.	1492.	376.	482.	20.	9586.	24737.	221.	60548.	13831.	0.	33.	465.
NATURAL GAS	1.	0.	207.	900.	0.	1524.	24207.	40.	8960.	13556.	0.	0.*	3001.
COAL	14.	10398.	2690.	9282.	1229.	318.	17078.	1830.	14.	13123.	992.	219.	10695.

NET EXPORTS OF RESOURCES

	AAF	ASC	ASL	EEM	JAP	LAT	NAH	OCH	OIL	RUH	SAF	TAF	WEU
COPPER	0.0	-0.1	0.2	-0.4	-2.8	3.2	-0.9	0.3	-0.3	-1.4	0.0	4.7	-4.4
BAUXITE	-0.0*	-0.2	0.0	0.0	-4.1	12.8	-5.3	5.0	-0.5	-3.0	-0.1	1.8	-6.2
NICKEL	0.0	-7.9	354.5	-27.1	-331.6	53.5	247.5	6.7	-6.8	6.7	-13.2	-0.1	-282.3
ZINC	0.0	-0.3	-0.2	-0.4	-2.5	-0.3	3.8	1.6	-0.4	-0.8	-0.0*	1.1	-2.1
LEAD	-0.0*	-0.1	-0.1	-0.7	-0.7	-0.3	7.3	-0.2	-0.7	-1.9	-0.0*	0.0	-2.9
IRON	4.1	0.0	65.7	-66.8	-183.7	127.3	20.5	24.6	-19.7	110.9	-29.7	57.5	-140.5
PETROLEUM	0.0	0.0	-148.4	-235.4	-1140.2	310.1	-366.1	-120.7	3955.1	232.7	0.0	-46.5	-2410.8
NATURAL GAS	-0.6	0.0	-23.0	-132.6	0.0	-17.5	0.0	-4.4	90.0	90.0	-0.0*	-0.0*	-2.0
COAL	-0.8	11.8	3.0	5.9	-205.9	-10.8	207.2	59.2	-24.4	8.9	0.0	0.0	-54.2
OTHER RESOURCES	0.2	0.3	0.3	-1.1	-1.6	0.6	2.1	0.2	0.8	0.4	0.3	0.2	-2.5
PETROL. REFINING	-0.0*	0.0*	-1.0	-1.9	-8.3	1.2	-1.1	-0.8	26.6	1.2	-0.1	-0.4	-15.4
PRIMARY METALS	-0.2	-1.1	-0.7	-3.3	-2.8	1.8	11.8	1.0	-1.6	-3.5	-0.0*	4.7	-6.1

BASE SCENARIO IN 1990

OUTPUT LEVELS

	AAF	ASC	ASL	EEM	JAP	LAT	NAH	OCH	OIL	RUH	SAF	TAF	WEU
ANIMAL PRODUCTS	5.5	37.7	28.8	20.0	16.4	36.5	60.6	8.9	18.5	46.8	3.4	9.3	73.6
HIGH PROT. CROPS	4.7	28.4	53.5	5.1	3.1	18.6	51.3	0.2	11.1	47.2	1.1	16.1	13.8
GRAINS	46.4	394.1	400.6	86.5	41.7	153.1	335.9	26.9	64.7	308.4	14.1	49.6	207.8
ROOTS	4.4	117.4	80.9	56.9	35.0	66.5	23.9	1.3	47.4	123.8	0.8	72.0	84.0
OTHER AGRICULT.	2.9	25.9	17.7	14.9	15.0	37.0	46.0	4.5	33.6	32.4	3.8	6.7	55.2
OTHER RESOURCES	0.5	1.9	1.4	1.2	2.7	2.0	11.7	0.8	3.6	8.8	0.5	0.3	7.3
FOOD PROCESSING	0.5	5.6	2.6	34.6	41.0	11.2	110.1	8.7	16.1	82.1	1.4	0.9	108.8
PETROL. REFINING	0.3	3.3	0.7	4.7	2.3	4.8	29.9	1.1	33.0	24.2	0.3	0.0*	12.7
PRIMARY METALS	0.3	6.7	2.4	17.7	28.7	6.9	82.5	5.0	10.8	63.1	0.7	5.2	65.5
TEXT. APPAREL	2.4	24.3	25.8	21.9	35.1	20.4	70.8	3.7	26.7	35.6	1.4	1.7	77.2
WOOD AND CORK	0.1	2.6	2.6	5.8	8.5	3.3	22.8	1.3	3.6	20.2	0.3	0.4	20.1
FURNITURE, FIXT.	0.6	7.4	3.9	9.9	5.8	10.5	15.5	1.9	19.5	10.2	1.1	1.3	18.9
PAPER	0.2	3.2	1.0	8.1	13.7	2.3	46.9	1.9	1.7	26.8	0.5	0.1	36.8
PRINTING	0.1	1.8	1.0	8.8	15.7	2.6	50.3	2.5	5.4	30.9	0.3	0.1	42.8
RUBBER	0.1	1.6	0.9	7.1	12.5	1.3	28.8	1.5	1.9	21.9	0.2	0.1	28.5
INDUSTRIAL CHEM.	0.8	8.2	4.5	9.5	19.0	5.4	44.0	1.7	7.5	30.8	0.5	0.5	45.0
FERTILIZERS	6.4	24.6	16.6	5.4	8.3	15.0	21.4	1.0	18.4	25.9	1.9	0.2	26.7
OTHER CHEMICALS	0.3	4.4	1.8	9.0	14.0	4.0	41.1	2.2	1.5	29.2	0.5	0.1	45.4
CEMENT	0.0*	0.4	0.2	0.9	2.2	0.4	4.2	2.3	0.6	3.6	0.0*	0.0*	4.5
GLASS	0.2	3.3	1.5	9.1	18.5	3.3	37.3	2.3	6.9	31.9	0.5	0.2	39.0
MOTOR VEHICLES	0.0*	2.0	0.2	22.3	39.0	0.9	72.6	3.0	5.1	64.4	0.1	0.0*	78.5
SHIPBUILDING	0.1	1.8	0.6	3.6	6.6	1.5	10.5	0.5	4.5	5.8	0.2	0.0*	9.2
AIRCRAFT	0.3	3.1	0.7	6.1	3.6	0.2	27.4	0.5	5.5	32.1	0.0*	0.0*	10.7
METAL PRODUCTS	0.7	8.8	4.2	24.2	41.9	6.9	88.0	5.9	17.3	85.1	0.9	0.6	95.4
MACHINERY	0.6	13.6	3.4	36.3	38.6	6.1	85.1	3.5	16.9	81.6	0.6	0.3	94.9
ELECTRICAL MACH.	0.3	6.3	1.4	23.4	37.6	2.0	71.6	3.4	5.4	64.8	0.3	0.0*	71.6
INSTRUMENTS	0.1	1.6	0.4	4.4	8.4	1.0	17.5	1.9	1.9	13.8	0.1	0.0*	16.4
OTHER MANUFACT.	0.4	3.9	3.6	4.7	9.1	3.8	19.1	1.0	5.9	13.0	1.1	0.9	22.4
UTILITIES	0.5	5.1	2.9	17.4	27.0	6.6	76.8	4.7	13.7	56.6	0.7	0.9	68.6
CONSTRUCTION	1.8	22.1	13.2	53.8	119.7	31.3	242.9	19.7	97.7	218.2	2.1	4.6	250.4
TRADE	2.7	30.4	17.3	86.5	139.1	43.9	377.0	24.0	89.2	267.2	4.8	5.6	351.8
TRANSPORTATION	1.6	18.8	10.7	23.6	28.7	17.5	100.5	5.0	31.9	70.5	2.0	2.7	100.1
COMMUNICATIONS	0.4	3.7	2.2	9.2	15.6	4.3	46.0	2.7	7.2	32.8	0.5	0.7	40.2
SERVICES	6.7	64.0	43.9	124.8	211.4	81.5	653.3	37.8	129.6	421.1	10.5	12.8	554.0

MILITARY OUTPUT LEVELS

	AAF	ASC	ASL	EEM	JAP	LAT	NAH	OCH	OIL	RUH	SAF	TAF	WEU
AIRCRAFT	0.2268	3.2310	0.5931	5.6318	1.8330	0.1333	19.0772	0.3988	-0.0000*	25.2683	0.3009	0.0000*	9.3429
SHIPS	0.0410	0.7371	0.0811	0.0968	0.5628	0.0470	2.7730	0.1471	0.0001	8.0783	0.0264	0.0000*	3.4263
ELECTRONIC EQUIP	0.1568	1.9171	0.4403	2.2484	0.7292	0.0977	10.4942	0.2260	0.0033	11.3397	0.2020	0.0001	3.7829
NEW CONSTRUCTION	0.0701	1.5850	0.1460	0.8244	0.2460	0.1003	1.9356	0.0774	1.5484	3.8557	0.0467	0.0419	1.5825
MAINTENANCE	0.0513	1.1590	0.1068	0.6028	0.1799	0.0733	1.4153	0.0566	1.1322	3.8193	0.0342	0.0306	1.1571
MISSILES	0.0491	0.5376	0.0752	0.4391	0.1263	0.0135	8.2565	0.0319	-0.0000*	11.2700	0.0327	-0.0000*	2.1948
AMMUNITION, NEC	0.0446	0.5592	0.1268	0.7089	0.2205	0.0288	3.0092	0.0668	-0.0000*	3.2593	0.0587	-0.0000*	1.1381
TANKS	0.1610	0.7450	0.2031	3.9048	0.1979	0.0343	1.8328	0.0474	-0.0000*	4.7102	0.0625	-0.0000*	2.4374
SMALL ARMS	0.0027	0.0349	0.0077	0.0463	0.0238	0.0023	0.2166	0.0058	0.0002	0.2270	0.0037	-0.0000*	0.0956
SM. ARMS AMMUN.	0.0075	0.0874	0.0207	0.1073	0.0432	0.0051	0.4920	0.0121	0.0002	0.5183	0.0094	-0.0000*	0.1933
OTHER ORDNANCE	0.0157	0.1891	0.0437	0.2301	0.0831	0.0102	1.0492	0.0241	-0.0000*	1.1282	0.0201	-0.0000*	0.3998
TOTAL OUTPUT	0.8266	10.7823	1.8446	14.8406	4.2457	0.5459	50.5515	1.0940	2.6844	72.4744	0.7974	0.0726	25.7506

	AAF	ASC	ASL	EEM	JAP	LAT	NAH	OCH	OIL	RUH	SAF	TAF	WEU
FISH													
FISH CATCH	0.6	7.9	9.3	0.8	8.2	14.4	3.8	0.2	0.4	6.7	2.2	1.9	9.6
NON-HUMAN USE	0.3	0.1	1.0	0.1	2.0	12.5	1.2	-0.0*	-0.1	0.6	2.0	0.6	1.7
FISH IMPORTS	0.1	0.0	0.3	0.2	0.2	0.1	1.3	0.0*	0.0*	0.4	0.0*	0.1	1.6
FISH EXPORTS	0.1	0.1	0.3	0.0*	0.5	0.1	0.4	0.0*	0.1	0.4	0.0*	0.1	2.0
EXPORTS													
LIVESTOCK	0.0*	0.0	0.1	1.9	0.0*	1.9	1.4	3.2	0.0*	0.2	0.1	0.1	7.6
HIGH PROT. CROPS	0.9	0.0	2.9	0.6	0.1	2.1	31.6	0.0*	2.1	1.2	0.2	1.7	4.3
GRAINS	1.2	0.0	7.4	6.1	3.2	15.7	96.9	13.5	0.3	8.1	1.6	0.6	27.5
ROOTS	0.6	0.0	1.2	2.6	0.1	0.7	3.5	1.5	0.3	0.3	0.4	0.5	8.9
OTHER AGRICULT.	1.1	0.7	5.9	1.9	0.4	5.5	3.9	1.5	1.1	1.3	0.4	3.1	9.5
FOOD PROCESSING	0.2	0.3	1.5	1.1	0.4	2.8	3.5	1.4	0.2	0.5	0.2	0.6	8.2
TEXT., APPAREL	0.5	2.1	12.3	8.6	13.6	1.5	4.5	0.8	1.8	2.7	0.2	0.2	58.2
WOOD AND CORK	0.0*	0.0*	1.4	0.7	0.7	0.5	3.3	0.0*	0.0*	2.7	0.0*	0.2	6.7
FURNITURE, FIXT.	0.0*	0.0*	0.0*	1.1	0.1	0.0*	0.1	0.0*	0.0*	0.0*	0.4	0.0*	1.4
PAPER	0.0*	0.2	0.2	0.4	1.2	0.4	12.4	0.3	0.1	0.9	0.4	0.0*	21.5
PRINTING	0.0*	0.0*	0.2	0.2	0.5	0.2	1.7	0.1	0.1	0.3	0.0*	0.0*	6.5
RUBBER	0.0*	0.0*	0.2	0.9	1.3	0.1	0.8	0.1	0.1	1.0	0.3	0.0*	5.6
INDUSTRIAL CHEM.	0.0*	0.3	0.3	1.4	5.3	0.7	6.9	0.4	0.0*	3.1	0.0*	0.1	26.0
FERTILIZERS	0.3	0.8	0.2	0.6	1.1	0.4	5.4	0.4	0.7	0.1	0.0*	0.0*	9.6
OTHER CHEMICALS	0.1	0.0*	0.7	0.6	1.1	0.6	4.3	0.0*	0.2	0.4	0.0*	0.0*	20.3
CEMENT	0.0*	0.2	0.1	0.1	0.2	0.1	0.1	0.0*	0.2	0.0*	0.0*	0.1	0.6
GLASS	0.0*	0.2	0.2	1.5	2.1	0.2	1.8	0.1	0.0*	0.2	0.3	0.1	12.9
MOTOR VEHICLES	0.0*	0.0*	0.5	8.9	10.1	0.3	16.1	0.4	0.2	5.7	0.1	0.0*	39.5
SHIPBUILDING	0.0*	0.0*	0.1	1.7	3.1	0.0*	1.5	0.0*	0.0*	1.5	0.1	0.0*	3.7
AIRCRAFT	0.0*	0.1	0.1	0.0*	0.1	0.0*	8.5	0.0*	0.1	4.9	0.0*	0.0*	4.4
METAL PRODUCTS	0.0*	0.1	0.4	0.3	2.2	0.1	2.7	0.1	0.0*	1.7	0.1	0.0*	9.8
MACHINERY	0.0*	0.1	0.6	20.6	8.4	0.6	15.4	0.3	0.1	8.2	0.3	0.0*	54.7
ELECTRICAL MACH.	0.0*	0.1	1.5	7.0	12.6	0.4	9.5	0.2	0.0*	0.4	0.1	0.0*	34.2
INSTRUMENTS	0.0*	0.0*	0.2	0.9	3.4	0.1	4.5	0.1	0.0*	0.4	0.1	0.0*	11.2
OTHER MANUFACT.	0.3	0.2	2.7	0.2	2.6	0.2	1.9	0.1	0.0*	0.8	0.8	0.4	12.2
SERVICES	0.4	0.0	1.0	0.0	4.6	4.2	7.4	0.3	0.6	0.8	2.6		24.3
TRANSPORT	0.3	0.0	2.7	0.0	0.5	2.3	11.5	1.6	0.8	0.0	0.7	0.9	44.4
AID INFLOW	2.8	0.0	14.9	0.0		7.3	6.5	1.1	2.7	0.0	1.1	2.1	25.7
CAPITAL INFLOW	0.1	0.0	3.3	0.0	10.5	5.9	25.8	0.5	3.3	0.0	0.2	0.5	34.5

MILITARY EXPORTS

	AAF	ASC	ASL	EEM	JAP	LAT	NAH	OCH	OIL	RUH	SAF	TAF	WEU
AIRCRAFT	0.0	0.0	0.0859	0.7732	0.0	0.0	3.4366	0.0	0.0	2.7492	0.0	0.0	1.4605
SHIPS	0.0	0.0	0.0	0.0	0.0	0.0	0.2601	0.0	0.0	0.3783	0.0	0.0	0.5320
ELECTRONIC EQUIP	0.0739	0.0369	0.0369	0.1478	0.0	0.0369	1.5517	0.0	0.0	0.8497	0.0	0.0	0.9606
MISSILES	0.0184	0.0105	0.0105	0.0419	0.0	0.0105	0.7729	0.0	0.0	0.7545	0.0	0.0	0.2944
AMMUNITION, NEC	0.0210	0.0	0.0105	0.2206	0.0	0.0	0.4403	0.0	0.0	0.2411	0.0	0.0	0.2726
TANKS	0.0	0.0	0.0	0.0027	0.0	0.0	1.2288	0.0	0.0	0.9137	0.0	0.0	0.7877
SMALL ARMS	0.0013	0.0007	0.0007	0.0072	0.0	0.0007	0.0283	0.0	0.0	0.0155	0.0	0.0	0.0175
SM. ARMS AMMUN.	0.0036	0.0018	0.0018	0.0150	0.0	0.0018	0.0758	0.0	0.0	0.0415	0.0	0.0	0.0469
OTHER ORDNANCE	0.0075	0.0037	0.0037	0.0	0.0	0.0037	0.1574	0.0	0.0	0.0862	0.0	0.0	0.0975
TOTAL EXPORTS	0.1257	0.1514	0.1396	1.2084	0.0	0.0537	7.9518	0.0	0.0	6.0298	0.0	0.0	4.4696
MIL. GRANTS INF.	0.0564	0.0811	0.1664	0.0036	0.0	0.0311	0.0	0.0	0.0	0.0	0.0	0.1214	0.0189

BASE SCENARIO IN 1990

IMPORTS	AAF	ASC	ASL	EEM	JAP	LAT	NAH	OCH	OIL	RUH	SAF	TAF	WEU
LIVESTOCK	0.1	0.0*	0.9	1.3	1.1	0.9	2.3	0.0*	1.1	0.3	0.1	0.4	7.9
HIGH PROT. CROPS	0.7	0.0*	2.1	3.3	13.7	1.4	2.4	0.3	2.4	0.2	0.0*	6.2	21.0
GRAINS	4.2	0.1	28.2	31.3	25.8	17.9	2.1	0.3	8.0	5.5	0.9	6.2	52.8
ROOTS	0.3	0.0*	1.5	3.0	1.6	1.9	0.5	0.1	1.1	0.0	0.0	0.3	8.6
OTHER AGRICULT.	0.2	1.0	2.1	2.9	2.6	1.2	7.3	0.2	5.4	1.5	0.2	0.3	11.0
FOOD PROCESSING	0.2	0.0*	1.9	1.4	0.9	1.2	3.3	0.2	4.1	0.8	0.1	0.6	6.2
TEXT., APPAREL	0.9	0.1	5.3	4.3	4.2	2.5	3.3	1.6	6.9	7.1	0.9	3.5	51.7
WOOD AND CORK	0.1	0.0	0.2	0.6	1.6	0.3	2.2	0.2	2.8	0.3	0.1	0.2	8.3
FURNITURE, FIXT.	0.0*	0.0*	0.0*	0.5	0.0*	0.1	0.6	0.0*	0.4	0.3	0.0*	0.4	0.7
PAPER	0.0*	0.0*	0.9	1.1	1.7	1.7	4.0	0.6	5.0	1.1	0.1	0.2	20.7
PRINTING	0.0*	0.0*	0.2	0.8	0.8	0.5	1.0	0.4	1.0	0.2	0.1	0.2	4.5
RUBBER	0.1	0.0*	0.3	0.2	0.1	0.5	0.9	0.2	2.0	0.2	0.1	0.2	4.2
INDUSTRIAL CHEM.	0.3	0.8	2.4	1.9	1.7	2.8	4.1	0.9	3.7	1.4	0.5	0.5	21.1
FERTILIZERS	0.8	1.1	6.4	0.9	0.8	4.8	1.6	0.1	3.1	0.6	0.0*	0.2	3.5
OTHER CHEMICALS	0.2	0.1	1.5	0.5	1.7	1.8	1.4	0.7	8.0	0.6	0.1	0.7	11.5
CEMENT	0.0*	0.0*	0.1	0.0	0.0*	0.1	0.1	0.0*	0.6	0.2	0.0	0.4	0.3
GLASS	0.1	0.0*	0.4	0.8	0.4	0.7	1.6	0.4	3.7	0.4	0.0	0.4	10.6
MOTOR VEHICLES	0.1	0.3	1.0	3.3	0.6	2.9	27.1	2.7	7.7	1.3	0.5	0.2	34.0
SHIPBUILDING	0.1	0.1	0.4	0.6	0.1	0.4	0.3	0.2	0.4	3.4	0.0*	0.3	4.2
AIRCRAFT	0.1	0.0*	0.4	0.0	1.9	0.7	3.0	0.8	0.8	0.5	0.2	0.2	10.3
METAL PRODUCTS	0.5	0.5	0.6	0.2	0.2	1.2	2.0	0.4	4.1	0.5	0.1	0.7	7.3
MACHINERY	0.5	0.5	4.7	7.2	2.7	7.9	11.7	2.5	21.1	6.8	1.1	2.4	40.4
ELECTRICAL MACH.	0.3	0.1	2.8	1.9	1.8	3.9	9.4	1.3	11.9	1.5	0.4	0.8	29.7
INSTRUMENTS	0.1	0.1	0.7	0.4	0.9	1.1	2.8	0.6	3.2	0.7	0.2	0.2	9.9
OTHER MANUFACT.	0.2	0.1	1.6	0.2	1.0	0.8	6.2	0.3	1.3	0.8	0.1	0.2	9.5
SERVICES	0.0	0.0	0.0*	0.0	2.0	3.0	11.0	0.9	2.0	0.0	0.3	0.1	22.0
TRANSPORT	0.6	0.0	3.2	0.0	9.2	4.5	8.3	2.4	6.0	0.0	0.7	1.6	33.1
AID OUTFLOW	0.5	0.3	1.9	0.0	2.7	2.8	15.6	1.4	12.0	1.9	0.3	1.3	24.0
CAPITAL OUTFLOW	0.1	0.0	2.3	0.0	6.1	9.6	10.1	5.8	21.0	0.0	0.7	1.0	27.9

MILITARY IMPORTS	AAF	ASC	ASL	EEM	JAP	LAT	NAH	OCH	OIL	RUH	SAF	TAF	WEU
AIRCRAFT	0.6455	0.0969	0.5694	0.9912	0.1815	0.4868	0.1927	0.0594	3.4755	0.5054	0.0530	0.3899	0.9443
SHIPS	0.0832	0.0074	0.0664	0.0242	0.0113	0.2150	0.0280	0.0046	0.5212	0.0*	0.0176	0.1357	0.0676
ELECTRONIC EQUIP	0.3184	0.0383	0.2272	0.3957	0.0634	0.2264	0.1060	0.0224	1.5576	0.1145	0.0224	0.1707	0.4314
MISSILES	0.1262	0.0285	0.1038	0.5356	0.0680	0.0387	0.0834	0.0171	0.5912	0.0387	0.0049	0.0230	0.2196
AMMUNITION, NEC	0.0906	0.0112	0.0654	0.1248	0.0192	0.0626	0.0304	0.0066	0.4244	0.0329	0.0065	0.0465	0.1273
TANKS	0.2990	0.0387	0.1730	0.2070	0.0527	0.1185	0.0185	0.0175	1.5455	0.0476	0.0208	0.1236	0.4883
SMALL ARMS	0.0054	0.0007	0.0040	0.0082	0.0021	0.0039	0.0022	0.0006	0.0248	0.0023	0.0004	0.0027	0.0100
SM. ARMS AMMUN.	0.0153	0.0017	0.0107	0.0189	0.0038	0.0112	0.0050	0.0012	0.0764	0.0052	0.0010	0.0084	0.0217
OTHER ORDNANCE	0.0318	0.0038	0.0226	0.0405	0.0072	0.0230	0.0106	0.0024	0.1571	0.0114	0.0022	0.0172	0.0451
TOTAL IMPORTS	1.6155	0.2273	1.2425	2.3460	0.4090	1.1861	0.4767	0.1318	8.3737	0.7193	0.1289	0.9178	2.3554
MIL. GRANTS OUTF	0.0	0.1034	0.0	0.0	0.0	0.0	0.1120	0.0	0.0	0.2180	0.0	0.0	0.0455

BASE SCENARIO IN 2000

	AAF	ASC	ASL	EEM	JAP	LAT	NAH	OCH	OIL	RUH	SAF	TAF	WEU
CONSUMPTION AND POPULATION													
GDP	44.5	463.9	291.8	596.4	895.1	427.7	2344.6	132.0	1225.8	1774.9	66.0	84.1	2062.1
PERSONAL CONSUMP	32.4	298.0	210.5	356.9	577.9	303.2	1504.2	99.6	791.0	1062.5	46.9	66.3	1359.1
GOVT.(CIVILIAN)	4.4	46.4	29.2	59.6	89.5	42.8	234.5	13.2	122.6	177.5	6.6	8.4	206.2
GOVT.(MILITARY)	6.7	43.6	11.7	40.0	26.9	8.8	174.4	3.3	79.7	174.4	3.6	3.3	71.0
POPULATION	285.7	1221.3	2048.9	125.7	132.9	615.8	300.0	24.5	309.8	315.0	50.0	331.8	487.1
URBAN POPULATION	168.4	508.9	704.4	90.1	98.5	465.0	258.9	22.4	148.2	245.2	32.0	109.4	382.4
EMPLOYMENT	22.3	193.5	139.5	63.8	67.6	146.7	133.9	10.2	217.5	151.8	12.9	43.3	168.1
GDP/HEAD	155.8	379.8	142.4	4744.9	6734.9	694.5	7815.2	5386.4	3956.6	5634.7	1320.0	253.3	4233.5
CONSUMPTION/HEAD	113.3	244.0	102.7	2839.4	4348.2	492.4	5013.9	4064.4	2553.3	3373.0	937.1	199.8	2790.2
CALORIES/HEAD	2122.6	2244.3	2084.0	3168.0	3244.7	2578.3	3181.5	3211.6	3334.8	3177.1	2940.8	2380.7	3131.6
PROTEINS/HEAD	61.8	69.4	54.1	107.0	122.9	67.1	99.2	99.9	117.3	106.8	91.4	69.6	101.8
INVESTMENT AND CAPITAL													
INVESTMENT	4.9	63.8	27.0	98.8	172.9	77.0	378.7	23.5	414.5	327.0	12.2	7.9	311.0
EQUIPMENT	2.4	37.6	14.2	41.9	56.0	41.1	137.6	7.7	145.9	119.6	5.6	4.0	124.5
PLANT	2.3	25.7	11.9	56.7	116.9	35.2	240.9	15.7	268.4	206.6	6.6	3.8	186.3
IRRIGATION	0.1	0.6	1.0	0.1	0.0*	0.2	0.1	0.0*	0.1	0.6	0.0*	0.0*	0.2
LAND (AREA)	0.9	0.9	1.3	0.1	5.2	2.8	0.8	0.6	0.5	0.6	0.1	1.7	0.1
INVENTORY CHANGE	0.5	9.1	3.4	3.2	5.2	6.0	10.0	0.5	21.6	8.7	1.3	1.4	10.1
CAPITAL STOCK	61.7	728.9	379.6	1276.4	2231.3	845.4	6317.7	362.1	2688.2	4153.2	114.9	115.0	5005.0
EQUIPMENT	27.5	367.8	179.0	420.7	570.2	354.4	1560.5	92.9	887.2	1255.5	46.0	54.6	1420.6
PLANT	34.2	361.1	200.6	855.6	1661.1	491.0	4757.2	269.2	1801.0	2897.7	69.0	60.4	3584.4
INVENTORY STOCK	15.4	164.5	101.7	117.5	156.0	133.3	397.4	24.7	260.9	335.5	16.8	28.5	391.2
CULTIVATED LAND	81.2	403.8	534.2	64.5	16.3	245.6	202.6	30.2	342.4	332.4	28.4	164.4	167.8
SURPLUS SAVINGS	3.3	-4.6	19.3	21.5	21.8	-10.7	38.0	-0.7	-245.3	11.5	1.6	0.7	141.9
INTERNATIONAL TRANSACTIONS													
IMPORTS	10.3	8.5	59.7	71.0	113.4	80.1	190.4	26.7	302.5	52.6	18.5	24.7	626.8
EXPORTS	5.9	11.4	69.7	107.8	135.1	68.8	229.8	18.4	98.1	74.1	13.9	21.4	728.7
PAYMENTS SURPLUS	0.0	0.3	0.0	-14.2	-84.8	12.0	22.6	-6.5	119.4	12.8	0.0	0.0	-56.6
FOR.INVEST.INFLO	-1.1	-3.7	32.3	-170.7	-1059.5	221.0	351.1	-244.9	2193.4	290.6	-25.1	-4.3	-1564.0
FOR.INC.OUTFLOW	-0.3	-0.3	1.8	-13.7	-85.1	15.1	33.0	-20.5	171.6	23.2	-2.5	-0.8	-120.3
LEVEL OF ABATEMENT ACTIVITIES													
AIR	0.0	0.0	0.0	6.49	6.90	2.67	79.66	0.83	11.48	21.39	0.66	0.0	24.02
PRIMARY WATER	0.0	0.0	0.0	3.92	3.27	0.82	9.20	0.71	3.62	12.19	-0.95	0.0	14.16
SECONDARY WATER	0.0	0.0	0.0	0.22	2.40	0.05	0.52	0.02	0.21	0.69	-0.50	0.0	0.81
TERTIARY WATER	0.0	0.0	0.0	0.05	0.53	0.01	0.11	0.01	0.05	0.15	-0.11	0.0	0.18
SOLID WASTE	0.0	0.0	0.0	111.59	129.78	332.12	393.49	30.06	147.28	320.62	31.19	0.0	481.07
NET TOTAL EMISSIONS													
PESTICIDES	0.53	0.52	2.10	0.50	1.35	1.47	2.39	0.03	3.98	0.78	0.04	0.51	1.65
PARTICULATES	0.31	3.41	1.44	0.53	0.23	1.37	4.21	0.05	3.18	1.17	0.06	0.39	1.45
BIOLOG. OXYGEN	1.30	8.61	5.75	2.41	1.66	5.73	11.58	0.35	7.03	7.26	0.88	0.54	10.24
NITROGEN (WATER)	0.01	0.08	0.04	0.12	0.08	0.06	0.23	0.01	0.11	0.43	0.04	0.00*	0.55
PHOSPHATES	0.01	0.05	0.02	0.06	0.04	0.04	0.19	0.01	0.07	0.21	0.02	0.00*	0.28
SUSPENDED SOLIDS	0.31	2.76	1.18	1.52	0.95	2.95	6.82	0.18	6.40	3.99	0.21	0.54	4.94
DISSOLVED SOLIDS	4.86	36.08	18.17	16.04	20.60	16.77	53.84	2.39	31.15	57.84	6.39	1.07	75.62
SOLID WASTE	65.52	276.71	295.07	0.0	0.0	53.05	0.0	0.0	0.0	0.0	0.0	37.16	0.0

BASE SCENARIO IN 2000

RESOURCE OUTPUTS

	AAF	ASC	ASL	EEM	JAP	LAT	NAH	OCH	OIL	RUH	SAF	TAF	WEU
COPPER	0.0*	0.0	0.1	0.4	0.3	7.7	4.8	0.5	0.0	2.3	0.1	5.2	0.6
BAUXITE	0.0	0.2	1.4	1.7	0.0	2.3	0.6	17.6	0.3	2.1	0.0	7.1	2.7
NICKEL	1.0	0.0	680.6	0.0	0.0	403.4	329.9	76.6	0.0	521.3	0.0	0.0*	0.0
ZINC	0.0*	0.8	0.4	1.4	3.4	0.4	2.0	0.2	1.3	2.3	0.1	0.0*	4.3
LEAD	0.0*	0.7	0.2	1.1	1.1	0.6	1.7	0.2	1.7	2.3	0.1	0.0*	3.9
IRON	1.8	123.1	104.6	20.1	2.0	209.4	183.1	41.2	24.4	515.3	17.4	73.9	165.3
PETROLEUM	76.0	210.4	75.0	24.1	1.0	758.5	2568.1	11.0	8128.7	2320.7	0.0	0.0	612.0
NATURAL GAS	0.0	0.0	13.0	0.0	0.0	259.1	1810.2	2.0	1247.6	1853.8	0.0	0.0*	349.6
COAL	1.7	1105.7	279.9	894.7	142.8	39.8	2607.2	167.7	1.7	1405.9	47.9	29.9	1010.9

CUMULATIVE RESOURCE OUTPUT AT END OF PERIOD

	AAF	ASC	ASL	EEM	JAP	LAT	NAH	OCH	OIL	RUH	SAF	TAF	WEU
COPPER	0.*	5.	6.	7.	6.	99.	99.	10.	0.*	48.	3.	99.	13.
BAUXITE	0.	5.	29.	32.	0.	250.	12.	187.	2.	38.	0.	64.	56.
NICKEL	13.	0.	10884.	84.	0.	3744.	12202.	1800.	0.	9707.	182.	145.	209.
ZINC	1.	10.	3.	19.	22.	21.	98.	30.	9.	31.	1.	15.	47.
LEAD	2.	1.	2.	10.	8.	13.	113.	12.	10.	20.	1.	1.	28.
IRON	135.	1801.	1563.	321.	39.	3347.	3732.	1252.	322.	7542.	229.	1305.	3129.
PETROLEUM	1448.	3134.	1126.	722.	30.	16796.	45984.	331.	128588.	34644.	0.	33.	3630.
NATURAL GAS	1.	0.	337.	1125.	0.	3535.	40624.	60.	20237.	29284.	0.	0.*	6174.
COAL	28.	19545.	5031.	17335.	2382.	639.	36026.	3369.	28.	25372.	1454.	472.	19531.

NET EXPORTS OF RESOURCES

	AAF	ASC	ASL	EEM	JAP	LAT	NAH	OCH	OIL	RUH	SAF	TAF	WEU
COPPER	0.0	-0.6	0.0	-0.7	-3.9	6.4	1.4	0.3	-0.9	-1.5	0.0	5.2	-5.6
BAUXITE	-0.0*	-0.4	0.0	0.0	-5.5	1.3	-6.8	16.7	-1.4	-3.4	-0.3	7.0	-7.2
NICKEL	0.0	-12.8	561.2	-38.0	-419.2	302.2	0.0	0.0	-19.9	0.0	-36.6	-0.1	-336.8
ZINC	0.0	0.0	0.0	0.0	0.0	0.0	0.0	0.0	0.0	0.0	0.0	0.0	0.0
LEAD	-0.0*	0.0	0.0	0.0	0.0	-0.0*	-0.0*	-0.0*	0.0	0.0	0.0	-0.0*	0.0
IRON	0.0	0.0	87.1	-88.8	-255.5	169.2	30.8	10.3	-68.1	143.5	-66.5	71.8	-100.2
PETROLEUM	0.0	0.0	-238.5	-372.9	-1497.8	168.2	0.0	-151.8	4442.0	149.7	0.0	-75.6	-2356.8
NATURAL GAS	-1.0	0.0	-43.6	-252.5	-257.6	-60.8	0.0	-5.8	183.7	183.7	0.0	-0.0*	-3.7
COAL	-0.1	18.2	3.6	0.0		-20.9	268.8	72.6	-76.1	0.0	0.4	0.0	-8.5
OTHER RESOURCES	0.3	0.2	0.4	-1.5	-2.2	0.8	2.8	0.3	0.8	0.5		0.2	-2.8
PETROL. REFINING	0.0	-0.0*	-2.2	-3.5	-14.1	1.6	0.0*	-1.4	41.7	1.4	-0.6	-0.7	-22.1
PRIMARY METALS	-0.2	-1.2	-0.3	-2.8	-1.2	5.4	1.3	-0.4	-1.5	-0.8	0.1	4.1	-2.6

OUTPUT LEVELS

	AAF	ASC	ASL	EEM	JAP	LAT	NAH	OCH	OIL	RUH	SAF	TAF	WEU
ANIMAL PRODUCTS	7.0	56.7	40.5	22.8	20.2	54.1	68.1	10.6	36.9	54.6	6.4	14.0	89.1
HIGH PROT. CROPS	6.1	39.4	69.2	6.3	4.2	28.8	63.6	0.2	20.7	58.1	2.1	30.2	20.3
GRAINS	63.1	541.1	522.4	108.2	52.2	256.3	434.4	36.7	127.0	359.9	26.8	80.3	275.8
ROOTS	5.1	142.2	108.2	63.3	41.0	85.6	26.6	1.3	92.5	138.5	1.2	100.9	97.5
OTHER AGRICULT.	4.0	57.8	24.2	15.1	20.9	55.7	58.3	6.0	62.6	44.4	6.6	12.6	71.1
OTHER RESOURCES	0.6	3.3	2.0	1.7	3.7	3.2	15.8	1.0	9.1	11.3	0.8	0.5	9.0
FOOD PROCESSING	0.6	11.4	3.5	37.6	52.2	20.8	132.1	11.1	70.8	104.6	3.1	0.1	130.6
PETROL. REFINING	0.4	6.2		6.4	0.1	8.3	39.1	1.0	60.2	32.3	0.5		13.0
PRIMARY METALS	0.7	13.7	4.6	29.1	42.5	16.7	97.3	4.1	45.1	87.7	2.1	5.0	87.2
TEXT., APPAREL	3.2	35.9	43.6	28.9	56.0	29.2	90.8	5.0	59.6	53.9	2.9	2.1	103.5
WOOD AND CORK	0.9	4.6	5.5	7.0	10.0	5.6	10.4	1.4	10.4	24.7	0.7	0.7	23.3
FURNITURE, FIXT.	0.9	13.2	2.0	6.1	8.1	15.9	19.9	1.2	48.3	14.3	2.6	2.2	23.7
PAPER	0.2	6.0	1.6	11.3	19.1	4.5	64.4	2.4	5.3	36.9	1.3	0.1	52.0
PRINTING	0.2	3.2	1.5	13.3	22.6	5.3	65.7	3.4	22.2	45.9	1.1	0.2	58.5
RUBBER	0.2			11.2	18.4	3.1	37.9	1.9	9.0	30.4	0.6	0.8	39.9
INDUSTRIAL CHEM.	1.2	14.8	7.3	13.3	28.7	10.0	58.3	2.3	23.0	43.6	1.4	1.0	62.8
FERTILIZERS	8.3	45.4	22.7	5.5	14.4	19.2	23.5	1.6	31.5	29.6	3.7	0.0*	29.9
OTHER CHEMICALS	0.4	8.2	3.0	13.4	18.8	7.2	53.6	2.8	5.1	38.5	1.2	0.3	63.3
CEMENT	0.1	0.7	0.5	1.4	3.1	0.9	6.2	0.3	2.4	4.8	0.1	0.0*	6.1
GLASS	0.3	6.1	2.5	13.8	25.2	6.3	52.3	2.5	24.6	41.6	1.5	0.0*	50.0
MOTOR VEHICLES	0.0*	3.6	0.5	37.0	59.0	3.3	92.8	3.6	25.2	88.7	0.6		104.9
SHIPBUILDING	0.3	3.6	0.9	4.9	9.6	3.0	14.5	0.6	10.4	7.7	0.5	0.9	11.8
AIRCRAFT	0.3	5.2	1.1	8.7	4.5	0.6	36.1	0.2	18.3	41.2	0.1	0.4	12.2
METAL PRODUCTS	1.1	16.3	6.5	35.3	55.6	14.4	117.4	6.6	67.0	110.2	2.9	0.0*	115.6
MACHINERY	1.1	27.3	6.0	54.7	53.4	16.8	113.1	3.5	55.6	103.7	2.2		122.2
ELECTRICAL MACH.	0.5	11.7	2.7	37.5	57.0	5.2	95.3	3.7	23.2	82.1	0.4		97.7
INSTRUMENTS	0.1	3.7	0.7	6.6	12.4	2.2	23.1	0.6	6.0	17.5	0.4		21.5
OTHER MANUFACT.	0.5	7.0	5.9	6.4	13.8	6.0	24.6	1.4	14.5	20.2	2.3	1.3	29.7
UTILITIES	0.7	8.7	4.4	24.8	35.3	11.8	94.7	5.9	50.6	76.4	1.9	1.5	82.9
CONSTRUCTION	3.4	36.3	19.6	75.1	146.9	51.7	338.7	20.1	309.1	270.6	8.8	6.3	257.0
TRADE	3.9	52.2	24.7	122.0	187.7	70.3	472.3	30.7	253.1	359.7	12.1	9.6	426.5
TRANSPORTATION	2.3	32.7	15.2	30.6	39.4	26.3	131.1	6.7	73.1	96.9	3.5	4.5	129.6
COMMUNICATIONS	0.5	6.7	3.1	14.7	21.3	7.2	58.0	3.4	22.0	44.8	1.2	1.1	49.8
SERVICES	10.9	120.2	66.1	192.1	305.0	134.8	852.7	51.4	411.0	628.6	22.2	23.2	717.4

MILITARY OUTPUT LEVELS

	AAF	ASC	ASL	EEM	JAP	LAT	NAH	OCH	OIL	RUH	SAF	TAF	WEU
AIRCRAFT	0.3106	5.1137	0.8433	8.2269	3.8542	0.1899	27.1500	0.4913	-0.0001	34.7716	0.6755	0.0000*	12.5873
SHIPS	0.0561	1.1642	0.1124	0.1355	1.1834	0.0670	3.7700	0.1812	0.0003	10.7704	0.0592	0.0000*	4.6021
ELECTRONIC EQUIP	0.2267	3.0295	0.6220	3.2141	1.5332	0.1507	14.6476	0.2783	0.0079	15.3460	0.4535	0.0001	5.2822
NEW CONSTRUCTION	0.0960	2.4957	0.2023	1.1546	0.5172	0.1530	2.5288	0.0953	3.6832	5.0374	0.1049	0.0568	1.9742
MAINTENANCE	0.0702	1.8249	0.1479	0.8442	0.3782	0.1119	1.8490	0.0697	2.6931	3.6833	0.0767	0.0416	1.4435
MISSILES	0.0692	0.8477	0.1046	0.6210	0.2657	0.0194	11.2256	0.0393	-0.0000*	15.1339	0.0735	0.0000*	2.9084
AMMUNITION, NEC	0.0645	0.8835	0.1790	1.0136	0.4534	0.0455	4.2097	0.0817	0.0098	4.4210	0.1324	-0.0000*	1.5908
TANKS	0.2205	1.1730	0.2813	5.5963	0.4128	0.0495	3.2789	0.0582	0.0043	6.8119	0.1404	0.0000*	3.5466
SMALL ARMS	0.0039	0.0551	0.0109	0.0665	0.0404	0.0046	0.2946	0.0066	0.0096	0.3075	0.0090	0.0000*	0.1295
SM. ARMS AMMUN.	0.0109	0.1381	0.0293	0.1534	0.0814	0.0089	0.6786	0.0143	0.0095	0.7008	0.0218	0.0000*	0.2667
OTHER ORDNANCE	0.0227	0.2988	0.0618	0.3294	0.1656	0.0167	1.4582	0.0291	0.0088	1.5279	0.0457	-0.0000*	0.5543
TOTAL OUTPUT	1.1513	17.0241	2.5949	21.3555	8.8854	0.8171	71.0911	1.3449	6.4264	98.5118	1.7924	0.0985	34.8857

BASE SCENARIO IN 2000

	AAF	ASC	ASL	EEM	JAP	LAT	NAH	OCH	OIL	RUH	SAF	TAF	WEU
FISH													
FISH CATCH	0.6	7.9	9.3	0.8	8.2	14.4	3.8	0.2	0.4	6.7	2.2	1.9	9.6
NON-HUMAN USE	0.3	0.1	1.0	0.1	2.0	12.5	1.2	-0.0*	-0.1	0.6	2.0	0.6	1.7
FISH IMPORTS	0.1	0.1	0.3	0.2	0.2	0.1	1.3	0.0*	0.0*	0.0*	0.0*	0.1	1.6
FISH EXPORTS	0.1	0.1	0.3	0.0*	0.5	0.1	0.4	0.0*	0.1	0.4	0.0*	0.1	2.0
EXPORTS													
LIVESTOCK	0.0*	0.0	0.1	2.3	0.0*	2.4	1.7	3.9	0.0*	0.3	0.1	0.1	9.5
HIGH PROT. CROPS	1.2	0.0	3.8	0.7	0.1	2.8	40.6	10.0*	2.7	1.5	0.3	2.2	5.6
GRAINS	1.6	0.0	9.8	8.2	4.2	20.9	129.2	18.0	0.4	10.8	2.2	0.6	36.7
ROOTS	0.8	0.0	1.4	3.1	0.1	0.8	4.2	0.3	0.4	0.4	0.6	0.6	10.6
OTHER AGRICULT.	1.5	1.0	8.2	2.7	0.0	7.7	5.5	2.1	1.6	1.8	0.6	4.3	13.3
FOOD PROCESSING	0.3	0.5	2.2	1.6	0.5	4.0	4.9	1.9	0.6	0.6	0.6	0.2	11.4
TEXT. APPAREL	0.9	5.2	26.5	16.3	25.8	3.9	7.8	1.5	4.9	1.5	0.6	0.2	109.4
WOOD AND CORK	0.0*	0.0*	2.5	1.2	1.2	1.1	4.8	0.1	0.6	4.3	0.0*	0.0*	10.8
FURNITURE, FIXT.	0.0*	0.6	0.1	1.6	0.1	0.0*	0.1	0.0*	0.0*	0.0*	0.0*	0.0*	2.1
PAPER	0.1	0.0*	0.4	0.8	2.3	1.3	20.6	0.5	0.2	1.6	1.2	0.0*	39.1
PRINTING	0.1	0.0*	0.5	0.4	0.9	0.6	3.0	0.1	0.0*	0.0*	0.1	0.0*	12.2
RUBBER	0.1	0.7	0.7	0.9	2.6	0.3	1.4	0.1	0.2	0.6	0.8	0.1	11.2
INDUSTRIAL CHEM.	0.4	0.7	0.7	1.5	8.7	1.9	9.9	0.7	0.1	1.6	0.0*	0.0*	40.4
FERTILIZERS	0.1	1.3	0.3	1.8	1.4	0.7	6.3	0.0*	1.3	4.0	0.0*	0.1	12.1
OTHER CHEMICALS	0.1	0.4	1.4	1.1	2.0	1.5	7.3	0.7	0.5	0.3	0.1	0.1	36.6
CEMENT	0.1	0.1	0.4	0.0	0.5	0.2	0.2	0.0*	0.6	0.1	0.8	0.1	1.6
GLASS	0.0*	0.5	0.4	2.9	4.0	0.5	3.2	0.1	0.6	0.3	0.7	0.0*	24.2
MOTOR VEHICLES	0.0*	0.1	1.5	16.8	19.0	1.1	25.2	0.7	0.6	11.0	0.5	0.0*	68.2
SHIPBUILDING	0.0*	0.0	0.1	2.4	4.5	0.0*	0.3	0.1	0.0*	2.3	0.0*	0.0*	6.1
AIRCRAFT	0.0*	0.0	0.2	0.0*	0.2	0.1	11.8	0.1	0.2	7.5	0.1	0.0*	6.5
METAL PRODUCTS	0.0*	0.1	0.8	0.4	3.1	0.3	3.4	0.2	0.1	2.4	0.1	0.1	13.6
MACHINERY	0.0*	0.2	1.7	34.7	14.1	2.1	21.6	0.5	0.3	14.1	1.1	0.1	84.9
ELECTRICAL MACH.	0.1	0.2	3.3	13.8	24.7	1.0	16.9	0.3	0.2	0.4	0.2	0.0*	65.0
INSTRUMENTS	0.0*	0.0*	0.5	1.5	6.0	0.3	6.6	0.2	0.1	0.8	0.3	0.0*	17.7
OTHER MANUFACT.	0.4	0.4	4.6	0.3	3.8	0.3	2.6	0.1	0.1	1.1	1.5	0.2	17.4
SERVICES	0.6	0.0	1.4	0.0	0.4	5.7	10.0	0.4	0.8	0.0	3.5	0.2	32.7
TRANSPORT	0.4	0.0	4.0	0.0	6.9	3.4	17.1	2.4	1.2	0.0	1.0	1.4	66.2
AID INFLOW	4.1	0.0	21.4	0.0	0.8	10.5	9.3	1.6	3.8	0.0	5.7	3.0	36.8
CAPITAL INFLOW	0.1	0.0	6.9	0.0	16.0	14.7	36.4	0.8	8.6	0.0	0.5	0.8	52.6
MILITARY EXPORTS													
AIRCRAFT	0.0	0.1568	0.1568	1.4115	0.0	0.0	6.2735	0.0	0.0	5.0188	0.0	0.0	2.6662
SHIPS	0.0	0.0221	0.0	0.0	0.0	0.0	0.4867	0.0	0.0	0.7080	0.0	0.0	0.9956
ELECTRONIC EQUIP	0.1366	0.0683	0.0683	0.2731	0.0	0.0683	2.8677	0.0	0.0	1.5704	0.0	0.0	1.7752
MISSILES	0.0320	0.0192	0.0192	0.0768	0.0	0.0192	1.3456	0.0	0.0	1.3136	0.0	0.0	0.5126
AMMUNITION, NEC	0.0384	0.0192	0.0192	0.0768	0.0	0.0192	0.8067	0.0	0.0	0.4418	0.0	0.0	0.4994
TANKS	0.0	0.0	0.0	0.4221	0.0	0.0	2.3515	0.0	0.0	1.7485	0.0	0.0	1.5073
SMALL ARMS	0.0024	0.0012	0.0012	0.0048	0.0	0.0012	0.0505	0.0	0.0	0.0277	0.0	0.0	0.0313
SM. ARMS AMMUN.	0.0067	0.0033	0.0033	0.0133	0.0	0.0033	0.1399	0.0	0.0	0.0766	0.0	0.0	0.0866
OTHER ORDNANCE	0.0138	0.0069	0.0069	0.0277	0.0	0.0069	0.2903	0.0	0.0	0.1590	0.0	0.0	0.1797
TOTAL EXPORTS	0.2299	0.2779	0.2558	2.2293	0.0	0.0989	14.6124	0.0	0.0	11.0643	0.0	0.0	8.2540
MIL. GRANTS INF.	0.0770	0.1107	0.2271	0.0049	0.0	0.0425	0.0	0.0	0.0	0.0		0.1656	0.0258

IMPORTS	AAF	ASC	ASL	EEM	JAP	LAT	NAH	OCH	OIL	RUH	SAF	TAF	WEU
LIVESTOCK	0.1	0.0*	1.3	1.5	1.4	1.3	2.6	0.0*	2.3	0.3	0.2	0.6	8.9
HIGH PROT. CROPS	0.9	0.0*	2.7	4.0	18.7	2.2	3.0	0.3	4.5	0.3	0.1	0.8	24.2
GRAINS	5.7	0.1	36.8	39.1	32.3	26.5	2.7	0.3	15.7	6.4	1.7	9.9	65.4
ROOTS	0.4	0.0*	2.0	3.3	1.9	2.3	0.6	0.1	2.1	0.0	0.0	0.5	9.4
OTHER AGRICULT.	0.3	2.3	2.9	3.0	3.6	1.9	9.2	0.3	10.1	2.1	0.3	0.5	13.9
FOOD PROCESSING	0.3	0.2	2.6	1.5	1.2	1.9	4.1	0.1	7.7	1.0	0.2	1.1	7.5
TEXT., APPAREL	1.5	0.0	7.5	8.8	10.4	4.0	25.5	3.0	20.1	16.2	2.4	5.4	99.6
WOOD AND CORK	0.1	0.0	0.2	0.8	2.3	0.5	2.7	0.3	8.6	0.4	0.3	0.3	10.6
FURNITURE, FIXT.	0.0*	0.0*	0.0*	0.3	0.0*	0.2	0.7	0.0*	1.0	0.5	0.0*	0.6	1.0
PAPER	0.2	0.0*	1.2	1.9	2.9	3.2	5.6	0.9	16.5	1.7	0.1	0.4	33.1
PRINTING	0.1	0.0*	0.4	0.3	1.3	1.0	1.3	0.6	4.5	0.0	0.0*	0.3	6.9
RUBBER	0.1	0.0*	0.4	1.4	0.1	1.0	1.9	0.3	7.4	0.3	0.3	0.8	6.3
INDUSTRIAL CHEM.	0.4	1.2	3.5	2.8	2.6	4.5	6.1	1.3	9.0	2.1	1.2	0.9	31.6
FERTILIZERS	1.0	1.7	7.9	0.9	2.4	5.4	1.9	0.9	4.2	0.8	0.0*	1.2	4.2
OTHER CHEMICALS	0.3	0.1	2.2	0.8	0.0*	2.8	2.0	0.9	21.3	0.2	0.2	0.1	17.3
CEMENT	0.0*	0.0*	0.2	0.0	0.7	0.1	0.1	0.0*	2.6	0.5	0.0	0.6	0.6
GLASS	0.2	0.0*	0.4	1.5	1.0	1.2	2.2	0.5	13.7	1.9	0.4	0.4	15.3
MOTOR VEHICLES	0.2	0.4	2.0	6.8	0.2	6.9	41.0	3.5	26.6	4.8	1.8	0.4	53.1
SHIPBUILDING	0.1	0.1	0.6	0.8		0.6	0.5	0.3	0.6	0.0	0.0*	0.2	6.7
AIRCRAFT	0.2	0.0*	0.5	0.0		1.8	4.7	0.9	1.9	1.9	0.5	0.9	13.6
METAL PRODUCTS	0.1	0.1	0.7	0.2	2.6	1.6	2.4	2.7	9.6	0.5	0.2	3.0	7.7
MACHINERY	0.9	0.7	6.8	11.5	0.3	13.6	18.1	1.6	44.9	9.0	2.7	1.0	57.1
ELECTRICAL MACH.	0.5	0.1	4.8	3.3	3.0	7.5	14.9	0.7	38.9	2.1	1.3	0.3	47.1
INSTRUMENTS	0.1	0.2	1.1	0.7	1.4	1.8	4.2	0.5	7.6	1.0	0.6	0.4	14.2
OTHER MANUFACT.	0.3	0.2	2.3	0.3	1.6	1.0	9.0		2.4	1.2	0.2	0.1	13.7
SERVICES	0.0	0.0	0.1	0.0	2.8	4.5	14.1	1.2	4.8	0.0	0.7	0.1	27.4
TRANSPORT	0.9	0.0	5.0	0.0	13.9	7.1	11.0	3.0	13.2	0.0	1.6	2.1	46.0
AID OUTFLOW	0.6	0.4	2.7	0.0	3.8	4.3	19.9	1.7	28.6	2.5	0.8	1.8	29.8
CAPITAL OUTFLOW	0.1	0.0	3.4	0.0	7.3	16.5	14.0	5.3	59.0	0.0	2.7	1.2	27.8

MILITARY IMPORTS

	AAF	ASC	ASL	EEM	JAP	LAT	NAH	OCH	OIL	RUH	SAF	TAF	WEU
AIRCRAFT	0.8841	0.1534	0.8095	1.4479	0.3816	0.7540	0.2742	0.0732	8.2670	0.6954	0.1189	0.5292	1.2952
SHIPS	0.1140	0.0116	0.0920	0.0339	0.0237	0.3335	0.0381	0.0056	1.2397	0.0	0.0395	0.1842	0.0967
ELECTRONIC EQUIP	0.4601	0.0606	0.3209	0.5657	0.1334	0.3545	0.1479	0.0276	3.7049	0.1550	0.0503	0.2317	0.6152
MISSILES	0.1780	0.0449	0.1445	0.7576	0.1429	0.0598	0.1134	0.0211	1.4063	0.0	0.0110	0.0312	0.2932
AMMUNITION, NEC	0.1309	0.0177	0.0924	0.1784	0.1098	0.0979	0.0425	0.0081	1.0095	0.0447	0.0147	0.0631	0.1815
TANKS	0.4096	0.0610	0.2397	0.2966		0.1837	0.0331	0.0215	3.6762	0.0688	0.0467	0.1678	0.7149
SMALL ARMS	0.0078	0.0011	0.0056	0.0117	0.0035	0.0060	0.0030	0.0007	0.0590	0.0031	0.0010	0.0037	0.0140
SM. ARMS AMMUN.	0.0221	0.0028	0.0151	0.0270	0.0071	0.0175	0.0069	0.0014	0.1817		0.0024	0.0114	0.0308
OTHER ORDNANCE	0.0460	0.0060	0.0319	0.0580	0.0144	0.0359	0.0147	0.0029	0.3737	0.0154	0.0051	0.0234	0.0640
TOTAL IMPORTS	2.2526	0.3591	1.7516	3.3767	0.8558	1.8429	0.6738	0.1620	19.9178	0.9895	0.2896	1.2458	3.3054
MIL. GRANTS OUTF	0.0	0.1628	0.0	0.0	0.0	0.0	0.1433	0.0	0.0	0.2911	0.0	0.0	0.0564

SCENARIO D1 IN 2000

	AAF	ASC	ASL	EEM	JAP	LAT	NAH	OCH	OIL	RUH	SAF	TAF	WEU
CONSUMPTION AND POPULATION													
GDP	50.5	454.5	300.5	615.1	904.0	432.7	2381.2	132.6	1200.0	1824.2	66.0	86.1	2086.5
PERSONAL CONSUMP	38.9	307.0	220.3	377.7	587.8	308.0	1566.1	100.7	791.0	1137.3	47.8	68.7	1392.7
GOVT.(CIVILIAN)	5.0	45.4	30.1	61.5	90.4	43.3	238.1	13.3	120.0	182.4	6.6	8.6	208.7
GOVT.(MILITARY)	4.5	25.6	7.2	24.7	16.3	5.4	116.2	2.0	46.8	116.2	2.2	2.0	43.1
POPULATION	285.7	1221.3	2048.9	125.7	132.9	615.8	300.0	24.5	309.8	315.0	50.0	331.8	487.1
URBAN POPULATION	168.4	508.9	704.4	90.1	98.5	465.0	258.9	22.4	148.2	245.2	32.0	109.4	382.4
EMPLOYMENT	24.5	187.2	139.9	63.8	67.6	147.1	133.9	10.2	213.0	151.8	12.9	44.2	167.9
GDP/HEAD	176.8	372.1	146.7	4893.7	6801.9	702.7	7937.4	5410.2	3873.6	5791.0	1320.0	259.5	4283.6
CONSUMPTION/HEAD	136.1	251.3	107.5	3005.0	4422.7	500.2	5220.3	4109.4	2553.3	3610.5	956.0	207.2	2859.1
CALORIES/HEAD	2167.6	2253.7	2092.7	3182.3	3250.3	2583.5	3192.2	3214.8	3334.8	3195.1	2945.9	2398.6	3137.0
PROTEINS/HEAD	63.6	69.8	54.4	108.0	123.5	67.2	99.8	100.1	117.3	108.2	91.6	70.4	102.2
INVESTMENT AND CAPITAL													
INVESTMENT	5.9	63.8	28.6	109.6	180.3	79.6	415.2	24.1	412.3	360.1	12.4	8.6	327.9
EQUIPMENT	2.8	37.1	15.0	44.3	57.5	42.2	141.6	7.8	144.7	124.9	5.6	4.3	127.5
PLANT	2.8	26.1	12.7	65.2	122.8	36.8	273.3	16.2	267.4	234.5	6.7	4.1	200.2
IRRIGATION	0.1	0.6	1.0	0.1	0.0*	0.2	0.2	0.0*	0.1	0.6	0.0*	0.0*	0.2
LAND (AREA)	0.9	0.9	1.3	0.1	0.0*	0.0*	0.8	0.6	0.5	0.0	0.1	1.7	0.1
INVENTORY CHANGE	0.6	9.2	3.6	3.5	5.5	6.2	10.3	0.5	21.6	9.3	1.3	1.5	10.6
CAPITAL STOCK	70.1	729.3	392.1	1359.7	2282.1	858.2	6697.8	367.4	2670.4	4464.1	116.3	119.2	5153.1
EQUIPMENT	31.2	365.0	184.0	435.6	579.0	359.0	1597.1	93.7	878.6	1297.5	46.2	56.3	1442.8
PLANT	38.9	364.3	207.4	924.1	1703.1	499.2	5100.7	273.7	1791.8	3166.6	70.0	62.9	3710.3
INVENTORY STOCK	16.8	165.4	104.2	121.7	158.8	134.8	406.7	24.9	259.3	347.5	16.9	29.1	397.3
CULTIVATED LAND	85.0	407.9	541.2	65.8	16.5	247.0	205.2	30.5	342.4	340.0	28.6	167.5	169.3
SURPLUS SAVINGS	2.8	-6.1	18.3	14.2	16.2	-13.0	7.2	-1.2	-247.4	-12.7	1.4	0.1	129.4
INTERNATIONAL TRANSACTIONS													
IMPORTS	10.4	8.3	60.6	71.7	114.6	80.6	194.4	26.9	291.1	55.0	18.4	24.9	635.7
EXPORTS	5.9	11.6	71.2	108.6	137.3	69.6	226.2	18.7	98.7	70.3	14.1	21.6	736.5
PAYMENTS SURPLUS	0.0	0.6	0.0	-13.7	-85.3	12.0	16.7	-6.4	129.0	9.8	0.0	0.0	-58.1
FOR.INVEST.INFLO	-1.3	-1.3	32.0	-162.8	-1056.7	221.4	329.2	-245.5	2242.5	259.0	-25.3	-5.0	-1573.6
FOR.INC.OUTFLOW	-0.3	-0.1	1.8	-13.0	-84.9	15.1	31.3	-20.6	175.5	20.7	-2.5	-0.8	-121.1
LEVEL OF ABATEMENT ACTIVITIES													
AIR	0.0	0.0	0.0	6.82	7.06	2.70	83.32	0.84	11.48	22.37	0.67	0.0	24.54
PRIMARY WATER	0.0	0.0	0.0	4.11	3.25	0.85	9.66	0.71	3.62	12.76	0.95	0.0	14.48
SECONDARY WATER	0.0	0.0	0.0	0.23	2.52	0.05	0.55	0.03	0.21	0.73	-0.50	0.0	0.83
TERTIARY WATER	0.0	0.0	0.0	0.05	0.55	0.01	0.12	0.01	0.05	0.16	-0.11	0.0	0.18
SOLID WASTE	0.0	0.0	0.0	111.59	129.78	332.12	393.49	30.06	147.28	320.62	31.19		481.07
NET TOTAL EMISSIONS													
PESTICIDES	0.58	0.53	2.14	0.51	1.36	1.49	2.44	0.03	3.98	0.80	0.04	0.52	1.67
PARTICULATES	0.35	3.39	1.48	0.53	0.23	1.41	4.21	0.05	3.07	1.17	0.06	0.40	1.45
BIOLOG. OXYGEN	1.38	8.67	5.83	2.44	1.65	5.74	11.60	0.35	6.98	7.37	0.88	0.55	10.28
NITROGEN (WATER)	0.01	0.08	0.04	0.12	0.08	0.04	0.24	0.01	0.11	0.44	0.04	0.00*	0.55
PHOSPHATES	0.01	0.05	0.02	0.06	0.04	0.04	0.19	0.01	0.07	0.22	0.02	0.00*	0.29
SUSPENDED SOLIDS	0.35	2.73	1.21	1.52	0.95	2.98	6.82	0.18	6.33	3.99	0.21	0.55	4.94
DISSOLVED SOLIDS	5.29	36.37	18.57	16.64	20.72	17.01	54.88	2.40	30.96	59.81	6.41	1.10	76.81
SOLID WASTE	65.52	276.71	295.07	0.0	0.0	53.05	0.0	0.0	0.0	0.0	0.0	37.16	0.0

RESOURCE OUTPUTS

	AAF	ASC	ASL	EEM	JAP	LAT	NAH	OCH	OIL	RUH	SAF	TAF	WEU
COPPER	0.0*	0.0	0.1	0.4	0.3	7.8	4.8	0.5	0.0	2.3	0.1	5.2	0.6
BAUXITE	0.0	0.2	1.5	1.6	0.0	2.3	0.6	17.6	0.3	2.1	0.0	7.1	2.8
NICKEL	0.8	0.0	677.3	0.0	0.0	401.4	319.6	77.0	0.0	513.3	0.0	0.0*	0.0
ZINC	0.0*	0.8	0.4	1.5	3.5	0.4	2.0	0.2	1.3	2.2	0.1	0.0*	4.3
LEAD	0.0*	0.7	0.2	1.1	1.1	0.6	1.7	0.2	1.6	2.4	0.1	0.0*	4.0
IRON	2.0	120.8	106.8	20.1	2.0	213.0	185.5	41.6	24.4	527.7	17.4	75.2	166.0
PETROLEUM	82.9	179.1	75.0	24.1	1.0	760.0	2492.9	11.0	8050.8	2286.8	0.0	0.0	612.0
NATURAL GAS	0.0	0.0	13.0	0.0	0.0	262.4	1855.4	2.0	1247.3	1920.9	0.0	0.0*	355.3
COAL	1.7	1108.4	292.2	922.9	142.8	39.8	2662.6	169.7	1.7	1444.5	48.3	30.8	1021.5

CUMULATIVE RESOURCE OUTPUT AT END OF PERIOD

	AAF	ASC	ASL	EEM	JAP	LAT	NAH	OCH	OIL	RUH	SAF	TAF	WEU
COPPER	0.*	5.	6.	7.	6.	99.	99.	10.	0*	48.	3.	99.	13.
BAUXITE	0.	5.	30.	31.	0.	250.	12.	187.	2.	38.	0.	65.	56.
NICKEL	11.	0.	10855.	84.	0.	3733.	12083.	1805.	0.	9613.	182.	145.	209.
ZINC	1.	10.	3.	19.	22.	21.	98.	30.	9.	31.	1.	15.	47.
LEAD	2.	10.	2.	10.	8.	13.	114.	12.	10.	21.	1.	1.	28.
IRON	138.	1781.	1581.	321.	39.	3376.	3765.	1258.	322.	7682.	229.	1316.	3135.
PETROLEUM	1513.	2854.	1126.	722.	30.	16714.	45608.	331.	127338.	34027.	0.	33.	3630.
NATURAL GAS	1.	0.	337.	1125.	0.	3545.	41186.	60.	20178.	29978.	0.	0.*	6226.
COAL	28.	19585.	5139.	17597.	2382.	639.	36454.	3394.	28.	25752.	1459.	479.	19584.

NET EXPORTS OF RESOURCES

	AAF	ASC	ASL	EEM	JAP	LAT	NAH	OCH	OIL	RUH	SAF	TAF	WEU
COPPER	0.0	-0.6	0.0	-0.6	-3.9	6.4	1.4	0.3	-0.9	-1.5	0.0	5.2	-5.7
BAUXITE	-0.0*	-0.3	0.0	0.0	-5.6	1.3	-6.8	16.7	-1.3	-3.3	-0.3	7.1	-7.3
NICKEL	0.0	-8.7	554.9	-32.6	-424.0	298.8	0.0	0.0	-19.1	0.0	-36.3	-0.1	-332.9
ZINC	0.0	0.0	0.0	0.0	0.0	0.0	0.0	0.0	0.0	0.0	0.0	-0.0*	0.0
LEAD	-0.0*	0.0	0.0	0.0	0.0	-0.0*	-0.0*	-0.0*	0.0	0.0	0.0	0.0	0.0
IRON	0.0	0.0	88.7	-91.6	-260.0	172.1	31.3	10.4	-67.2	146.0	-64.8	-73.0	-102.6
PETROLEUM	-1.1	0.0	-243.5	-362.2	-1506.7	166.6	0.0	-151.6	4450.3	150.0	0.0	-76.3	-2361.8
NATURAL GAS	-0.4	0.0	-45.4	-262.6	0.0	-62.7	0.0	-5.9	190.8	190.8	0.0	-0.0*	-3.9
COAL	0.3	18.5	3.7	-1.6	-262.5	-21.7	273.8	74.0	-73.6	0.5	0.4	0.2	-11.9
OTHER RESOURCES	0.0	0.2	0.4	-3.4	-2.2	0.8	2.8	0.3	0.9	1.4	-0.6	-0.7	-2.9
PETROL. REFINING	0.0*	0.0*	-2.3		-14.1	1.6	0.0*	-1.4	41.8	-0.8			-22.2
PRIMARY METALS	-0.2	-1.1	-0.3	-2.9	-1.3	5.5	1.4	-0.4	-1.5		0.1	4.1	-2.7

101

SCENARIO D1 IN 2000

OUTPUT LEVELS

	AAF	ASC	ASL	EEM	JAP	LAT	NAH	OCH	OIL	RUH	SAF	TAF	WEU
ANIMAL PRODUCTS	7.7	57.6	41.3	23.3	20.4	54.4	68.7	10.7	36.9	55.9	6.4	14.3	89.7
HIGH PROT. CROPS	6.4	39.8	70.0	6.4	4.2	28.9	64.2	0.2	20.7	59.5	2.2	30.9	20.4
GRAINS	65.5	546.4	527.8	110.1	52.8	257.5	438.6	37.0	127.0	367.7	27.0	81.6	277.8
ROOTS	5.2	142.8	110.1	64.1	41.4	85.8	26.5	1.3	92.4	140.8	1.2	101.3	97.8
OTHER AGRICULT.	4.5	58.7	25.2	15.8	21.4	56.3	60.6	6.1	62.6	47.4	6.7	13.0	72.8
OTHER RESOURCES	0.7	3.3	2.0	1.8	3.8	3.3	16.6	1.2	9.0	12.0	0.8	0.5	9.3
FOOD PROCESSING	0.8	11.9	3.7	39.0	52.9	21.2	135.6	11.2	70.8	109.4	3.1	1.5	132.9
PETROL. REFINING	0.5	6.1	0.4	6.9	0.3	8.4	39.9	1.1	60.0	33.4	0.5	0.1	13.5
PRIMARY METALS	0.8	12.9	4.7	29.6	43.1	16.9	98.9	4.1	44.4	88.7	2.1	5.0	87.9
TEXT.. APPAREL	3.7	36.9	45.4	30.7	57.6	29.7	94.9	5.1	59.6	58.9	3.0	2.2	107.3
WOOD AND CORK	0.2	4.6	4.4	7.4	10.3	5.7	30.6	1.4	10.4	26.2	0.7	0.7	24.0
FURNITURE, FIXT.	1.1	13.7	5.9	6.4	8.3	16.2	20.5	1.3	48.2	15.3	2.7	2.3	24.4
PAPER	0.3	6.1	2.0	11.8	19.5	4.6	66.2	2.5	5.3	38.7	1.4	0.1	52.9
PRINTING	0.3	3.3	1.7	14.0	23.0	5.4	67.8	3.4	22.0	48.5	1.1	0.2	59.7
RUBBER	0.2	3.0	1.5	11.6	18.7	3.1	38.9	1.9	8.9	31.7	0.6	0.1	40.6
INDUSTRIAL CHEM.	1.3	14.7	7.5	13.7	29.1	10.2	59.0	2.3	22.7	44.8	1.4	0.8	63.7
FERTILIZERS	9.0	46.0	23.1	5.6	14.6	19.4	24.1	1.6	31.5	30.4	3.7	1.1	30.3
OTHER CHEMICALS	0.5	8.3	3.1	13.9	19.0	7.3	55.1	2.8	5.0	40.1	1.3	0.2	64.2
CEMENT	0.1	0.7	0.5	1.5	3.2	0.9	6.6	0.3	2.4	5.2	0.2	0.0*	6.3
GLASS	0.4	6.0	2.6	14.7	26.0	6.5	55.8	3.6	24.3	44.8	1.5	0.3	51.6
MOTOR VEHICLES	0.0*	3.6	0.5	38.6	60.2	3.3	95.6	3.6	25.0	93.5	0.6	0.0*	107.2
SHIPBUILDING	0.1	3.5	1.0	5.2	10.0	3.1	15.1	0.6	10.4	8.3	0.5	0.1	12.2
AIRCRAFT	0.3	4.4	1.0	8.3	4.4	0.6	32.9	0.2	17.0	38.1	0.1	0.0*	11.7
METAL PRODUCTS	1.3	15.8	6.7	37.1	56.9	14.7	122.2	6.6	66.1	114.9	2.9	1.0	118.1
MACHINERY	1.3	26.5	6.3	55.9	54.3	17.1	114.6	3.6	54.9	105.2	2.2	0.4	123.5
ELECTRICAL MACH.	0.5	11.0	2.7	38.0	57.3	5.2	95.1	3.7	22.8	82.5	1.0	0.1	97.9
INSTRUMENTS	0.1	3.5	0.7	6.7	12.5	2.2	23.1	0.6	5.8	17.7	0.4	0.0*	21.6
OTHER MANUFACT.	0.6	7.1	6.1	6.9	14.1	6.0	25.4	1.4	14.3	21.5	2.3	1.4	30.5
UTILITIES	0.8	8.6	4.5	25.7	35.7	12.0	96.7	5.9	50.1	79.0	2.0	1.6	84.2
CONSTRUCTION	4.0	36.4	20.6	83.8	152.9	53.4	370.8	20.6	307.1	298.6	8.9	6.7	271.1
TRADE	4.7	53.7	26.1	128.2	191.0	71.8	490.0	31.0	252.2	380.3	12.4	10.1	436.2
TRANSPORTATION	2.7	32.5	15.7	31.8	40.0	26.7	134.3	6.8	72.1	100.6	3.6	4.6	131.4
COMMUNICATIONS	0.6	6.6	3.2	15.1	21.5	7.3	58.8	3.5	21.5	45.9	1.2	1.1	50.4
SERVICES	12.4	121.2	68.5	202.2	310.3	136.7	883.6	52.0	407.6	663.0	22.4	24.0	733.4

MILITARY OUTPUT LEVELS

	AAF	ASC	ASL	EEM	JAP	LAT	NAH	OCH	OIL	RUH	SAF	TAF	WEU
AIRCRAFT	0.2115	3.0093	0.5200	5.0709	2.3356	0.1155	17.6182	0.2961	-0.0000*	22.8004	0.4053	0.0000*	7.6329
SHIPS	0.0382	0.6846	0.0695		0.7171	0.0407	2.4817	0.1092	-0.0000*	7.1337	0.0355	0.0000*	2.7881
ELECTRONIC EQUIP	0.1508	1.7821	0.3837	1.9849	0.9291	0.0914	9.5639	0.1677	0.0047	10.1166	0.2721	0.0001	3.2004
NEW CONSTRUCTION	0.0654	1.4671	0.1250	0.7145	0.3134	0.0929	1.6858	0.0574	2.1635	3.3583	0.0629	0.0349	1.1982
MAINTENANCE	0.0478	1.0727	0.0914	0.5224	0.2292	0.0679	1.2327	0.0420	1.5820	2.4556	0.0460	0.0255	0.8761
MISSILES	0.0465	0.4984	0.0646	0.3839	0.1610	0.0118	7.3807	0.0237	-0.0000*	9.9926	0.0441	-0.0000*	1.7640
AMMUNITION, NEC	0.0429	0.5198	0.1105	0.6298	0.2802	0.0285	2.7572	0.0499	-0.0098	2.9251	0.0798	-0.0000*	0.9786
TANKS	0.1502	0.6895	0.1739	3.4564	0.2520	0.0306	2.0114	0.0352	0.0043	4.4106	0.0843	-0.0000*	2.1485
SMALL ARMS	0.0026	0.0325	0.0068	0.0446	0.0296	0.0036	0.2039	0.0046	0.0094	0.2147	0.0057	0.0000*	0.0924
SM. ARMS AMMUN.	0.0072	0.0812	0.0181	0.0982	0.0543	0.0061	0.4545	0.0092	0.0093	0.4739	0.0134	-0.0000*	0.1751
OTHER ORDNANCE	0.0151	0.1758	0.0381	0.2068	0.1052	0.0109	0.9630	0.0181	0.0088	1.0186	0.0277	-0.0000*	0.3491
TOTAL OUTPUT	0.7782	10.0131	1.6017	13.1963	5.4067	0.4998	46.3530	0.8132	3.7919	64.9000	1.0768	0.0606	21.2036

FISH

	AAF	ASC	ASL	EEM	JAP	LAT	NAH	OCH	OIL	RUH	SAF	TAF	WEU
FISH CATCH	0.6	7.9	9.3	0.8	8.2	14.4	3.8	0.2	0.4	6.7	2.2	1.9	9.6
NON-HUMAN USE	0.3	0.1	1.0	0.1	2.0	12.5	1.2	-0.0*	-0.1	0.6	2.0	0.6	1.7
FISH IMPORTS	0.1	0.0	0.3	0.2	0.2	0.1	1.3	-0.0*	0.0*	0.1	0.0*	0.1	1.6
FISH EXPORTS	0.1	0.1	0.3	0.0*	0.5	0.1	0.4	-0.0*	0.1	0.4	0.0*	0.1	2.0

EXPORTS

	AAF	ASC	ASL	EEM	JAP	LAT	NAH	OCH	OIL	RUH	SAF	TAF	WEU
LIVESTOCK	0.0*	0.0	0.1	2.3	0.0*	2.4	1.8	4.0	0.0*	0.3	0.1	0.1	9.6
HIGH PROT. CROPS	1.2	0.0	3.8	0.7	0.1	2.8	41.0	0.0*	2.7	1.5	0.3	2.3	5.6
GRAINS	1.6	0.0	9.9	8.3	4.3	21.1	130.6	18.2	0.4	10.9	2.2	0.8	37.1
ROOTS	0.8	0.0	1.4	3.2	0.1	0.8	4.2	2.2	1.6	1.9	0.0	0.6	10.6
OTHER AGRICULT.	1.6	1.1	8.4	2.7	0.0	7.9	5.7	1.9	0.2	0.6	0.6	4.4	13.7
FOOD PROCESSING	0.3	0.5	2.3	1.6	0.5	4.0	5.0	1.6	0.2	0.6	0.3	0.8	11.7
TEXT., APPAREL	0.9	5.4	27.5	17.0	26.8	4.1	8.1	1.6	5.1	1.6	0.6	0.2	113.7
WOOD AND CORK	0.0*	0.0*	2.6	1.2	1.2	1.2	4.9	0.0*	0.7	4.4	0.0*	0.2	11.0
FURNITURE, FIXT.	0.0*	0.0*	0.1	1.7	0.1	0.0*	0.1	0.0*	0.0*	0.0*	0.0*	0.0*	2.2
PAPER	0.1	0.6	0.5	0.9	2.3	1.4	21.0	0.5	0.2	1.7	1.2	0.0*	39.7
PRINTING	0.1	0.0*	0.4	0.4	0.9	0.6	3.0	0.1	0.0*	0.1	0.1	0.0*	12.4
RUBBER	0.1	0.0*	0.5	0.9	2.6	0.4	1.4	0.1	0.2	0.6	0.1	0.0*	11.3
INDUSTRIAL CHEM.	0.1	0.7	0.7	1.5	8.8	1.9	10.0	0.7	0.1	1.6	0.8	0.1	40.9
FERTILIZERS	0.4	1.4	1.4	1.8	1.4	0.7	6.4	0.0*	1.4	4.1	0.1	0.1	12.3
OTHER CHEMICALS	0.1	0.4	0.4	1.1	2.0	1.5	7.3	0.0*	0.7	0.3	0.0*	0.1	37.6
CEMENT	0.1	0.1	0.4	0.0	0.5	0.5	3.3	0.1	0.7	0.1	0.1	0.1	1.6
GLASS	0.0*	0.5	0.4	3.0	4.1	0.5	3.3	0.1	0.1	0.4	0.7	0.0*	24.7
MOTOR VEHICLES	0.0*	0.1	1.5	17.1	19.4	1.2	25.7	0.7	0.6	11.3	0.5	0.0*	69.5
SHIPBUILDING	0.0*	0.0	0.1	2.6	4.7	0.0*		0.1	0.0*	2.4	0.0*	0.0*	6.4
AIRCRAFT	0.0*	0.0	0.2	0.0*	0.2	0.0*	11.2	0.1	0.2	7.2	0.1	0.0*	6.2
METAL PRODUCTS	0.0*	0.1	1.7	0.4	3.2	2.1	3.4	0.2	0.1	2.4	1.1	0.1	13.7
MACHINERY	0.1	0.2	3.3	35.0	14.2	1.0	21.8	0.5	0.3	14.2	0.2	0.0*	85.6
ELECTRICAL MACH.	0.1	0.2	0.5	13.7	24.7	0.2	16.8	0.3	0.2	0.4	0.3	0.0*	64.8
INSTRUMENTS	0.0*	0.0*	4.7	1.5	6.0	0.3	6.6	0.2	0.1	0.8	1.5	0.0*	17.7
OTHER MANUFACT.	0.4	0.4	1.4	0.4	3.9	0.3	2.7	0.1	0.1	1.2		0.6	18.0
SERVICES	0.6	0.0	4.0	0.0	0.4	5.7	10.2	0.4	0.8	0.0	3.5	0.2	33.0
TRANSPORT	0.4	0.0		0.0	6.9	3.4	17.2	2.4	1.2	0.0	1.0	1.4	66.7
AID INFLOW	4.1	0.0	21.5	0.0	0.8	10.5	9.3	1.6	3.8	0.0	5.7	3.0	37.0
CAPITAL INFLOW	0.1	0.0	7.1	0.0	16.5	15.1	37.5	0.8	8.9	0.0	0.5	0.9	54.1

MILITARY EXPORTS

	AAF	ASC	ASL	EEM	JAP	LAT	NAH	OCH	OIL	RUH	SAF	TAF	WEU
AIRCRAFT	0.0	0.0949	0.0949	0.8542	0.0	0.0	3.7963	0.0	0.0	3.0370	0.0	0.0	1.6134
SHIPS	0.0	0.0133	0.0	0.0	0.0	0.0	0.2929	0.0	0.0	0.4260	0.0	0.0	0.5990
ELECTRONIC EQUIP	0.0825	0.0412	0.0412	0.1649	0.0	0.0412	1.7317	0.0	0.0	0.9483	0.0	0.0	1.0720
MISSILES	0.0194	0.0	0.0	0.0466	0.0	0.0116	0.8163	0.0	0.0	0.7968	0.0	0.0	0.3110
AMMUNITION, NEC	0.0233	0.0116	0.0116	0.2539	0.0	0.0	0.4888	0.0	0.0	0.2677	0.0	0.0	0.3026
TANKS	0.0	0.0	0.0	0.0030	0.0	0.0	1.4146	0.0	0.0	1.0519	0.0	0.0	0.9068
SMALL ARMS	0.0015	0.0008	0.0008	0.0082	0.0	0.0008	0.0318	0.0	0.0	0.0174	0.0	0.0	0.0197
SM. ARMS AMMUN.	0.0041	0.0020	0.0020	0.0168	0.0	0.0020	0.0856	0.0	0.0	0.0469	0.0	0.0	0.0530
OTHER ORDNANCE	0.0084	0.0042	0.0042	0.0	0.0	0.0042	0.1765	0.0	0.0	0.0966	0.0	0.0	0.1092
TOTAL EXPORTS	0.1392	0.1681	0.1548	1.3475	0.0	0.0599	8.8343	0.0	0.0	6.6886	0.0	0.0	4.9867
MIL. GRANTS INF.	0.0779	0.1119	0.2298	0.0050	0.0	0.0430	0.0	0.0	0.0	0.0	0.0	0.1676	0.0261

IMPORTS	AAF	ASC	ASL	EEM	JAP	LAT	NAH	OCH	OIL	RUH	SAF	TAF	WEU
LIVESTOCK	0.1	0.0*	1.3	1.5	1.4	1.3	2.6	0.0*	2.3	0.3	0.2	0.6	9.0
HIGH PROT. CROPS	0.9	0.0*	2.7	4.1	18.9	2.2	3.0	0.3	4.5	0.3	0.1	0.8	24.4
GRAINS	5.9	0.1	37.2	39.8	32.6	26.7	2.7	0.3	15.7	6.5	1.8	10.1	65.9
ROOTS	0.4	0.0*	2.0	3.4	1.9	2.3	0.6	0.1	2.1	0.0	0.0	0.5	9.4
OTHER AGRICULT.	0.3	2.4	3.0	3.1	3.7	1.9	9.6	0.3	10.1	2.3	0.3	1.1	14.3
FOOD PROCESSING	0.3	0.2	2.7	1.5	1.2	1.9	4.3	0.1	7.7	1.1	0.3	5.6	7.6
TEXT. APPAREL	1.8	0.0	7.8	9.3	10.7	4.0	26.6	3.0	20.1	17.7	2.4	0.3	103.1
WOOD AND CORK	0.2	0.0	0.2	0.8	2.3	0.5	2.9	0.3	8.5	0.4	0.3	0.3	10.9
FURNITURE, FIXT.	0.0*	0.0*	0.0*	0.4	0.0*	0.2	0.7	0.0*	1.0	0.6	0.0*	0.6	1.0
PAPER	0.3	0.0*	1.3	1.9	2.9	3.2	5.8	0.9	16.4	1.8	0.2	0.4	33.7
PRINTING	0.1	0.0	0.2	1.5	1.3	1.1	1.1	0.6	4.4	0.0	1.1	0.3	7.1
RUBBER	0.1	0.0	0.4	2.9	2.7	1.0	1.3	0.3	7.3	0.3	0.3	1.0	6.4
INDUSTRIAL CHEM.	0.5	1.2	3.6	1.0	1.4	4.6	6.1	1.3	8.9	2.1	1.2	1.2	32.0
FERTILIZERS	1.0	1.8	8.1	0.8	0.0*	5.5	1.9	0.2	4.2	0.8	0.0*	0.6	4.2
OTHER CHEMICALS	0.3	0.1	2.3	0.0	2.4	2.8	2.0	0.9	21.2	0.3	0.2	0.4	17.5
CEMENT	0.0*	0.0*	0.4	1.6	0.0*	0.1	0.1	0.0*	2.5	0.6	0.4	0.4	0.6
GLASS	0.2	0.0*	2.1	6.2	0.7	1.2	2.4	0.5	13.6	2.0	1.9	0.9	15.8
MOTOR VEHICLES	0.2	0.4	0.6	0.9	1.0	7.1	42.2	3.5	26.4	5.2	0.0*	3.1	54.3
SHIPBUILDING	0.2	0.1	0.5	0.0	0.2	0.6	0.5	0.3	0.6	0.6	0.4	1.0	6.9
AIRCRAFT	0.1	0.0*	0.7	0.3	2.5	1.7	4.3	0.9	1.8	0.2	0.2	0.4	13.0
METAL PRODUCTS	1.0	0.7	7.0	11.7	0.3	1.7	2.5	0.4	9.5	9.1	2.7	0.1	7.8
MACHINERY	0.5	0.1	4.8	3.4	4.0	13.9	18.4	2.7	44.3	2.1	1.3	2.1	58.3
ELECTRICAL MACH.	0.1	0.2	1.1	0.7	3.0	7.6	14.9	1.6	38.2	1.3	0.5	1.3	47.2
INSTRUMENTS	0.4	0.0	2.4	0.4	1.4	1.9	4.2	0.7	7.5	0.0	0.2		14.3
OTHER MANUFACT.	0.4	0.0	0.1	0.0	1.6	1.0	9.4	0.5	2.4	0.0	0.7		14.1
SERVICES	0.0	0.0	5.2	0.0	2.8	4.5	14.3	1.2	4.7	0.0	1.6		27.7
TRANSPORT	0.9	0.4	2.8	0.0	14.0	7.2	11.1	3.0	12.8	0.0	0.8		46.5
AID OUTFLOW	0.7	0.0	3.6	0.0	3.9	4.3	20.2	1.7	28.0	2.6	2.7		30.2
CAPITAL OUTFLOW	0.1			0.0	7.6	17.1	15.4	5.5	58.7	0.0			29.4

MILITARY IMPORTS	AAF	ASC	ASL	EEM	JAP	LAT	NAH	OCH	OIL	RUH	SAF	TAF	WEU
AIRCRAFT	0.6020	0.0903	0.4992	0.8925	0.2312	0.4573	0.1779	0.0441	4.8561	0.4560	0.0713	0.3253	0.7874
SHIPS	0.0776	0.0068	0.0568	0.0210	0.0143	0.2022	0.0251	0.0034	0.7282		0.0237	0.1132	0.0588
ELECTRONIC EQUIP	0.3061	0.0356	0.1980	0.3493	0.0808	0.2149	0.0966	0.0166	2.1763	0.1022	0.0302	0.1424	0.3738
MISSILES	0.1194	0.0264	0.0893	0.4684	0.0866	0.0363	0.0745	0.0127	0.8260	0.0295	0.0066	0.0192	0.1781
AMMUNITION. NEC	0.0871	0.0104	0.0570	0.1108	0.0244	0.0595	0.0278	0.0049	0.5930	0.0445	0.0089	0.0388	0.1116
TANKS	0.2789	0.0359	0.1482	0.1832	0.0670	0.1115	0.0203	0.0130	2.1594	0.0022	0.0281	0.1031	0.4341
SMALL ARMS	0.0052	0.0006	0.0095	0.0073	0.0026	0.0038	0.0021	0.0005	0.0346	0.0048	0.0006	0.0070	0.0098
SM. ARMS AMMUN.	0.0147	0.0016	0.0093	0.0173	0.0047	0.0107	0.0046	0.0009	0.1067	0.0103	0.0015	0.0144	0.0199
OTHER ORDNANCE	0.0306	0.0035	0.0197	0.0364	0.0092	0.0219	0.0097	0.0018	0.2195		0.0031	0.0023	0.0401
TOTAL IMPORTS	1.5218	0.2112	1.0810	2.0867	0.5209	1.1182	0.4387	0.0980	11.6999	0.6495	0.1739	0.7657	2.0136
MIL. GRANTS OUTF	0.0	0.1595	0.0	0.0	0.0	0.0	0.1455	0.0	0.0	0.2992	0.0	0.0	0.0570

	AAF	ASC	ASL	EEM	JAP	LAT	NAH	OCH	OIL	RUH	SAF	TAF	WEU
CONSUMPTION AND POPULATION													
GDP	103.7	454.6	399.2	614.8	904.5	472.1	2381.1	132.6	1206.2	1823.7	66.0	126.7	2093.5
PERSONAL CONSUMP	80.8	306.6	301.7	374.3	584.7	335.4	1560.9	100.3	791.0	1134.8	47.5	105.8	1382.9
GOVT.(CIVILIAN)	10.4	45.5	39.9	61.5	90.4	47.2	238.1	13.3	120.6	182.4	6.6	12.7	209.3
GOVT.(MILITARY)	9.3	25.6	9.6	24.7	16.3	5.8	116.2	2.0	47.0	116.2	2.2	3.0	43.2
POPULATION	285.7	1221.3	2048.4	125.7	132.9	615.8	300.0	24.5	309.8	315.0	50.0	331.8	487.1
URBAN POPULATION	168.4	508.9	704.4	90.1	98.5	465.0	258.9	22.4	148.2	245.2	32.0	109.4	382.4
EMPLOYMENT	49.7	187.2	181.4	63.8	67.6	156.2	133.9	10.2	214.9	151.8	12.9	68.0	168.7
GDP/HEAD	362.9	372.2	194.8	4891.1	6805.8	766.6	7937.0	5411.5	3893.4	5789.6	1320.0	381.7	4297.9
CONSUMPTION/HEAD	282.7	251.3	147.3	2977.8	4399.5	544.7	5202.9	4092.8	2553.3	3602.4	950.4	318.5	2839.0
CALORIES/HEAD	2457.3	2253.3	2164.0	3180.0	3248.5	2610.7	3191.3	3213.6	3334.8	3194.5	2944.4	2672.2	3136.1
PROTEINS/HEAD	75.4	69.8	57.1	107.9	123.3	68.3	99.7	100.1	117.3	108.1	91.6	82.2	102.1
INVESTMENT AND CAPITAL													
INVESTMENT	15.3	63.8	45.2	108.5	179.2	90.7	412.5	24.0	415.8	359.2	12.4	19.4	325.4
EQUIPMENT	7.5	37.2	23.6	44.3	57.7	46.8	141.9	7.8	146.2	125.0	5.6	8.8	129.0
PLANT	7.6	26.1	20.7	64.0	121.5	43.2	270.4	16.0	269.4	233.5	6.7	10.3	196.2
IRRIGATION	0.1	0.6	1.0	0.1	0.0*	0.2	0.1	0.0*	0.1	0.6	0.0*	0.0*	0.2
LAND (AREA)	0.9	0.9	1.3	0.0	0.0	2.8	0.8	0.6	0.5	0.0	0.1	1.7	0.1
INVENTORY CHANGE	1.5	9.2	5.3	3.6	5.5	7.0	10.4	0.5	21.9	9.4	1.3	1.0	11.0
CAPITAL STOCK	139.3	729.3	512.3	1350.3	2272.4	930.6	6674.6	366.5	2687.2	4456.5	116.2	185.3	5125.3
EQUIPMENT	62.8	365.2	241.3	435.9	580.0	386.0	1599.4	94.1	885.7	1297.7	46.3	83.0	1452.3
PLANT	76.6	364.1	271.0	914.4	1692.4	544.6	5075.2	272.4	1801.5	3158.9	69.9	102.3	3673.0
INVENTORY STOCK	27.3	165.5	122.6	122.8	159.8	142.5	408.4	25.1	261.8	348.1	17.0	38.0	403.1
CULTIVATED LAND	109.6	407.8	595.6	66.0	16.5	254.1	207.3	31.2	343.2	340.2	28.7	210.2	170.4
SURPLUS SAVINGS	-2.3	-6.0	7.3	15.2	18.1	-19.9	11.7	-1.0	-250.1	-11.9	1.6	-9.5	136.4
INTERNATIONAL TRANSACTIONS													
IMPORTS	19.8	8.3	76.3	72.4	115.3	86.8	195.2	27.0	293.4	55.1	18.5	38.6	645.6
EXPORTS	6.1	12.0	73.7	113.5	142.6	71.6	234.6	19.3	102.4	73.5	14.5	22.0	764.3
PAYMENTS SURPLUS	0.0	-1.9	0.0	-13.9	-82.6	12.0	133.7	-5.7	141.7	98.9	0.0	0.0	-49.2
FOR. INVEST.(INF	-3.3	-21.3	14.9	-167.7	-1071.5	204.8	1087.2	-251.0	2248.8	992.0	-25.5	-19.3	-1554.9
FOR. INCOME (OUT	-0.4	-1.7	0.4	-13.4	-86.1	13.8	91.9	-21.0	176.0	79.4	-2.5	-2.0	-119.6
LEVEL OF ABATEMENT ACTIVITIES													
AIR	0.0	0.0	0.0	6.83	7.09	2.94	83.60	0.84	11.48	22.38	0.67	0.0	24.79
PRIMARY WATER	0.0	0.0	0.0	4.14	3.24	1.06	9.71	0.71	3.62	12.78	0.95	0.0	14.69
SECONDARY WATER	0.0	0.0	0.0	0.24	2.55	0.06	0.55	0.04	0.21	0.73	-0.50	0.0	0.84
TERTIARY WATER	0.0	0.0	0.0	0.05	0.56	0.01	0.12	0.01	0.05	0.16	-0.11	0.0	0.18
SOLID WASTE	0.0	0.0	0.0	111.59	129.78	332.12	393.49	30.06	147.28	320.62	31.19	0.0	481.07
NET TOTAL EMISSIONS													
PESTICIDES	0.89	0.53	2.43	0.51	1.37	1.54	2.46	0.03	3.99	0.80	0.04	0.67	1.68
PARTICULATES	0.66	3.39	1.82	0.53	0.23	1.53	4.21	0.05	3.26	1.17	0.06	0.55	1.45
BIOLOG. OXYGEN	1.87	8.69	6.40	2.45	1.66	5.71	11.65	0.35	7.05	7.38	0.87	0.65	10.34
NITROGEN (WATER)	0.02	0.08	0.05	0.12	0.08	0.05	0.24	0.01	0.11	0.44	0.04	0.00*	0.57
PHOSPHATES	0.02	0.05	0.03	0.06	0.04	0.04	0.19	0.01	0.07	0.22	0.02	0.00*	0.29
SUSPENDED SOLIDS	0.64	2.74	1.52	1.52	0.95	3.07	6.82	0.18	6.39	3.99	0.21	0.68	4.94
DISSOLVED SOLIDS	8.16	36.47	21.44	16.77	20.95	18.25	55.54	2.43	31.20	60.04	6.40	1.41	78.58
SOLID WASTE	65.52	276.71	295.07	0.0	0.0	53.05	0.0	0.0	0.0	0.0	0.0	37.16	0.0

SCENARIO D2 IN 2000

RESOURCE OUTPUTS

	AAF	ASC	ASL	EEM	JAP	LAT	NAH	OCH	OIL	RUH	SAF	TAF	WEU
COPPER	0.1	0.0	0.2	0.4	0.3	8.0	4.8	0.5	0.0	2.3	0.1	5.3	0.6
BAUXITE	0.0	0.2	1.9	1.7	0.0	2.4	0.6	17.8	0.3	2.1	0.0	7.2	2.8
NICKEL	1.6	0.0	722.6	0.0	0.0	418.1	321.7	77.2	0.0	515.0	0.0	0.0	0.0
ZINC	0.1	0.8	0.6	1.5	3.5	0.5	2.0	0.2	1.3	2.3	0.1	0.0*	4.4
LEAD	0.1	0.7	0.2	1.2	1.1	0.7	1.7	0.2	1.6	2.4	0.1	0.0*	4.1
IRON	4.8	120.9	116.3	20.1	2.0	219.8	186.6	41.8	24.4	530.7	17.4	78.0	167.2
PETROLEUM	171.4	179.1	75.0	24.1	1.0	792.5	2494.7	11.0	8264.9	2291.5	0.0	0.0	612.0
NATURAL GAS	0.0	0.0	13.0	0.0	0.0	275.1	1857.9	2.0	1276.3	1936.8	0.0	0.0	355.9
COAL	1.7	1109.2	408.0	923.6	142.8	39.8	2675.8	172.6	1.7	1445.0	48.3	46.0	1023.8

CUMULATIVE RESOURCE OUTPUT AT END OF PERIOD

	AAF	ASC	ASL	EEM	JAP	LAT	NAH	OCH	OIL	RUH	SAF	TAF	WEU
COPPER	1.	5.	7.	7.	6.	101.	100.	10.	0.*	48.	3.	100.	13.
BAUXITE	0.	5.	34.	31.	0.	252.	12.	188.	2.	38.	0.	65.	56.
NICKEL	18.	0.	11246.	84.	0.	3858.	12116.	1807.	0.	9629.	182.	145.	209.
ZINC	1.	10.	4.	19.	22.	22.	98.	31.	9.	31.	1.	15.	47.
LEAD	3.	10.	2.	10.	8.	14.	115.	12.	10.	21.	1.	2.	29.
IRON	161.	1782.	1662.	321.	39.	3431.	3774.	1260.	322.	7706.	229.	1339.	3143.
PETROLEUM	2254.	2854.	1126.	722.	30.	16994.	45617.	331.	129099.	34081.	0.	33.	3630.
NATURAL GAS	1.	0.	337.	1125.	0.	3633.	41209.	60.	20426.	30108.	0.	0.*	6232.
COAL	28.	19590.	6112.	17597.	2382.	639.	36554.	3419.	28.	25757.	1458.	602.	19595.

NET EXPORTS OF RESOURCES

	AAF	ASC	ASL	EEM	JAP	LAT	NAH	OCH	OIL	RUH	SAF	TAF	WEU
COPPER	0.0	-0.6	0.0	-0.7	-4.0	6.5	1.4	0.4	-0.9	-1.5	0.0	5.3	-5.8
BAUXITE	-0.1	-0.3	0.0	-0.0	-5.6	1.3	-6.8	16.9	-1.4	-3.4	-0.3	7.1	-7.4
NICKEL	0.0	-8.7	561.9	-32.9	-428.3	302.6	0.0	0.0	-19.3	0.0	-36.5	-0.2	-338.5
ZINC	-0.0*		0.0	0.0	0.0	-0.0*	0.0	0.0	0.0	0.0	0.0	-0.0*	0.0
LEAD	-0.0*		0.0	0.0	0.0	-0.0*	-0.0*	-0.0*	0.0	0.0	0.0	-0.0*	0.0
IRON	0.0		89.9	-93.0	-262.3	174.4	31.7	-10.6	-67.8	148.0	0.0	74.0	-105.4
PETROLEUM	0.0		-354.4	-360.0	-1505.3	150.9	0.0	-151.8	4618.8	155.7	-64.8	-119.6	-2368.6
NATURAL GAS	-2.2		-60.7	-262.3	-263.2	-77.8	0.0	-5.9	206.5	206.5	0.0	-0.0*	-4.1
COAL	-4.1		3.8	0.0	-2.2	-27.0	284.2	76.8	-74.0		0.0	0.0	-15.6
OTHER RESOURCES	0.3	19.2	0.3	-1.6		0.8	2.9	0.3	0.9	0.5	0.4	0.2	-2.9
PETROL. REFINING	0.0	0.0*	-3.3	-3.4	-14.1	1.4	0.0*	-1.4	43.3	1.5	-0.6	-1.1	-22.2
PRIMARY METALS	-0.2	-1.1	-0.3	-2.9	-1.4	5.6	1.5	-0.3	-1.5	-0.8	0.1	4.2	-2.8

OUTPUT LEVELS

	AAF	ASC	ASL	EEM	JAP	LAT	NAH	OCH	OIL	RUH	SAF	TAF	WEU
ANIMAL PRODUCTS	11.7	57.6	47.9	23.3	20.4	55.9	68.7	10.8	37.0	55.9	6.4	19.9	90.0
HIGH PROT. CROPS	8.3	39.8	76.3	6.4	4.2	29.5	64.9	0.2	20.8	59.5	2.2	40.2	20.5
GRAINS	81.2	546.3	571.7	110.5	52.9	264.0	443.8	37.9	127.3	368.0	27.0	102.0	279.9
ROOTS	6.2	142.8	125.6	64.3	41.3	86.9	26.6	1.4	92.6	140.7	1.2	107.0	98.2
OTHER AGRICULT.	8.0	58.7	31.9	15.8	21.3	59.1	60.6	6.2	62.7	47.3	6.7	16.9	73.1
OTHER RESOURCES	0.9	3.3	2.3	1.8	3.8	3.5	16.7	1.0	9.1	12.0	0.8	0.6	9.4
FOOD PROCESSING	1.5	11.9	4.9	38.9	52.7	23.0	135.6	11.2	70.9	109.3	3.1	2.6	132.9
PETROL. REFINING	1.0	6.1	0.2	6.9	0.3	8.8	39.9	1.1	61.7	33.5	0.5	0.1	13.5
PRIMARY METALS	2.0	12.9	6.4	30.0	43.3	18.1	99.3	4.2	44.9	89.0	2.1	5.5	89.0
TEXT.. APPAREL	7.0	37.0	54.4	31.0	58.3	32.5	94.8	5.2	59.8	58.8	3.0	3.3	109.3
WOOD AND CORK	0.4	4.6	5.2	7.4	10.3	6.2	30.6	1.4	10.4	26.3	0.7	1.0	24.2
FURNITURE, FIXT.	2.9	13.7	9.3	6.5	8.3	17.9	20.5	1.2	48.3	15.2	2.7	4.3	24.6
PAPER	0.5	6.1	2.7	11.8	19.5	5.1	67.7	2.5	5.3	38.7	1.4	0.2	53.7
PRINTING	0.3	3.3	2.2	13.9	22.9	5.9	39.0	3.4	22.1	48.4	1.1	0.3	59.8
RUBBER	0.3	3.0	1.8	11.7	18.8	3.4	59.6	1.9	9.0	31.7	0.6	0.2	41.0
INDUSTRIAL CHEM.	2.3	14.8	9.0	13.9	29.6	11.0		2.3	22.9	44.9	1.4	1.1	65.3
FERTILIZERS	13.4	46.1	26.3	5.8	14.7	20.8	24.7	1.6	31.6	30.8	3.8	1.3	31.4
OTHER CHEMICALS	1.1	8.3	4.0	13.9	19.1	8.0	55.4	2.9	5.1	40.1	1.3	0.3	65.7
CEMENT	0.1	0.7	0.6	1.5	3.2	1.0	6.6	0.3	2.4	5.2	0.2	0.0*	6.3
GLASS	0.8	6.0	3.6	14.7	26.0	7.2	55.7	2.6	24.6	44.7	1.5	0.6	52.0
MOTOR VEHICLES	0.1	3.6	0.6	38.7	60.4	3.8	95.8	3.6	25.1	93.6	0.6	0.1	107.8
SHIPBUILDING	0.4	3.5	1.5	5.3	10.3	3.4	15.1	0.6	10.4	8.4	0.5	0.0*	12.4
AIRCRAFT	0.6	4.4	1.4	8.4	4.5	0.7	33.5	0.2	17.2	38.5	0.1	0.0*	11.9
METAL PRODUCTS	2.8	15.8	9.2	37.1	57.0	16.3	122.3	6.6	66.7	115.0	2.9	1.6	119.0
MACHINERY	3.1	26.6	9.0	57.8	55.3	18.9	116.0	3.6	55.6	106.2	2.2	0.7	127.9
ELECTRICAL MACH.	1.2	11.0	3.4	38.6	58.3	6.0	95.8	3.7	23.0	82.6	1.0	0.2	100.0
INSTRUMENTS	0.3	3.5	0.9	6.7	12.7	2.4	23.4	0.6	5.9	17.7	0.4	0.1	22.2
OTHER MANUFACT.	1.8	8.6	7.4	6.8	14.2	6.6	25.4	5.9	14.4	21.5	2.4	2.0	30.9
UTILITIES			6.1	25.6	35.7	13.6	96.6	5.9	50.4	79.0	1.9	2.5	84.1
CONSTRUCTION	9.8	36.4	30.5	82.6	151.6	61.0	368.1	20.5	309.8	297.7	8.9	13.7	267.5
TRADE	11.0	53.6	37.9	127.4	190.4	79.8	488.9	30.9	252.9	379.7	12.3	18.3	434.6
TRANSPORTATION	5.6	32.5	20.9	31.7	40.0	29.0	134.6	6.8	72.6	100.5	3.6	7.0	133.1
COMMUNICATIONS	1.3	6.5	4.5	15.0	21.5	7.9	58.8	3.5	21.6	45.9	1.2	1.8	50.3
SERVICES	24.8	121.1	90.2	200.9	309.1	148.1	881.6	51.9	410.6	662.1	22.4	37.6	730.1

MILITARY OUTPUT LEVELS

	AAF	ASC	ASL	EEM	JAP	LAT	NAH	OCH	OIL	RUH	SAF	TAF	WEU
AIRCRAFT	0.4343	3.0229	0.6790	5.1665	2.3369	0.1314	18.1431	0.2961	-0.0000*	23.2152	0.4053	0.0000*	7.8441
SHIPS	0.0785	0.6866	0.0923	0.0838	0.7175	0.0463	2.5199	0.1092	0.0002	7.1999	0.0355	0.0000*	2.8706
ELECTRONIC EQUIP	0.2835	1.7874	0.5034	2.0016	0.9296	0.1031	9.7733	0.1678	0.0047	10.2353	0.2721	0.0001	3.3189
NEW CONSTRUCTION	0.1342	1.4675	0.1661	0.7141	0.3136	0.1000	1.6858	0.0575	2.1746	3.3583	0.0629	0.0514	1.2011
MAINTENANCE	0.0982	1.0730	0.1214	0.5221	0.2293	0.0731	1.2327	0.0420	1.5901	2.4556	0.0460	0.0376	0.8783
MISSILES	0.0899	0.4991	0.0856	0.3855	0.1611	0.0134	7.4733	0.0237	-0.0000*	10.0787	0.0441	-0.0000*	1.7988
AMMUNITION, NEC	0.0806	0.5213	0.1449	0.6352	0.2804	0.0322	2.8227	0.0499	0.0098	2.9623	0.0798	-0.0000*	1.0160
TANKS	0.3083	0.6897	0.2310	0.4893	0.2522	0.0347	2.2140	0.0352	0.0043	4.5612	0.0843	-0.0000*	2.2570
SMALL ARMS	0.0048	0.0326	0.0089	0.0450	0.0297	0.0041	0.2081	0.0046	0.0094	0.2171	0.0057	-0.0000*	0.0951
SM. ARMS AMMUN.	0.0136	0.0815	0.0237	0.0990	0.0544	0.0071	0.4638	0.0092	0.0093	0.4790	0.0134	-0.0000*	0.1809
OTHER ORDNANCE	0.0284	0.1763	0.0500	0.2086	0.1053	0.0124	0.9839	0.0182	0.0088	1.0305	0.0277	-0.0000*	0.3612
TOTAL OUTPUT	1.5543	10.0378	2.1062	13.3509	5.4099	0.5578	47.5207	0.8134	3.8111	65.7829	1.0768	0.0891	21.8221

SCENARIO D2 IN 2000

	AAF	ASC	ASL	EEM	JAP	LAT	NAH	OCH	OIL	RUH	SAF	TAF	WEU
FISH													
FISH CATCH	0.6	7.9	9.3	0.8	8.2	14.4	3.8	0.2	0.4	6.7	2.2	1.9	9.6
NON-HUMAN USE	0.3	0.1	1.0	0.1	2.0	12.5	1.2	-0.0*	-0.1	0.6	2.0	0.6	1.7
FISH IMPORTS	0.1	0.0	0.3	0.2	0.2	0.1	1.3	0.0*	0.0*	0.1	0.0*	0.1	1.6
FISH EXPORTS	0.1	0.1	0.3	0.0*	0.5	0.1	0.4	0.0*	0.1	0.4	0.0*	0.1	2.0
EXPORTS													
LIVESTOCK	0.0*	0.0	0.1	2.4	0.0*	2.5	1.8	4.1	0.0*	0.3	0.1	0.1	9.9
HIGH PROT. CROPS	1.2	0.1	3.9	0.8	0.1	2.8	41.6	8.0*	2.8	1.6	0.3	2.3	5.7
GRAINS	1.6	0.0	10.3	8.6	4.4	21.9	135.1	18.8	0.4	11.3	2.3	0.9	38.4
ROOTS	0.8	0.0	1.4	3.2	0.1	0.8	4.3	0.3	0.4	0.4	0.6	0.6	10.9
OTHER AGRICULT.	1.6	1.1	8.7	2.8	0.5	8.1	5.8	2.2	1.7	1.9	0.3	4.5	14.0
FOOD PROCESSING	0.3	0.5	2.4	1.7	0.5	4.2	5.2	1.6	0.7	0.7	0.6	0.8	12.1
TEXT., APPAREL	1.0	5.6	28.6	17.6	27.8	1.2	8.4	0.1	5.3	1.6	0.7	0.2	118.1
WOOD AND CORK	0.0*	0.1	2.6	1.2	1.2	1.2	5.0	0.1	0.7	4.5	1.3	0.2	11.2
FURNITURE, FIXT.	0.0*	0.0*	0.1	1.8	1.2	1.4	0.2	0.0*	0.0*	0.0*	0.0*	0.0*	2.3
PAPER	0.1	0.6	0.6	0.9	2.4	0.6	21.5	0.5	0.2	1.7	0.1	0.0*	40.8
PRINTING	0.1	0.0*	0.4	0.4	0.9	0.4	3.1	0.1	0.0*	0.1	0.8	0.0*	12.8
RUBBER	0.1	0.0*	0.5	0.9	2.7	0.4	1.4	0.1	0.2	0.6	0.1	0.0*	11.6
INDUSTRIAL CHEM.	0.4	1.5	0.7	1.6	9.2	2.0	10.4	0.7	0.2	1.7	0.7	0.1	42.5
FERTILIZERS	0.1	0.4	0.4	2.0	1.5	0.5	6.9	0.0*	1.5	4.4	0.0*	0.1	13.2
OTHER CHEMICALS	0.1	0.1	1.5	1.2	2.1	1.5	7.7	0.8	0.6	0.3	0.6	0.1	38.8
CEMENT	0.1	0.5	0.4	0.0	0.5	0.2	0.3	0.0*	0.7	0.1	0.0*	0.0*	1.7
GLASS	0.1	0.1	0.5	3.1	4.2	0.5	3.4	0.1	0.6	0.4	0.1	0.0*	25.4
MOTOR VEHICLES	0.0*	0.0*	1.5	17.4	19.7	1.2	26.1	0.7	0.6	11.4	0.6	0.0*	70.6
SHIPBUILDING	0.0*	0.0*	0.1	2.8	5.1	0.0*	0.3	0.1	0.0*	2.6	0.0*	0.0*	6.9
AIRCRAFT	0.0*	0.1	0.2	0.0*	0.2	0.1	11.6	0.1	0.2	7.4	0.0*	0.0*	6.4
METAL PRODUCTS	0.0*	0.2	0.9	0.4	3.3	0.4	3.6	0.1	0.4	2.6	0.1	0.0*	14.5
MACHINERY	0.1	0.2	1.8	37.3	15.2	2.2	23.2	0.5	0.2	15.2	1.2	0.1	91.2
ELECTRICAL MACH.	0.1	0.4	3.4	14.3	25.7	1.1	17.5	0.3	0.1	10.4	0.2	0.0*	67.5
INSTRUMENTS	0.4	0.0*	0.5	1.6	6.2	0.2	6.9	0.2	0.1	0.8	0.4	0.0*	18.5
OTHER MANUFACT.	0.6	0.0	4.9	0.4	4.4	0.3	2.8	0.1	0.1	1.2	1.6	0.6	18.6
SERVICES	0.4	0.0	1.4	0.0	0.4	5.8	10.1	0.4	0.8	0.0	3.6	0.2	33.3
TRANSPORT		0.0	4.1	0.0	7.2	3.5	17.9	2.5	1.3	0.0	1.0	1.4	69.2
AID INFLOW	4.2	0.0	22.2	0.0	0.8	10.8	9.6	1.7	3.9	0.0	5.9	3.1	38.1
ADD. AID REC'D	8.2	0.0	24.7	0.0	0.0	5.5	0.0	0.0	0.0	0.0	0.0	16.4	0.0
CAPITAL INFLOW	0.1	0.0	7.4	0.0	17.2	15.8	39.2	0.8	9.3	0.0	0.5	0.9	56.5
MILITARY EXPORTS													
AIRCRAFT	0.0	0.1054	0.1054	0.9488	0.0	0.0	4.2169	0.0	0.0	3.3735	0.0	0.0	1.7922
SHIPS	0.0914	0.0150	0.0	0.1828	0.0	0.0	0.3310	0.0	0.0	0.4815	0.0	0.0	0.6771
ELECTRONIC EQUIP	0.0211	0.0457	0.0457	0.0516	0.0	0.0457	1.9191	0.0	0.0	1.0509	0.0	0.0	1.1880
MISSILES	0.0258	0.0129	0.0129	0.2845	0.0	0.0129	0.8849	0.0	0.0	0.8638	0.0	0.0	0.3355
AMMUNITION, NEC	0.0	0.0	0.0	0.0	0.0	0.0	0.5420	0.0	0.0	0.2968	0.0	0.0	1.0161
TANKS	0.0017	0.0008	0.0008	0.0033	0.0	0.0008	1.5852	0.0	0.0	1.1787	0.0	0.0	
SMALL ARMS	0.0045	0.0023	0.0023	0.0090	0.0	0.0023	0.0350	0.0	0.0	0.0192	0.0	0.0	0.0217
SM. ARMS AMMUN.	0.0093	0.0047	0.0047	0.0186	0.0	0.0047	0.0947	0.0	0.0	0.0518	0.0	0.0	0.0586
OTHER ORDNANCE	0.0	0.0	0.0	0.0	0.0	0.0	0.1953	0.0	0.0	0.1070	0.0	0.0	0.1209
TOTAL EXPORTS	0.1537	0.1868	0.1718	1.4987	0.0	0.0663	9.8041	0.0	0.0	7.4233	0.0	0.0	5.5473
MIL. GRANTS INF.	0.0779	0.1119	0.2298	0.0050	0.0	0.0430	0.0	0.0	0.0	0.0	0.0	0.1676	0.0261

IMPORTS	AAF	ASC	ASL	EEM	JAP	LAT	NAH	OCH	OIL	RUH	SAF	TAF	WEU
LIVESTOCK	0.2	0.0*	1.5	1.5	1.4	1.4	2.6	0.0*	2.3	0.3	0.2	0.8	9.0
HIGH PROT. CROPS	1.2	0.0*	3.0	4.1	18.8	2.2	3.0	0.4	4.5	0.3	0.1	1.0	24.5
GRAINS	7.3	0.1	40.2	39.9	32.7	27.3	2.8	0.4	15.8	6.5	1.8	12.6	66.5
ROOTS	0.4	0.0*	2.3	3.4	1.9	2.4	0.6	0.1	2.1	2.0	0.0	0.6	9.5
OTHER AGRICULT.	0.6	0.0*	3.8	3.1	3.7	2.0	9.6	0.3	10.1	2.3	0.3	1.5	14.3
FOOD PROCESSING	0.5	0.2	3.3	1.5	1.2	2.0	4.3	0.1	7.7	1.1	0.2	8.4	7.6
TEXT., APPAREL	3.4	0.0	9.4	9.4	10.8	4.3	26.6	0.3	20.2	17.7	2.4	0.5	104.8
WOOD AND CORK	0.4	0.0	0.2	0.4	2.3	0.6	2.9	0.3	8.6	0.6	0.3	1.0	11.0
FURNITURE, FIXT.	0.1	0.0*	0.1	0.8	0.0*	0.2	0.7	0.0*	1.0	0.6	0.0*	0.5	1.0
PAPER	0.5	0.0*	1.6	1.9	3.0	3.4	5.8	0.9	16.5	1.8	1.1	1.0	34.2
PRINTING	0.2	0.0*	0.3	1.5	1.3	1.1	1.3	0.6	4.4	0.0	0.3	0.7	7.1
RUBBER	0.2	0.2	0.5	0.3	0.1	1.1	1.3	0.3	7.3	0.3	0.2	0.4	6.5
INDUSTRIAL CHEM.	0.8	1.2	4.3	2.9	2.7	4.9	6.2	1.3	9.0	2.1	1.2	1.1	32.9
FERTILIZERS	1.6	1.8	9.2	1.0	1.4	5.7	2.0	0.9	4.2	0.0	0.0*	1.2	4.4
OTHER CHEMICALS	0.6	0.1	3.0	0.8	2.4	3.0	2.0	0.2	21.3	0.8	0.2	2.0	17.9
CEMENT	0.0*	0.0*	0.2	0.0	0.0*	0.1	0.1	0.0*	2.6	0.3	0.0	0.1	0.6
GLASS	0.4	0.4	0.6	1.6	0.7	1.3	2.3	0.5	13.7	0.6	0.4	1.0	15.9
MOTOR VEHICLES	0.4	0.0*	2.4	6.3	1.0	7.9	42.3	3.5	26.5	2.0	1.9	0.7	54.7
SHIPBUILDING	0.4	0.0*	0.9	0.9	0.9	0.7	0.5	0.3	0.6	5.3	0.0*	0.3	7.2
AIRCRAFT	0.3	0.0*	0.6	0.3	2.6	1.9	4.3	0.9	1.8	0.6	0.4	1.5	13.3
METAL PRODUCTS	0.3	0.7	1.0	0.3	0.3	1.8	2.5	0.4	9.5	0.6	0.2	1.5	7.9
MACHINERY	2.4	1.1	10.0	12.1	4.1	15.1	18.6	2.7	44.8	9.2	2.7	5.6	60.4
ELECTRICAL MACH.	1.1	0.1	6.2	3.4	3.1	8.3	15.0	1.6	38.5	2.1	1.3	0.7	48.2
INSTRUMENTS	0.3	0.2	1.5	1.5	1.5	2.0	4.3	0.7	7.5	1.0	0.6	0.5	14.6
OTHER MANUFACT.	0.7	0.0	2.9	0.4	1.6	1.1	9.4	0.5	2.4	1.3	0.2	0.5	14.3
SERVICES	0.0	0.0	0.1	0.0	2.8	4.9	14.3	1.2	4.7	0.0	0.7	1.0	27.7
TRANSPORT	1.5	0.0	6.1	0.0	14.2	7.6	11.2	3.1	13.0	0.0	1.7	2.9	47.3
AID OUTFLOW	1.5	0.4	3.7	0.0	3.9	4.6	20.2	1.7	28.1	2.6	0.8	2.7	30.2
ADD. AID GIVEN	0.0	4.5	0.0	3.8	2.6	0.0	14.5	0.3	8.1	14.5	0.0	0.0	6.3
CAPITAL OUTFLOW	0.4	0.0	5.7	0.0	7.5	19.2	15.3	5.4	59.2	0.0	2.7	3.0	29.2

MILITARY IMPORTS	AAF	ASC	ASL	EEM	JAP	LAT	NAH	OCH	OIL	RUH	SAF	TAF	WEU
AIRCRAFT	1.2361	0.0907	0.6518	0.9093	0.2314	0.4864	0.1832	0.0441	4.8809	0.4643	0.0713	0.4784	0.8143
SHIPS	0.1594	0.0069	0.0755	0.0210	0.0144	0.2149	0.0255	0.0034	0.7319	0.0	0.0237	0.1665	0.0618
ELECTRONIC EQUIP	0.5754	0.0357	0.2597	0.3523	0.0809	0.2289	0.0987	0.0166	2.1874	0.1034	0.0302	0.2095	0.3904
MISSILES	0.2312	0.0265	0.1182	0.4703	0.0867	0.0387	0.0755	0.0127	0.8303	0.0	0.0066	0.0282	0.1821
AMMUNITION, NEC	0.1636	0.0104	0.0748	0.1118	0.0244	0.0636	0.0285	0.0049	0.5960	0.0299	0.0089	0.0571	0.1167
TANKS	0.5726	0.0359	0.1968	0.1849	0.0671	0.1186	0.0224	0.0130	2.1704	0.0461	0.0281	0.1517	0.4571
SMALL ARMS	0.0098	0.0007	0.0046	0.0079	0.0026	0.0042	0.0021	0.0005	0.0348	0.0022	0.0006	0.0033	0.0102
SM. ARMS AMMUN.	0.0276	0.0016	0.0122	0.0174	0.0047	0.0116	0.0047	0.0009	0.1073	0.0048	0.0015	0.0103	0.0208
OTHER ORDNANCE	0.0576	0.0035	0.0258	0.0367	0.0092	0.0234	0.0099	0.0018	0.2206	0.0104	0.0031	0.0211	0.0418
TOTAL IMPORTS	3.0331	0.2119	1.4194	2.1116	0.5212	1.1903	0.4505	0.0980	11.7596	0.6611	0.1739	1.1262	2.0953
MIL. GRANTS OUTF	0.0	0.1596	0.0	0.0	0.0	0.0	0.1455	0.0	0.0	0.2991	0.0	0.0	0.0571

SCENARIO D3 IN 2000

	AAF	ASC	ASL	EEM	JAP	LAT	NAH	OCH	OIL	RUH	SAF	TAF	WEU
CONSUMPTION AND POPULATION													
GDP	107.8	454.6	401.4	614.8	904.5	475.7	2383.5	132.6	1213.8	1824.4	66.0	128.8	2094.5
PERSONAL CONSUMP	83.3	306.6	303.1	373.9	584.2	337.8	1564.8	100.2	791.0	1137.0	47.4	107.3	1383.8
GOVT.(CIVILIAN)	10.8	45.5	40.1	61.5	90.4	47.6	238.3	13.3	121.4	182.4	6.6	12.9	209.5
GOVT.(MILITARY)	9.7	25.6	9.6	24.7	16.3	5.8	116.2	2.0	47.3	116.2	2.2	3.0	43.3
POPULATION	285.7	1221.3	2048.9	125.7	132.9	615.0	300.0	24.5	309.8	315.0	50.0	331.8	487.1
URBAN POPULATION	168.4	508.9	704.4	90.1	98.5	465.0	258.9	22.4	148.2	245.2	32.0	109.4	382.4
EMPLOYMENT	51.6	187.2	182.3	63.8	67.6	157.1	133.9	10.2	215.9	151.8	12.9	69.1	168.8
GDP/HEAD	377.3	372.2	195.9	4891.0	6805.8	772.5	7944.9	5411.0	3918.1	5791.7	1320.0	388.1	4300.0
CONSUMPTION/HEAD	291.5	251.0	147.9	2974.2	4395.8	548.5	5215.9	4090.1	2553.3	3610.6	948.6	323.2	2840.0
CALORIES/HEAD	2474.6	2253.3	2165.3	3179.7	3248.3	2613.5	3192.0	3213.4	3334.8	3195.1	2943.9	2682.8	3136.2
PROTEINS/HEAD	76.2	69.8	57.2	107.8	123.3	68.4	99.8	100.0	117.3	108.2	91.5	82.6	102.1
INVESTMENT AND CAPITAL													
INVESTMENT	16.2	63.8	45.6	108.4	179.0	91.4	415.1	24.0	416.2	360.3	12.4	19.6	325.9
EQUIPMENT	7.9	37.2	23.3	44.3	57.7	47.0	142.1	7.8	146.6	125.1	5.6	8.9	129.1
PLANT	8.0	26.1	20.9	63.9	121.3	43.7	272.8	16.0	269.4	234.6	6.7	10.5	196.6
IRRIGATION	0.1	0.6	1.0	0.1	0.0*	0.2	0.1	0.0*	0.5	0.6	0.0*	0.0*	0.2
LAND (AREA)	0.9	0.9	1.3	0.1	0.0*	2.8	0.8	0.6	0.5	0.4	0.1	1.7	0.1
INVENTORY CHANGE	1.6	9.2	5.3	3.6	5.6	2.0	10.5	0.5	21.9	9.4	1.3	2.4	11.0
CAPITAL STOCK	145.1	729.3	515.1	1349.3	2270.7	937.8	6697.5	366.2	2696.6	4465.8	116.1	188.6	5129.0
EQUIPMENT	65.5	365.2	242.7	435.9	580.0	388.5	1601.0	94.1	890.8	1298.2	46.3	84.4	1452.9
PLANT	79.5	364.1	272.4	913.4	1690.6	549.3	5096.5	272.2	1805.8	3167.6	69.8	104.2	3676.1
INVENTORY STOCK	28.0	165.5	123.0	122.8	159.9	143.0	409.0	25.1	262.5	348.5	17.0	38.3	403.6
CULTIVATED LAND	111.1	407.8	596.6	66.0	16.5	254.5	207.5	31.2	343.2	340.5	28.7	211.7	170.5
SURPLUS SAVINGS	-2.8	-6.0	7.1	15.2	18.4	-20.2	9.5	-1.0	-249.0	-12.9	1.7	-9.6	136.4
INTERNATIONAL TRANSACTIONS													
IMPORTS	19.8	8.2	76.2	71.7	115.2	86.8	195.2	26.9	287.3	54.8	18.5	38.5	645.5
EXPORTS	6.0	11.9	73.8	113.2	143.2	71.7	230.3	19.3	102.5	70.1	14.5	22.2	763.7
PAYMENTS SURPLUS	0.0	-1.9	0.0	-14.1	-84.8	12.0	100.3	-6.3	140.8	2.5	0.0	0.0	-54.5
FOR. INVEST.(INF	-3.4	-21.0	14.9	-161.5	-1035.7	207.2	724.3	-243.0	2346.9	173.1	-25.1	-19.2	-1497.8
FOR. INCOME (OUT	-0.4	-1.7	0.4	-12.9	-83.2	14.0	62.9	-20.4	183.9	13.9	-2.5	-2.0	-115.0
LEVEL OF ABATEMENT ACTIVITIES													
AIR	0.0	0.0	0.0	6.83	7.09	2.95	83.86	0.84	11.48	22.41	0.67	0.0	24.82
PRIMARY WATER	0.0	0.0	0.0	4.14	3.24	1.07	9.72	0.71	3.62	12.77	-0.95	0.0	14.71
SECONDARY WATER	0.0	0.0	0.0	0.24	2.55	0.06	0.55	0.04	0.21	0.73	-0.50	0.0	0.84
TERTIARY WATER	0.0	0.0	0.0	0.05	0.56	0.01	0.12	0.01	0.05	0.16	-0.11	0.0	0.18
SOLID WASTE	0.0	0.0	0.0	111.59	129.78	332.12	393.49	30.06	147.28	320.62	31.19	0.0	481.07
NET TOTAL EMISSIONS													
PESTICIDES	0.91	0.53	2.43	0.51	1.36	1.54	2.46	0.03	3.99	0.80	0.04	0.68	1.68
PARTICULATES	0.69	3.39	1.83	0.53	0.23	1.56	4.21	0.05	3.33	1.17	0.06	0.56	1.45
BIOLOG. OXYGEN	1.90	8.69	6.41	2.45	1.66	5.73	11.66	0.35	7.09	7.39	0.87	0.65	10.35
NITROGEN (WATER)	0.02	0.08	0.05	0.12	0.08	0.05	0.24	0.01	0.11	0.44	0.04	0.00*	0.57
PHOSPHATES	0.01	0.05	0.03	0.06	0.04	0.04	0.19	0.01	0.07	0.22	0.02	0.00*	0.29
SUSPENDED SOLIDS	0.67	2.74	1.53	1.52	0.95	3.09	6.82	0.18	6.48	3.99	0.21	0.69	4.94
DISSOLVED SOLIDS	8.35	36.48	21.50	16.78	20.96	18.31	55.65	2.43	31.26	60.11	6.39	1.42	78.72
SOLID WASTE	65.52	276.71	295.07	0.0	0.0	53.05	0.0	0.0	0.0	0.0	0.0	37.16	0.0

RESOURCE OUTPUTS

	AAF	ASC	ASL	EEM	JAP	LAT	NAH	OCH	OIL	RUH	SAF	TAF	WEU
COPPER	0.1	0.0	0.2	0.4	0.3	8.0	4.8	0.5	0.0	2.3	0.1	5.3	0.6
BAUXITE	0.0	0.2	1.9	1.7	0.0	2.4	0.6	17.8	0.3	2.1	0.0	7.2	2.8
NICKEL	2.3	0.0	728.8	0.0	0.0	421.6	317.8	77.2	0.0	512.1	0.0	0.0	0.0
ZINC	0.1	0.8	0.6	1.5	3.5	0.5	2.0	0.2	1.3	2.2	0.1	0.0*	4.4
LEAD	0.1	0.7	0.2	1.2	1.1	0.7	1.7	0.2	1.7	2.4	0.1	0.0*	4.1
IRON	5.1	120.9	116.9	20.1	2.0	221.0	186.1	41.8	24.4	530.9	17.5	78.5	167.2
PETROLEUM	178.1	179.1	75.0	24.1	1.0	796.8	2497.8	11.0	8280.0	2294.0	0.0	0.0	612.0
NATURAL GAS	0.0	0.0	13.0	0.0	0.0	278.0	1861.0	2.0	1279.4	1939.0	0.0	0.0	356.1
COAL	1.7	1109.3	410.7	923.7	142.8	39.8	2680.6	173.0	1.7	1445.4	48.3	46.8	1024.0

CUMULATIVE RESOURCE OUTPUT AT END OF PERIOD

	AAF	ASC	ASL	EEM	JAP	LAT	NAH	OCH	OIL	RUH	SAF	TAF	WEU
COPPER	1.	5.	7.	7.	6.	101.	99.	10.	0.*	48.	3.	100.	13.
BAUXITE	0.	5.	34.	31.	0.	252.	12.	188.	2.	38.	0.	65.	57.
NICKEL	23.	0.	11307.	84.	0.	3887.	12093.	1808.	0.	9599.	182.	145.	209.
ZINC	1.	10.	4.	19.	22.	22.	98.	31.	9.	31.	1.	15.	47.
LEAD	3.	10.	2.	10.	8.	14.	115.	12.	10.	21.	1.	2.	29.
IRON	164.	1782.	1669.	321.	39.	3444.	3769.	1261.	322.	7709.	229.	1345.	3144.
PETROLEUM	2305.	2854.	1126.	722.	30.	17046.	45632.	331.	129296.	34105.	0.	33.	3630.
NATURAL GAS	1.	0.	337.	1125.	0.	3660.	41240.	60.	20487.	30127.	0.	0.*	6234.
COAL	28.	19592.	6137.	17597.	2382.	639.	36591.	3423.	28.	25759.	1458.	611.	19596.

NET EXPORTS OF RESOURCES

	AAF	ASC	ASL	EEM	JAP	LAT	NAH	OCH	OIL	RUH	SAF	TAF	WEU
COPPER	0.0	-0.6	0.0	-0.7	-4.0	6.5	1.4	0.4	-1.0	-1.5	0.0	5.3	-5.8
BAUXITE	-0.1	-0.3	0.0	0.0	-5.7	1.3	-6.8	16.9	-1.5	-3.3	-0.3	7.1	-7.4
NICKEL	0.0	-8.7	566.7	-32.9	-429.1	305.1	0.0	0.0	-26.1	0.0	-36.6	-0.8	-337.5
ZINC	0.0	0.0	0.0	0.0	0.0	0.0	-0.0*	-0.0*	0.0	0.0	0.0	-0.0*	0.0
LEAD	-0.0*	0.0	0.0	-93.1	0.0	-0.0*	0.0	0.0	0.0	0.0	0.0	0.0	0.0
IRON	0.0	0.0	90.2	-360.7	-262.6	175.1	31.8	10.6	-69.7	148.6	-64.7	74.3	-105.3
PETROLEUM	0.0	0.0	-356.7	-262.3	-1504.7	151.0	0.0	-151.8	4623.5	155.8	0.0	-121.5	-2370.2
NATURAL GAS	-2.3	0.0	-61.1	0.0	-263.3	-78.0	0.0	-5.9	206.8	206.8	0.0	-0.0*	-4.1
COAL	-4.5	19.3	3.9	-1.6	-2.2	-27.6	285.7	77.2	-74.8	0.5	0.4	0.2	-15.9
OTHER RESOURCES	0.3	0.2	0.3	-3.4	-14.1	1.4	2.9	-1.4	0.9	1.5	-0.6	-1.1	-2.9
PETROL. REFINING	0.0	0.0*	-3.3	-2.9	-1.4	5.6	0.0*	-0.3	43.4	-0.8	0.1	4.2	-22.2
PRIMARY METALS	-0.2	-1.1	-0.3				1.5		-1.5				-2.8

111

SCENARIO D3 IN 2000

OUTPUT LEVELS

	AAF	ASC	ASL	EEM	JAP	LAT	NAH	OCH	OIL	RUH	SAF	TAF	WEU
ANIMAL PRODUCTS	11.9	57.6	48.0	23.3	20.3	56.0	68.8	10.8	37.0	55.9	6.4	20.1	90.0
HIGH PROT. CROPS	8.4	39.8	76.4	6.4	4.2	29.6	64.9	0.2	20.8	59.5	2.2	40.5	20.5
GRAINS	82.2	546.3	572.4	110.5	52.9	264.2	444.2	37.9	127.3	368.3	27.0	102.7	280.0
ROOTS	6.3	142.8	125.9	64.3	41.3	86.9	26.6	1.4	92.6	140.8	1.2	107.1	98.2
OTHER AGRICULT.	8.2	58.7	32.0	15.8	21.3	59.2	60.8	6.2	62.7	47.4	6.7	17.0	73.2
OTHER RESOURCES	0.9	3.3	2.3	1.8	3.8	3.5	16.8	1.0	9.1	12.0	0.8	0.6	9.4
FOOD PROCESSING	1.5	11.9	4.9	38.9	52.7	23.1	135.8	11.2	70.9	109.5	3.1	2.6	133.0
PETROL. REFINING	1.0	6.1	0.2	6.9	0.3	8.8	40.0	1.1	61.8	33.5	0.5	0.1	13.5
PRIMARY METALS	2.1	12.9	6.5	30.0	43.4	18.3	99.0	4.2	45.8	88.7	2.1	5.6	89.0
TEXT., APPAREL	7.2	37.1	54.6	31.0	58.4	32.7	95.1	5.2	59.8	58.9	3.0	3.3	109.5
WOOD AND CORK	0.4	4.6	5.2	7.4	10.3	6.2	30.7	1.4	10.4	26.3	0.7	1.0	24.2
FURNITURE, FIXT.	3.0	13.7	9.4	6.5	8.3	18.1	20.5	2.5	48.3	15.3	2.6	4.3	24.7
PAPER	0.5	6.1	2.7	11.8	19.5	5.1	66.9	3.4	5.3	38.8	1.4	0.2	53.8
PRINTING	0.5	3.3	2.2	13.9	22.9	6.0	67.9	1.9	22.1	48.5	1.1	0.3	59.9
RUBBER	0.3	3.0	1.9	11.7	18.9	3.5	39.0	1.9	9.0	31.7	0.6	0.2	41.1
INDUSTRIAL CHEM.	2.3	14.8	9.1	13.9	29.6	11.0	59.7	1.4	23.0	44.9	1.4	1.1	65.4
FERTILIZERS	13.7	46.1	26.4	5.8	14.7	20.8	24.8	1.6	31.7	30.8	3.7	1.3	31.4
OTHER CHEMICALS	1.1	8.3	4.1	13.9	19.1	8.0	55.5	2.9	5.1	40.2	1.3	0.3	65.8
CEMENT	0.1	0.7	0.6	1.5	3.2	1.0	6.6	0.3	2.4	5.2	0.6	0.3	6.3
GLASS	0.9	6.0	3.6	14.7	26.0	7.3	56.0	2.6	24.6	44.8	1.5	0.0*	52.1
MOTOR VEHICLES	0.1	3.6	0.6	38.8	60.5	3.8	96.0	3.6	25.2	93.7	0.6	0.1	107.9
SHIPBUILDING	0.7	3.5	1.5	5.3	10.4	3.4	15.1	0.6	10.5	8.4	0.5	0.0*	12.5
AIRCRAFT	0.7	4.4	1.4	8.4	4.5	0.7	33.4	0.2	17.4	38.5	0.1	0.0*	11.9
METAL PRODUCTS	3.0	15.8	9.3	37.1	57.1	16.4	122.6	6.6	67.1	115.1	2.9	1.7	119.1
MACHINERY	3.2	26.6	9.0	58.0	55.4	19.0	116.1	3.6	55.9	106.1	2.2	0.7	128.2
ELECTRICAL MACH.	1.0	11.0	3.4	38.7	58.5	6.0	95.7	3.7	23.2	82.5	1.0	0.3	100.3
INSTRUMENTS	0.4	3.5	0.9	6.8	12.8	2.5	23.4	1.4	14.4	17.7	0.4	0.1	22.2
OTHER MANUFACT.	1.2	7.1	7.4	6.8	14.2	6.6	25.5	1.4	17.7	21.6	2.4	2.1	30.9
UTILITIES	1.8	8.6	6.1	25.6	35.7	13.3	96.7	5.9	50.6	79.0	1.9	2.5	84.2
CONSTRUCTION	10.3	36.4	30.7	82.5	151.4	61.5	370.4	20.5	310.0	298.8	8.9	13.9	267.9
TRADE	11.4	53.6	38.2	127.4	190.3	80.5	490.0	30.9	253.2	380.4	12.3	18.6	434.9
TRANSPORTATION	5.9	32.5	21.0	31.7	39.9	29.2	134.9	6.8	72.9	100.6	3.6	7.1	133.1
COMMUNICATIONS	1.4	6.5	4.6	15.0	21.5	8.0	58.8	3.5	21.8	45.9	1.2	1.9	50.3
SERVICES	25.6	121.1	90.6	200.7	308.9	149.1	883.7	51.9	411.5	663.2	22.4	38.2	730.6

MILITARY OUTPUT LEVELS

	AAF	ASC	ASL	EEM	JAP	LAT	NAH	OCH	OIL	RUH	SAF	TAF	WEU
AIRCRAFT	0.7418	3.0137	0.8986	5.1438	2.4745	0.4819	15.6096	0.3216	3.6953	21.3991	0.4459	0.3659	7.2296
SHIPS	0.1230	0.6818	0.1200	0.0932	0.7247	0.1754	2.3519	0.1109	0.4601	6.9255	0.0445	0.1057	2.5354
ELECTRONIC EQUIP	0.4221	1.7787	0.5963	2.0701	0.9733	0.2443	8.6141	0.1766	1.6953	9.6128	0.2880	0.1631	2.8072
NEW CONSTRUCTION	0.1396	1.4675	0.1670	0.7141	0.3136	0.1009	1.6858	0.0575	1.1884	3.3583	0.0629	0.0522	1.2017
MAINTENANCE	0.1021	1.0730	0.1221	0.5221	0.2293	0.0738	1.2327	0.0420	1.6002	2.4556	0.0460	0.0382	0.8787
MISSILES	0.1167	0.4986	0.0903	0.3858	0.1649	0.0453	7.1414	0.0244	0.6615	9.7853	0.0457	0.0303	1.6884
AMMUNITION, NEC	0.1366	0.5202	0.1817	0.6715	0.2974	0.0738	2.4541	0.0533	0.5035	2.7644	0.0859	0.0474	0.8639
TANKS	0.4896	0.7106	0.3109	3.4214	0.2870	0.1218	1.2242	0.0416	1.6785	3.8428	0.0983	0.1183	1.8804
SMALL ARMS	0.0105	0.0325	0.0122	0.0494	0.0320	0.0067	0.1819	0.0050	0.0363	0.2034	0.0063	0.0029	0.0872
SM. ARMS AMMUN.	0.0283	0.0812	0.0315	0.1065	0.0582	0.0137	0.4000	0.0100	0.0844	0.4459	0.0146	0.0075	0.1559
OTHER ORDNANCE	0.0595	0.1759	0.0669	0.2245	0.1131	0.0271	0.8453	0.0197	0.1747	0.9569	0.0303	0.0163	0.3074
TOTAL OUTPUT	2.3697	10.0337	2.5976	13.4025	5.6679	1.3648	41.7411	0.8625	12.7780	61.7500	1.1684	0.9480	19.6356

112

FISH

	AAF	ASC	ASL	EEM	JAP	LAT	NAH	OCH	OIL	RUH	SAF	TAF	WEU
FISH CATCH	0.6	7.9	9.3	0.8	8.2	14.4	3.8	0.2	0.4	6.7	2.2	1.9	9.6
NON-HUMAN USE	0.3	0.1	1.0	0.1	2.0	12.5	1.2	-0.0*	-0.1	0.6	2.0	0.6	1.7
FISH IMPORTS	0.1	0.0	0.3	0.2	0.2	0.1	1.3	-0.0*	-0.0*	0.1	0.0*	0.1	1.6
FISH EXPORTS	0.1	0.1	0.3	0.0*	0.5	0.1	0.4	0.0*	0.1	0.4	0.0*	0.1	2.0

EXPORTS

	AAF	ASC	ASL	EEM	JAP	LAT	NAH	OCH	OIL	RUH	SAF	TAF	WEU
LIVESTOCK	0.0*	0.0	0.1	2.4	0.0*	2.5	1.8	4.1	0.0*	0.3	0.1	0.1	9.9
HIGH PROT. CROPS	1.3	0.0	3.9	0.8	0.1	2.8	41.6	0.0*	2.8	1.6	0.3	2.3	5.7
GRAINS	1.6	0.0	10.3	8.6	4.4	21.9	135.3	18.8	0.4	11.3	2.3	0.9	38.4
ROOTS	0.8	0.0	1.4	3.2	0.1	0.8	4.3	0.3	0.4	0.4	0.0	0.6	10.9
OTHER AGRICULT.	1.6	1.1	8.7	2.8	0.0	8.1	5.8	2.2	1.7	1.9	0.6	4.5	14.1
FOOD PROCESSING	0.3	0.5	2.4	1.7	0.5	4.2	5.2	2.0	5.3	0.7	0.3	0.8	12.2
TEXT. APPAREL	1.0	5.6	28.6	17.7	27.9	4.2	8.4	1.6	0.7	1.6	0.7	0.2	118.4
WOOD AND CORK	0.0*	0.1	2.7	1.2	1.2	1.2	5.0	0.1	0.0*	4.5	0.0*	0.2	11.3
FURNITURE, FIXT.	0.0*	0.0*	0.1	1.8	0.1	0.0*	0.2	0.0*	0.0*	0.0*		0.0*	2.4
PAPER	0.1	0.6	0.6	0.9	2.4	1.4	21.6	0.5	0.2	1.7	1.3	0.1*	40.9
PRINTING	0.1	0.0*	0.4	0.4	0.9	0.6	3.1	0.1	0.0*	0.6	0.0*	0.0*	12.8
RUBBER	0.1	0.0*	0.5	0.9	2.7	0.4	1.5	0.1	0.2	0.6	0.1	0.0*	11.7
INDUSTRIAL CHEM.	0.1	0.8	0.8	1.6	9.2	2.0	10.4	0.7	0.1	1.7	0.8	0.1	42.6
FERTILIZERS	0.4	1.5	0.4	2.0	1.5	0.8	6.9	0.0*	0.6	4.4	0.0*	0.0*	13.3
OTHER CHEMICALS	0.1	0.4	1.5	1.2	2.2	1.5	7.7	0.8	0.7	0.3	0.1	0.1	38.9
CEMENT	0.1	0.1	0.4	0.0	0.5	0.2	0.3	0.0*	0.7	0.1	0.0	0.1	1.7
GLASS	0.1	0.5	0.5	3.1	4.3	0.5	3.4	0.7	0.6	0.4	0.6	0.1	25.5
MOTOR VEHICLES	0.0*	0.1	1.5	17.4	19.7	1.2	26.1	0.7	0.6	11.5	0.6	0.0*	70.7
SHIPBUILDING	0.0*	0.0	0.1	2.8	5.1	0.0*	0.3	0.1	0.0*	2.6	0.0*	0.0*	7.0
AIRCRAFT	0.0*	0.0	0.2	0.4*	0.2	0.1	11.6	0.1	0.2	7.4	0.1	0.0*	6.4
METAL PRODUCTS	0.0*	0.1	0.9	0.4	3.3	0.4	3.6	0.1	0.4	2.6	1.2	0.0*	14.6
MACHINERY	0.0*	0.2	1.8	37.4	15.2	2.2	23.3	0.5	0.4	15.2	0.2	0.1	91.7
ELECTRICAL MACH.	0.1	0.0*	3.5	14.4	25.8	1.1	17.6	0.3	0.3	0.4	0.2	0.0*	67.9
INSTRUMENTS	0.0*	0.4	0.5	1.6	6.3	0.2	6.9	0.2	0.1	0.8	1.6	0.6	18.6
OTHER MANUFACT.	0.4	0.0	4.9	0.4	4.1	0.3	2.8	0.4	0.8	1.2	1.6	0.2	18.7
SERVICES	0.6	0.0	1.4	0.0	0.4	5.8	10.2	2.5	1.3	0.0	3.6	1.4	33.4
TRANSPORT	0.4	0.0	4.1	0.0	7.2	3.5	17.8	1.7	4.0	0.0	1.0	3.1	69.1
AID INFLOW	4.2	0.0	22.3	0.0	0.8	10.9	9.6			0.0	5.9	3.1	38.3
ADD. AID REC'D	8.2	0.0	24.6	0.0	0.0	5.5	0.0			0.0	0.0	16.4	0.0
CAPITAL INFLOW		0.0	7.4	0.0	17.3	15.8	39.3	0.8	9.3	0.0	0.5	0.9	56.7

MILITARY EXPORTS

	AAF	ASC	ASL	EEM	JAP	LAT	NAH	OCH	OIL	RUH	SAF	TAF	WEU
AIRCRAFT	0.0	0.0527	0.0527	0.4743	0.0	0.0	2.1079	0.0	0.0	1.6863	0.0	0.0	0.8958
SHIPS	0.0	0.0069	0.0	0.0	0.0	0.0	0.1514	0.0	0.0	0.2202	0.0	0.0	0.3096
ELECTRONIC EQUIP	0.0393	0.0196	0.0196	0.0785	0.0	0.0196	0.8246	0.0	0.0	0.4516	0.0	0.0	0.5105
MISSILES	0.0160	0.0053	0.0053	0.0212	0.0	0.0053	0.6712	0.0	0.0	0.6552	0.0	0.0	0.2557
AMMUNITION, NEC	0.0106	0.0003	0.0003	0.1337	0.0	0.0003	0.2226	0.0	0.0	0.1219	0.0	0.0	0.1378
TANKS	0.0006	0.0007	0.0007	0.0	0.0	0.0007	0.7451	0.0	0.0	0.5541	0.0	0.0	0.4777
SMALL ARMS	0.0013	0.0014	0.0014	0.0012	0.0	0.0014	0.0121	0.0	0.0	0.0066	0.0	0.0	0.0075
SM. ARMS AMMUN.	0.0028	0.0	0.0	0.0027	0.0	0.0	0.0283	0.0	0.0	0.0155	0.0	0.0	0.0175
OTHER ORDNANCE	0.0	0.0	0.0	0.0056	0.0	0.0	0.0588	0.0	0.0	0.0322	0.0	0.0	0.0364
TOTAL EXPORTS	0.0706	0.0869	0.0800	0.7172	0.0	0.0273	4.8219	0.0	0.0	3.7435	0.0	0.0	2.6484
MIL. GRANTS INF.	0.0779	0.1120	0.2299	0.0050	0.0	0.0430	0.0	0.0	0.0	0.0	0.0	0.1676	0.0261

SCENARIO D3 IN 2000

IMPORTS

	AAF	ASC	ASL	EEM	JAP	LAT	NAH	OCH	OIL	RUH	SAF	TAF	WEU
LIVESTOCK	0.2	0.0*	1.5	1.5	1.4	1.4	2.6	0.0*	2.3	0.3	0.2	0.8	9.0
HIGH PROT. CROPS	1.2	0.0*	3.0	4.1	18.8	2.3	3.0	0.4	4.5	0.3	0.1	1.0	24.5
GRAINS	7.4	0.1	40.3	39.9	32.7	27.3	2.8	0.4	15.8	6.5	1.8	12.7	66.5
ROOTS	0.4	0.0*	2.3	3.4	1.9	2.4	0.6	0.1	2.1	0.0	0.0	0.5	9.5
OTHER AGRICULT.	0.6	2.4	3.8	3.1	3.7	2.0	9.6	0.3	10.1	2.3	0.2	0.7	14.3
FOOD PROCESSING	0.5	0.0*	3.3	1.5	1.2	2.0	4.3	0.1	7.7	1.1	0.2	1.5	7.6
TEXT.. APPAREL	3.5	0.2	9.4	9.4	10.8	4.3	26.7	3.0	20.2	17.8	2.4	8.5	105.0
WOOD AND CORK	0.4	0.0	0.1	0.4	2.3	0.6	2.9	0.3	8.6	0.4	0.0	0.4	11.0
FURNITURE. FIXT.	0.1	0.0	0.1	0.4	0.0*	0.2	0.7	0.0*	1.0	0.6	0.3*	1.0	1.0
PAPER	0.6	0.0*	1.7	1.9	3.0	3.5	5.9	0.9	16.5	1.8	1.1	0.7	34.2
PRINTING	0.2	0.0*	0.3	1.5	1.3	1.1	1.3	0.6	4.4	0.0	0.2	1.1	7.1
RUBBER	0.2	0.0*	0.5	0.9	0.1	1.1	1.3	0.3	7.4	0.3	0.3	1.2	6.5
INDUSTRIAL CHEM.	0.9	1.2	4.3	2.9	2.7	4.9	6.2	1.3	9.0	2.1	1.2	2.0	32.9
FERTILIZERS	1.6	1.8	9.2	1.0	1.4	5.8	2.0	0.2	4.2	0.0	0.0*	1.0	4.4
OTHER CHEMICALS	0.7	0.1	3.0	0.8	2.4	3.0	2.0	0.2	21.4	0.8	0.2	0.7	17.9
CEMENT	0.0*	0.0*	0.2	0.2	0.0*	0.1	0.1	0.0*	2.6	0.3	0.0	0.8	0.6
GLASS	0.4	0.0*	0.6	1.6	0.7	1.3	2.4	0.5	13.7	0.6	0.4	1.6	15.9
MOTOR VEHICLES	0.4	0.4	2.4	6.3	1.0	7.9	42.4	3.5	26.6	2.0	1.9	1.0	54.8
SHIPBUILDING	0.4	0.1	0.1	0.9	0.2	0.7	0.5	0.3	0.6	5.3	0.0*	0.7	7.2
AIRCRAFT	0.3	0.0*	0.6	0.0	2.6	1.9	4.3	0.9	1.8	0.0	0.2	0.8	13.3
METAL PRODUCTS	0.3	0.0*	1.0	0.3	0.3	1.8	2.5	0.4	9.6	0.6	0.2	1.6	7.9
MACHINERY	2.6	0.7	10.1	12.4	4.1	15.2	18.6	2.7	45.1	9.2	2.7	5.7	60.5
ELECTRICAL MACH.	1.2	0.1	6.2	3.4	3.1	8.4	15.0	1.6	39.0	2.1	1.3	2.0	48.3
INSTRUMENTS	0.3	0.1	1.5	0.7	1.5	2.1	4.3	0.7	7.6	1.0	0.6	0.7	14.6
OTHER MANUFACT.	0.7	0.2	2.9	0.4	1.6	1.1	9.4	0.5	2.4	1.3	0.2	0.6	14.3
SERVICES	0.0	0.0	0.1	0.0	2.8	5.0	14.3	1.2	4.7	0.0	0.7	0.2	27.7
TRANSPORT	1.5	0.0	6.1	0.0	14.2	7.7	11.1	3.1	12.9	0.0	1.7	2.9	47.3
AID OUTFLOW	1.5	0.4	3.7	0.0	3.9	4.7	20.3	1.7	28.3	2.6	0.8	2.8	30.2
ADD. AID GIVEN	0.0	4.5	0.0	3.8	2.6	0.0	14.5	0.3	8.1	14.5	0.0	0.0	6.3
CAPITAL OUTFLOW	0.4	0.0	5.7	0.0	7.5	19.4	15.4	5.4	59.3	0.0	2.7	3.0	29.3

MILITARY IMPORTS

	AAF	ASC	ASL	EEM	JAP	LAT	NAH	OCH	OIL	RUH	SAF	TAF	WEU
AIRCRAFT	1.0555	0.0452	0.4314	0.4527	0.1225	0.2149	0.0788	0.0240	1.9881	0.2140	0.0392	0.1969	0.4066
SHIPS	0.1248	0.0034	0.0491	0.0117	0.0072	0.0899	0.0119	0.0017	0.2820	0.0	0.0148	0.0648	0.0266
ELECTRONIC EQUIP	0.4284	0.0178	0.1538	0.1822	0.0423	0.0794	0.0435	0.0087	0.6917	0.0485	0.0160	0.0665	0.1844
MISSILES	0.2250	0.0264	0.1247	0.4707	0.0887	0.0244	0.0721	0.0131	0.3559	0.0	0.0068	0.0163	0.1738
AMMUNITION. NEC	0.1109	0.0042	0.0375	0.0907	0.0103	0.0225	0.0099	0.0021	0.2054	0.0112	0.0038	0.0193	0.0454
TANKS	0.4546	0.0185	0.1324	0.0473	0.0382	0.0475	0.0062	0.0077	0.7906	0.0194	0.0164	0.0557	0.2328
SMALL ARMS	0.0043	0.0001	0.0013	0.0017	0.0006	0.0017	0.0004	0.0001	0.0148	0.0004	0.0001	0.0012	0.0022
SM. ARMS AMMUN.	0.0115	0.0003	0.0032	0.0037	0.0010	0.0036	0.0008	0.0002	0.0344	0.0009	0.0003	0.0031	0.0043
OTHER ORDNANCE	0.0242	0.0007	0.0069	0.0079	0.0020	0.0072	0.0017	0.0004	0.0713	0.0019	0.0007	0.0067	0.0086
TOTAL IMPORTS	2.4392	0.1166	0.9403	1.2685	0.3129	0.4910	0.2253	0.0580	4.4341	0.2964	0.0982	0.4305	1.0847
MIL. GRANTS OUTF	0.0	0.1596	0.0	0.0	0.0	0.0	0.1456	0.0	0.0	0.2992	0.0	0.0	0.0571

SCENARIO A1 IN 2000

	AAF	ASC	ASL	EEM	JAP	LAT	NAH	OCH	OIL	RUH	SAF	TAF	WEU
CONSUMPTION AND POPULATION													
GDP	31.0	488.9	264.0	554.2	873.6	412.5	2233.3	130.5	1290.7	1627.1	66.0	78.7	1999.5
PERSONAL CONSUMP	18.9	274.0	182.2	308.7	553.9	289.0	1314.5	96.8	791.0	836.7	44.8	59.8	1271.0
GOVT.(CIVILIAN)	3.1	48.9	26.4	55.4	87.4	41.2	223.3	13.1	129.1	162.7	6.6	7.9	199.9
GOVT.(MILITARY)	9.3	91.9	21.1	74.3	52.4	17.1	348.7	6.5	167.8	348.7	7.3	6.1	137.5
POPULATION	285.7	1221.3	2048.9	125.7	132.9	615.8	300.0	24.5	309.8	315.0	50.0	331.8	487.1
URBAN POPULATION	168.4	508.9	704.4	90.1	98.5	465.0	258.9	22.4	148.2	245.2	32.0	109.4	382.4
EMPLOYMENT	17.0	210.7	135.2	63.8	67.6	145.2	133.9	10.2	228.8	151.8	13.0	40.8	168.0
GDP/HEAD	108.6	400.3	128.8	4408.7	6573.6	669.8	7444.3	5327.4	4166.4	5165.5	1320.0	237.1	4104.8
CONSUMPTION/HEAD	66.1	224.4	88.9	2455.5	4167.5	469.3	4381.7	3952.0	2553.3	2656.0	895.8	180.3	2609.0
CALORIES/HEAD	2029.3	2219.2	2059.2	3134.7	3231.3	2563.1	3148.8	3203.6	3334.8	3122.9	2929.7	2332.9	3117.1
PROTEINS/HEAD	57.9	68.2	53.1	104.7	121.6	66.5	97.5	99.5	117.3	102.7	90.8	67.5	100.9
INVESTMENT AND CAPITAL													
INVESTMENT	3.5	63.8	23.5	79.1	157.1	70.6	268.7	22.4	415.7	227.7	11.9	6.7	277.0
EQUIPMENT	1.7	38.5	12.4	37.9	52.9	38.6	125.7	7.5	146.7	103.8	5.5	3.5	118.5
PLANT	1.6	24.8	10.2	41.1	104.2	31.3	142.8	14.8	268.9	123.2	6.4	3.0	158.3
IRRIGATION	0.1	0.6	0.1	0.1	0.0*	0.2	0.1	0.0*	0.1	0.6	0.0*	0.0*	0.2
LAND (AREA)	0.9	0.9	1.3	0.0	0.0	2.8	0.8	0.6	0.5	0.0	0.1	1.7	0.1
INVENTORY CHANGE	0.4	9.1	3.0	2.8	4.7	5.6	9.2	0.5	21.4	7.0	1.2	1.3	9.5
CAPITAL STOCK	43.3	727.6	342.1	1085.2	2108.6	808.4	5156.4	348.9	2730.7	3216.0	111.9	104.3	4624.1
EQUIPMENT	19.5	375.0	161.8	387.4	549.2	341.3	1450.4	91.0	907.4	1129.4	45.3	50.4	1365.2
PLANT	23.9	352.6	180.4	697.9	1559.4	467.1	3706.1	258.0	1823.3	2086.5	66.6	53.9	3259.3
INVENTORY STOCK	12.4	162.2	94.7	108.3	149.5	129.1	369.6	24.0	264.1	299.5	16.4	26.7	374.7
CULTIVATED LAND	74.0	393.4	515.0	61.8	15.9	241.7	195.7	29.6	341.6	309.4	28.1	156.5	164.2
SURPLUS SAVINGS	3.3	-0.9	20.5	32.8	33.0	-5.9	131.3	0.3	-234.5	83.6	1.9	1.6	163.3
INTERNATIONAL TRANSACTIONS													
IMPORTS	10.1	9.9	57.8	73.7	111.9	78.8	179.7	26.6	331.5	47.5	19.1	24.0	609.1
EXPORTS	5.9	10.9	65.4	106.5	129.2	66.7	245.4	17.6	96.5	88.7	13.3	20.7	710.7
PAYMENTS SURPLUS	0.0	-0.5	0.0	-16.7	-84.6	12.0	40.6	-7.0	96.7	21.1	-0.5	3.0	-55.6
FOR.INVEST.INFLO	-0.5	-15.4	33.8	-218.0	-1080.3	220.2	458.4	-245.5	2039.3	405.8	-24.7	-2.6	-1547.8
FOR.INC.OUTFLOW	-0.2	-1.2	1.9	-17.4	-86.8	15.0	41.6	-20.6	159.2	32.5	-2.5	-0.7	-119.0
LEVEL OF ABATEMENT ACTIVITIES													
AIR	0.0	0.0	0.0	5.80	6.53	2.59	68.93	0.80	11.48	18.43	0.64	0.0	22.77
PRIMARY WATER	0.0	0.0	0.0	3.51	3.33	0.73	7.85	0.72	3.62	10.50	-0.95	0.0	13.39
SECONDARY WATER	0.0	0.0	0.0	0.20	2.12	0.04	0.45	0.00*	0.21	0.60	-0.51	0.0	0.76
TERTIARY WATER	0.0	0.0	0.0	0.04	0.46	0.01	0.10	0.00*	0.05	0.13	-0.11	0.0	0.17
SOLID WASTE	0.0	0.0	0.0	111.59	129.78	332.12	393.49	30.06	147.28	320.62	31.19	0.0	481.07
NET TOTAL EMISSIONS													
PESTICIDES	0.43	0.51	1.99	0.46	1.31	1.43	2.23	0.03	3.97	0.72	0.04	0.48	1.62
PARTICULATES	0.23	3.49	1.31	0.53	0.23	1.27	4.21	0.05	3.42	1.17	0.06	0.36	1.45
BIOLOG. OXYGEN	1.15	8.44	5.51	2.32	1.67	5.70	11.55	0.35	7.14	6.91	0.88	0.52	10.13
NITROGEN (WATER)	0.01	0.08	0.04	0.11	0.07	0.05	0.22	0.01	0.11	0.39	0.04	0.00*	0.53
PHOSPHATES	0.01	0.05	0.02	0.06	0.04	0.03	0.18	0.01	0.08	0.19	0.02	0.00*	0.27
SUSPENDED SOLIDS	0.23	2.85	1.08	1.52	0.95	2.86	6.82	0.18	6.56	3.99	0.21	0.52	4.94
DISSOLVED SOLIDS	4.00	35.35	17.05	14.71	20.31	16.13	50.78	2.37	31.58	51.95	6.39	1.02	72.61
SOLID WASTE	65.52	276.71	295.07	0.0	0.0	53.05	0.0	0.0	0.0	0.0	0.0	37.16	0.0

SCENARIO A1 IN 2000

RESOURCE OUTPUTS

	AAF	ASC	ASL	EEM	JAP	LAT	NAH	OCH	OIL	RUH	SAF	TAF	WEU
COPPER	0.0*	0.0	0.1	0.4	0.3	7.6	4.9	0.5	0.0	2.3	0.1	5.2	0.6
BAUXITE	0.0	0.2	1.3	1.7	0.0	2.2	0.6	17.4	0.3	2.1	0.0	7.0	2.6
NICKEL	0.9	0.0	682.8	0.0	0.0	406.0	363.1	75.5	0.0	545.8	0.0	0.0*	0.0
ZINC	0.0*	0.9	0.4	1.4	3.3	0.4	2.1	0.2	1.3	2.3	0.1	0.0*	4.2
LEAD	0.0*	0.8	0.2	1.1	1.1	0.6	1.6	0.2	1.7	2.2	0.1	0.0*	3.8
IRON	1.2	128.8	99.1	20.1	2.0	200.7	176.6	40.2	24.4	480.0	17.2	70.8	163.2
PETROLEUM	59.4	294.9	75.0	24.1	1.0	752.2	2792.6	11.0	8319.6	2421.9	0.0	0.0	612.0
NATURAL GAS	0.0	0.0	13.0	0.0	0.0	249.6	1673.9	2.0	1247.6	1656.8	0.0	0.0	335.8
COAL	1.7	1097.7	242.5	831.3	142.8	39.8	2441.7	162.4	1.7	1290.2	47.0	27.5	985.0

CUMULATIVE RESOURCE OUTPUT AT END OF PERIOD

	AAF	ASC	ASL	EEM	JAP	LAT	NAH	OCH	OIL	RUH	SAF	TAF	WEU
COPPER	0.*	5.	6.	7.	6.	98.	100.	10.	0.*	48.	3.	99.	13.
BAUXITE	0.	5.	28.	32.	0.	248.	12.	185.	2.	38.	0.	64.	55.
NICKEL	11.	0.	10911.	84.	0.	3752.	12624.	1782.	9.	10020.	182.	145.	209.
ZINC	1.	10.	3.	19.	21.	21.	98.	30.	9.	31.	1.	15.	46.
LEAD	2.	10.	2.	9.	8.	13.	111.	12.	11.	20.	1.	1.	28.
IRON	126.	1864.	1502.	321.	39.	3260.	3644.	1233.	322.	7128.	227.	1271.	3108.
PETROLEUM	1245.	4084.	1126.	722.	30.	17024.	47106.	331.	132433.	36472.	0.	33.	3630.
NATURAL GAS	1.	0.	337.	1125.	0.	3497.	38899.	60.	20444.	27189.	0.	0.*	6012.
COAL	28.	19392.	4647.	16567.	2382.	639.	34698.	3286.	28.	24231.	1439.	449.	19401.

NET EXPORTS OF RESOURCES

	AAF	ASC	ASL	EEM	JAP	LAT	NAH	OCH	OIL	RUH	SAF	TAF	WEU
COPPER	-0.0*	-0.7	0.0	-0.7	-3.8	6.4	1.4	0.3	-1.0	-1.5	0.0	5.2	-5.5
BAUXITE	-0.0*	-0.5	0.0	0.0	-5.3	1.3	-6.7	16.6	-1.4	-3.5	-0.3	7.0	-7.1
NICKEL	0.0	-23.3	573.6	-47.8	-406.9	308.8	0.0	0.0	-21.9	0.0	-37.1	-0.1	-345.4
ZINC	-0.0*	0.0	0.0	0.0	0.0	0.0*	-0.0*	-0.0*	0.0	0.0	0.0	-0.0*	0.0
LEAD	0.0	0.0	0.0	0.0	0.0	-0.0*	0.0*	0.0*	0.0	0.0	0.0	-0.0*	0.0
IRON	-0.0*	0.0	83.7	-82.8	-244.8	162.5	29.5	9.8	-69.8	137.9	0.0	68.9	-95.0
PETROLEUM	-0.7	0.0	-219.9	-397.5	-1478.1	173.1	0.0	-152.4	4412.1	148.7	-71.0	-73.4	-2341.6
NATURAL GAS	-0.7	0.0	-38.5	-230.5	0.0	-55.5	0.0	-5.7	167.0	167.0	0.0	-0.0*	-3.1
COAL	0.8	17.3	3.5	-1.3	-245.7	-18.7	255.3	69.0	-82.8	0.0	0.4	0.2	1.4
OTHER RESOURCES	0.3	0.2	0.4		-2.0	0.7	2.6	0.0	0.7	0.4	0.0		-2.7
PETROL. REFINING	0.0	-0.0*	-2.1	-3.7	-13.9	1.6	-0.0*	-1.4	41.4	1.4	-0.7	-0.7	-22.0
PRIMARY METALS	-0.2	-1.3	-0.3	-2.7	-1.0	5.4	1.2	-0.4	-1.7	-0.9	0.1	4.1	-2.4

OUTPUT LEVELS

	AAF	ASC	ASL	EEM	JAP	LAT	NAH	OCH	OIL	RUH	SAF	TAF	WEU
ANIMAL PRODUCTS	5.8	54.5	38.3	21.9	19.6	53.3	66.1	10.5	36.9	50.5	6.3	13.0	87.5
HIGH PROT. CROPS	5.5	38.4	67.0	6.0	4.1	28.4	62.1	0.2	20.6	53.9	2.1	28.6	20.0
GRAINS	58.8	527.7	508.0	104.4	51.0	253.2	423.0	36.0	126.7	336.4	26.5	77.0	271.4
ROOTS	5.1	140.9	103.3	61.4	40.2	85.0	26.8	1.3	92.6	131.9	1.2	100.1	96.9
OTHER AGRICULT.	2.8	55.5	21.3	13.3	20.0	53.9	51.1	0.9	62.4	35.6	6.4	11.6	66.8
OTHER RESOURCES	0.6	3.4	1.8	1.5	3.5	3.0	13.4	1.0	9.1	9.2	0.8	0.5	8.4
FOOD PROCESSING	0.4	10.2	3.1	34.4	50.7	19.7	121.4	10.8	70.9	90.2	2.9	1.2	124.6
PETROL. REFINING	0.3	6.4	0.3	5.3	-0.1	8.1	36.8	1.0	60.6	28.8	0.4	0.0*	11.7
PRIMARY METALS	0.5	15.6	4.2	28.0	41.2	16.1	92.9	4.1	46.5	84.7	2.2	4.9	85.7
TEXT., APPAREL	2.1	33.2	38.4	24.4	51.9	27.5	78.6	4.8	59.5	39.0	2.8	1.9	93.5
WOOD AND CORK	0.1	4.6	3.8	6.0	9.3	5.3	24.4	1.3	10.6	20.1	0.7	0.6	21.7
FURNITURE, FIXT.	0.4	12.1	4.4	5.3	7.8	15.0	18.3	1.2	48.5	11.4	2.5	1.8	21.9
PAPER	0.1	5.9	1.7	10.1	18.3	4.3	59.2	2.4	22.6	31.4	1.3	0.1	49.5
PRINTING	0.2	3.1	1.5	11.7	21.7	5.0	59.5	1.9	9.3	38.1	1.0	0.7	55.3
RUBBER	0.1	3.2	1.4	10.2	17.7	2.9	35.1	1.5	23.9	26.6	0.6	0.1	38.3
INDUSTRIAL CHEM.	0.9	14.9	6.7	12.4	27.6	9.7	55.9	2.8	31.3	40.2	1.3	1.0	60.5
FERTILIZERS	6.9	44.1	21.5	5.1	14.0	18.4	21.7	0.3	5.1	27.3	3.7	0.1	28.9
OTHER CHEMICALS	0.3	8.1	2.6	12.2	18.1	6.9	49.2	2.4	2.4	33.5	1.2	0.1	61.0
CEMENT	0.2	0.8	0.4	1.2	2.9	0.9	4.9	0.3	2.4	3.7	0.1	0.0*	5.7
GLASS	0.2	6.4	2.3	11.8	23.5	5.9	41.6	3.5	25.1	32.1	1.4	0.3	46.4
MOTOR VEHICLES	0.0*	3.7	0.4	33.4	56.1	3.1	84.4	0.5	25.6	74.5	0.6	0.0*	99.0
SHIPBUILDING	0.1	3.6	0.8	4.2	8.7	2.8	12.7	0.2	10.6	6.1	0.4	0.0*	10.7
AIRCRAFT	0.3	7.3	1.3	9.4	4.8	0.7	45.3	6.4	21.5	50.2	0.2	0.0*	13.5
METAL PRODUCTS	0.8	17.6	5.8	31.7	52.9	13.7	102.9	3.5	68.9	96.0	2.9	0.8	110.1
MACHINERY	0.8	29.2	5.5	52.4	51.6	16.0	108.9	3.7	56.8	99.0	2.2	0.4	119.3
ELECTRICAL MACH.	0.4	13.7	2.6	36.6	56.3	5.0	95.8	1.3	24.1	81.0	1.1	0.1	97.2
INSTRUMENTS	0.1	4.0	0.6	6.3	12.2	2.1	22.9	0.3	6.3	17.1	0.4	0.0*	21.3
OTHER MANUFACT.	0.4	6.8	5.3	5.5	13.0	5.7	22.0	1.3	14.8	15.9	2.1	1.2	27.5
UTILITIES	0.5	8.7	3.9	22.9	34.2	11.2	88.6	5.8	51.8	68.6	1.9	1.4	79.5
CONSTRUCTION	2.4	36.4	17.4	58.8	134.0	47.5	241.7	19.2	311.8	186.7	8.6	5.5	228.0
TRADE	2.1	48.2	20.9	108.2	180.0	66.1	418.0	29.9	255.5	297.6	11.7	8.2	402.0
TRANSPORTATION	1.4	33.3	13.7	27.9	38.0	25.3	121.4	6.6	75.8	85.9	3.5	4.1	124.9
COMMUNICATIONS	0.4	7.0	2.8	13.7	20.8	6.9	55.4	3.4	23.1	41.2	1.2	1.0	48.2
SERVICES	7.5	117.6	59.1	168.8	292.2	129.2	758.4	50.0	419.4	524.7	21.6	20.9	675.9

MILITARY OUTPUT LEVELS

	AAF	ASC	ASL	EEM	JAP	LAT	NAH	OCH	OIL	RUH	SAF	TAF	WEU
AIRCRAFT	0.243	10.472	1.026	13.729	6.771	0.259	57.507	0.839	-0.000*	70.902	1.143	0.000*	23.810
SHIPS	0.047	2.432	0.140	0.210	2.265	0.093	7.578	0.348	0.001	21.710	0.084	0.000*	9.053
ELECTRONIC EQUIP	0.217	6.274	0.850	5.263	2.743	0.243	30.517	0.500	0.017	31.212	0.817	0.000*	10.263
NEW CONSTRUCTION	0.134	5.261	0.366	2.146	1.010	0.296	5.058	0.189	7.757	10.075	0.210	0.106	3.833
MAINTENANCE	0.098	3.847	0.268	1.569	0.738	0.216	3.698	0.138	5.672	7.367	0.153	0.078	2.803
MISSILES	0.060	1.688	0.113	0.722	0.367	0.025	22.897	0.055	-0.000*	30.860	0.122	-0.000*	5.407
AMMUNITION, NEC	0.061	1.827	0.241	1.640	0.796	0.071	8.769	0.145	0.010	8.969	0.236	-0.000*	3.049
TANKS	0.182	2.335	0.338	10.041	0.645	0.069	7.492	0.088	0.004	14.217	0.218	0.000*	6.516
SMALL ARMS	0.004	0.114	0.015	0.101	0.061	0.006	0.581	0.010	0.010	0.590	0.015	0.000*	0.217
SM. ARMS AMMUN.	0.010	0.286	0.040	0.247	0.136	0.013	1.378	0.025	0.010	1.390	0.039	-0.000*	0.487
OTHER ORDNANCE	0.022	0.619	0.085	0.534	0.286	0.026	3.008	0.051	0.009	3.074	0.082	-0.000*	1.044
TOTAL OUTPUT	1.077	35.154	3.481	36.201	15.818	1.317	148.484	2.386	13.489	200.366	3.120	0.184	66.480

117

SCENARIO A1 IN 2000

	AAF	ASC	ASL	EEM	JAP	LAT	NAH	OCH	OIL	RUH	SAF	TAF	WEU
FISH													
FISH CATCH	0.6	7.9	9.3	0.8	8.2	14.4	3.8	0.2	0.4	6.7	2.2	1.9	9.6
NON-HUMAN USE	0.3	0.1	1.0	0.1	2.0	12.5	1.2	-0.0*	-0.1	0.6	2.0	0.6	1.7
FISH IMPORTS	0.1	0.0	0.3	0.2	0.2	0.1	1.3	0.0*	0.0*	0.1	0.0*	0.1	1.6
FISH EXPORTS	0.1	0.1	0.3	0.0*	0.5	0.1	0.4	0.0*	0.1	0.4	0.0*	0.1	2.0
EXPORTS													
LIVESTOCK	0.0*	0.0	0.1	2.2	0.0*	2.3	1.7	3.8	0.0*	0.3	0.1	0.1	9.2
HIGH PROT. CROPS	1.2	0.0	3.7	0.7	0.1	2.7	39.7	0.0*	2.7	1.5	0.3	2.2	5.4
GRAINS	1.5	0.0	9.6	8.0	4.1	20.4	125.9	17.5	0.4	10.5	2.1	0.8	35.8
ROOTS	0.7	0.0	1.4	3.1	0.1	0.8	4.1	0.3	0.4	0.4	0.0	0.6	10.4
OTHER AGRICULT.	1.4	1.0	7.6	2.5	0.0	7.2	5.1	2.0	1.5	1.7	0.6	4.0	12.4
FOOD PROCESSING	0.3	0.4	2.1	1.5	0.5	3.7	4.7	1.8	4.4	0.6	0.3	0.7	10.8
TEXT., APPAREL	0.8	4.7	23.6	14.6	23.0	3.5	6.9	1.3	0.6	1.3	0.5	0.2	97.7
WOOD AND CORK	0.0*	0.0*	2.4	1.1	1.1	1.1	4.5	0.1	0.6	4.0	0.0*	0.2	10.2
FURNITURE, FIXT.	0.0*	0.5	0.1	1.5	0.1	1.3	0.1	0.0*	0.2	1.6	0.0*	0.0*	1.9
PAPER	0.1	0.5	0.5	0.4	2.2	0.5	19.8	0.4	0.0*	0.1	1.2	0.0*	37.5
PRINTING	0.1	0.0*	0.4	0.9	0.8	0.5	2.8	0.1	0.0*	0.6	0.0*	0.0*	11.6
RUBBER	0.1	0.7	0.5	1.5	2.5	1.9	1.4	0.7	0.2	1.5	0.8	0.1	11.0
INDUSTRIAL CHEM.	0.1	1.3	0.7	1.7	8.4	0.7	9.6	0.0*	0.2	3.8	0.0*	0.0*	39.1
FERTILIZERS	0.4	0.4	1.4	1.1	1.3	1.4	6.0	0.7	1.3	0.3	0.1	0.1	11.6
OTHER CHEMICALS	0.1	0.1	0.4	2.8	2.0	0.7	7.1	0.0*	0.5	0.3	0.0*	0.1	35.7
CEMENT	0.0*	0.1	0.4	0.5	0.5	1.4	3.0	0.0*	0.6	0.1	0.6	0.1	1.6
GLASS	0.0*	0.5	0.4	1.2	3.8	0.5	3.0	0.1	0.6	0.3	0.5	0.1	22.9
MOTOR VEHICLES	0.0*	0.1	1.4	15.8	17.9	1.1	23.8	0.7	0.6	10.4	0.0*	0.0*	64.4
SHIPBUILDING	0.0*	0.0	0.1	2.1	3.9	0.0*	0.2	0.0*	0.0*	2.0	0.1	0.0*	5.3
AIRCRAFT	0.0*	0.0*	0.2	0.4	0.2	0.3	13.3	0.1	0.2	8.5	0.0*	0.0*	7.3
METAL PRODUCTS	0.0*	0.2	0.8	3.1	3.0	2.0	13.3	0.5	0.3	2.3	0.1	0.1	13.2
MACHINERY	0.1	0.2	1.6	33.9	13.8	1.0	21.1	0.3	0.2	13.8	0.2	0.0*	82.9
ELECTRICAL MACH.	0.0*	0.0*	3.3	13.8	24.9	0.3	17.0	0.2	0.1	0.4	0.3	0.0*	65.4
INSTRUMENTS	0.0*	0.4	0.5	1.5	5.9	0.3	6.5	0.1	0.7	0.8	1.4	0.1	17.7
OTHER MANUFACT.	0.3	0.0	4.2	0.3	3.5	0.3	2.4	0.4	0.7	1.0	0.2	0.5	16.0
SERVICES	0.6	0.0	1.3	0.0	0.4	5.5	9.7	0.4	0.7	0.0	3.4	0.2	31.8
TRANSPORT	0.4	0.0	3.9	0.0	6.7	3.3	16.8	2.4	1.2	0.0	1.0	1.3	65.2
AID INFLOW	4.0	0.0	21.2	0.0	0.8	10.3	9.1	1.6	3.8	0.0	5.6	2.9	36.3
CAPITAL INFLOW	0.1	0.0	6.4	0.0	14.8	13.6	33.7	0.7	8.0	0.0	0.5	0.8	48.7
MILITARY EXPORTS													
AIRCRAFT	0.0	0.3924	0.3924	3.5320	0.0	0.0	15.6976	0.0	0.0	12.5581	0.0	0.0	6.6715
SHIPS	0.0	0.0495	0.0	0.0	0.0	0.0	1.0884	0.0	0.0	1.5831	0.0	0.0	2.2262
ELECTRONIC EQUIP	0.3399	0.1699	0.1699	0.6798	0.0	0.1699	7.1376	0.0	0.0	3.9087	0.0	0.0	4.4185
MISSILES	0.0768	0.0480	0.0480	0.1921	0.0	0.0480	3.2261	0.0	0.0	3.1493	0.0	0.0	1.2290
AMMUNITION, NEC	0.0961	0.0030	0.0030	1.0022	0.0	0.0030	2.0175	0.0	0.0	1.1048	0.0	0.0	1.2489
TANKS	0.0059	0.0082	0.0082	0.0119	0.0	0.0082	5.5837	0.0	0.0	4.1520	0.0	0.0	3.5793
SMALL ARMS	0.0164	0.0171	0.0171	0.0327	0.0	0.0171	0.1246	0.0	0.0	0.0682	0.0	0.0	0.0771
SM. ARMS AMMUN.	0.0343			0.0685	0.0		0.3436	0.0	0.0	0.1882	0.0	0.0	0.2127
OTHER ORDNANCE					0.0		0.7194	0.0	0.0	0.3940	0.0	0.0	0.4454
TOTAL EXPORTS	0.5693	0.6882	0.6387	5.5192	0.0	0.2463	35.9386	0.0	0.0	27.1064	0.0	0.0	20.1087
MIL. GRANTS INF.	0.0742	0.1066	0.2189	0.0047	0.0	0.0409	0.0	0.0	0.0	0.0	0.0	0.1596	0.0249

IMPORTS

IMPORTS	AAF	ASC	ASL	EEM	JAP	LAT	NAH	OCH	OIL	RUH	SAF	TAF	WEU
LIVESTOCK	0.1	0.0*	1.2	1.4	1.3	1.3	2.5	0.0*	2.3	0.3	0.2	0.5	8.7
HIGH PROT. CROPS	0.8	0.0*	2.6	3.9	18.2	2.2	2.9	0.3	4.4	0.2	0.1	0.7	23.8
GRAINS	5.3	0.1	35.8	37.7	31.5	26.1	2.6	0.3	15.7	6.0	1.7	9.5	64.3
ROOTS	0.4	0.0*	1.9	3.2	1.9	2.3	0.6	0.3	2.1	1.7	0.0	0.5	9.4
OTHER AGRICULT.	0.2	2.2	2.6	2.6	3.4	1.8	8.1	0.1	10.1	0.9	0.3	0.4	13.1
FOOD PROCESSING	1.0	0.0*	2.4	1.3	1.1	1.9	3.7	0.1	7.6	11.7	0.2	1.0	7.1
TEXT., APPAREL	0.2	0.1	6.6	7.4	9.6	3.8	22.1	2.8	20.1	0.4	2.3	4.9	90.2
WOOD AND CORK	1.0	0.0	0.7	0.7	2.1	0.5	2.3	0.3	8.7	1.5	0.0*	0.2	9.9
FURNITURE, FIXT.	0.0*	0.0*	0.0*	0.3	0.0*	0.2	0.6	0.0*	0.3	0.0	1.0*	0.2	0.9
PAPER	0.2	0.0*	1.1	1.7	2.8	3.0	5.2	0.9	16.7	1.9	0.2	0.5	31.5
PRINTING	0.1	0.0*	0.2	1.2	1.2	0.9	1.1	0.6	4.5	0.0	0.2	0.4	6.5
RUBBER	0.3	0.0*	0.4	0.3	0.1	1.0	1.2	1.2	7.6	0.7	0.3	0.3	6.0
INDUSTRIAL CHEM.	0.8	1.2	3.2	2.6	2.5	4.4	5.8	1.2	9.4	0.4	1.2	0.7	30.5
FERTILIZERS	0.2	1.7	7.5	0.7	1.4	5.2	1.7	0.2	4.2	1.9	0.0*	0.9	4.0
OTHER CHEMICALS	0.2	0.1	2.0	0.7	2.3	2.6	1.8	0.9	21.7	0.0	0.2	1.1	16.6
CEMENT	0.0*	0.0*	0.2	0.0	0.0*	0.1	0.1	0.0*	2.6	0.7	0.2	0.1	0.5
GLASS	0.1	0.0*	0.4	1.3	0.7	1.1	1.8	0.5	14.0	0.4	0.4	0.5	14.2
MOTOR VEHICLES	0.2	0.4	1.9	5.4	0.9	6.5	37.3	3.4	27.0	1.6	1.8	0.3	50.0
SHIPBUILDING	0.1	0.5	0.5	0.7	0.2	0.6	0.4	0.9	0.6	3.8	0.0*	0.4	15.0
AIRCRAFT	0.1	0.0*	0.6	0.0	2.8	1.8	5.9	0.3	2.2	2.2	0.6	0.3	7.3
METAL PRODUCTS	0.1	0.1	0.6	0.2	0.2	1.6	2.1	0.4	9.9	0.5	0.2	0.8	56.3
MACHINERY	0.6	0.7	6.1	11.0	3.8	12.8	17.4	2.6	45.8	8.6	2.7	2.7	46.8
ELECTRICAL MACH.	0.4	0.1	4.7	3.3	3.0	7.2	15.0	1.6	40.5	2.1	1.4	0.9	14.1
INSTRUMENTS	0.1	0.2	1.0	0.7	1.4	1.8	4.2	0.7	8.0	0.9	0.6	0.3	12.7
OTHER MANUFACT.	0.2	0.2	2.1	0.3	1.5	1.0	8.1	0.5	2.4	1.0	0.2	0.3	26.6
SERVICES	0.0	0.0	0.1	0.0	2.7	4.3	13.4	1.1	5.0	0.0	0.7	0.1	44.7
TRANSPORT	0.9	0.0	4.8	0.0	13.5	6.9	10.8	3.0	14.0	0.0	1.6	2.0	29.0
AID OUTFLOW	0.4	0.4	2.4	0.0	3.8	4.1	19.0	1.7	30.1	2.3	0.8	1.7	24.7
CAPITAL OUTFLOW	0.1	0.0	3.0	0.0	6.6	15.0	10.0	5.1	59.2	0.0	2.6	1.0	

MILITARY IMPORTS

MILITARY IMPORTS	AAF	ASC	ASL	EEM	JAP	LAT	NAH	OCH	OIL	RUH	SAF	TAF	WEU
AIRCRAFT	1.3830	0.6283	1.9692	4.8328	1.3406	1.5425	1.1616	0.2500	17.4106	2.8361	0.4024	0.9905	4.4966
SHIPS	0.1900	0.0486	0.2290	0.1048	0.0906	0.6807	0.1531	0.0216	2.6109	0.6305	0.1126	0.3448	0.3603
ELECTRONIC EQUIP	0.8802	0.2509	0.8768	1.8526	0.4773	0.7660	0.6164	0.0990	7.8026	0.0	0.1813	0.4337	2.1269
MISSILES	0.3074	0.1789	0.3122	1.7621	0.3954	0.1226	0.4625	0.0587	2.9616		0.0365	0.0584	1.0250
AMMUNITION, NEC	0.2476	0.0731	0.2490	0.5774	0.1385	0.2120	0.1771	0.0286	2.1260	0.1812	0.0524	0.1182	0.6226
TANKS	0.6755	0.2429	0.5761	1.0643	0.3431	0.3760	0.1513	0.0648	7.7422	0.2872	0.1454	0.3140	2.3344
SMALL ARMS	0.0148	0.0046	0.0151	0.0354	0.0105	0.0129	0.0117	0.0020	0.1242	0.0119	0.0034	0.0069	0.0431
SM. ARMS AMMUN.	0.0424	0.0115	0.0417	0.0868	0.0236	0.0375	0.0278	0.0049	0.3826	0.0281	0.0086	0.0213	0.1014
OTHER ORDNANCE	0.0682	0.0248	0.0873	0.1879	0.0497	0.0773	0.0608	0.0101	0.7870	0.0621	0.0181	0.0437	0.2160
TOTAL IMPORTS	3.8291	1.4635	4.3565	10.5042	2.8694	3.8275	2.8225	0.5397	41.9476	4.0370	0.9606	2.3316	11.3262
MIL. GRANTS OUTF	0.0	0.1716	0.0	0.0	0.0	0.0	0.1365	0.0	0.0	0.2668	0.0	0.0	0.0549

SCENARIO A2 IN 2000

	AAF	ASC	ASL	EEM	JAP	LAT	NAH	OCH	OIL	RUH	SAF	TAF	WEU
CONSUMPTION AND POPULATION													
GDP	33.5	409.1	270.5	554.1	873.6	427.6	2241.9	130.5	1322.4	1629.4	66.0	83.6	2003.4
PERSONAL CONSUMP	20.2	273.7	186.4	306.2	551.8	298.2	1328.8	96.5	791.0	845.8	44.4	63.0	1273.5
GOVT.(CIVILIAN)	3.4	48.9	27.0	55.4	87.4	42.8	224.2	13.0	132.2	162.9	6.6	8.4	200.3
GOVT.(MILITARY)	10.1	91.9	21.6	74.2	52.4	17.8	348.7	6.5	171.9	348.7	7.3	6.5	137.8
POPULATION	285.7	1221.3	2048.9	125.7	132.9	615.8	300.0	24.5	309.8	315.0	50.0	331.8	487.1
URBAN POPULATION	168.4	508.9	704.4	90.1	98.5	465.0	258.9	22.4	148.2	245.2	32.0	109.4	382.4
EMPLOYMENT	18.3	210.7	138.1	63.8	67.6	149.1	133.9	10.2	233.1	151.8	13.0	43.3	168.4
GDP/HEAD	117.4	400.5	132.0	4408.1	6573.1	694.3	7472.9	5325.0	4268.6	5172.7	1320.0	252.1	4113.0
CONSUMPTION/HEAD	70.7	224.1	91.0	2436.2	4152.3	484.2	4429.2	3939.9	2553.3	2685.1	887.1	189.8	2614.4
CALORIES/HEAD	2038.4	2218.9	2062.9	3133.0	3230.2	2573.9	3151.2	3202.7	3334.8	3125.1	2927.3	2356.3	3117.7
PROTEINS/HEAD	58.3	68.1	53.3	104.6	121.5	66.9	97.7	99.5	117.3	102.9	90.6	68.5	100.9
INVESTMENT AND CAPITAL													
INVESTMENT	3.8	63.8	24.1	78.6	156.3	74.4	278.0	22.4	419.1	231.8	11.9	7.4	278.4
EQUIPMENT	1.8	38.5	12.7	37.9	52.9	40.0	126.6	7.5	149.0	104.1	5.5	3.8	118.8
PLANT	1.7	24.8	10.5	40.6	103.4	33.7	151.3	14.7	269.9	127.0	6.3	3.4	159.4
IRRIGATION	0.1	0.6	1.0	0.1	0.0*	0.2	0.1	0.0*	0.1	0.6	0.0*	0.0*	0.2
LAND (AREA)	0.9	0.9	1.3	0.0	0.0	2.8	0.8	0.5	0.6		1.2	1.7	0.1
INVENTORY CHANGE	0.4	9.1	3.0	2.8	4.7	5.8	9.3	0.6	21.5	7.1		1.4	9.5
CAPITAL STOCK	46.8	727.6	349.9	1078.3	2101.3	837.0	5240.0	347.9	2768.4	3248.9	111.5	111.8	4633.7
EQUIPMENT	21.1	375.1	165.6	387.4	549.2	351.4	1456.1	91.0	927.5	1131.5	45.3	53.7	1367.6
PLANT	25.7	352.5	184.3	690.9	1552.1	485.5	3783.9	256.9	1840.8	2117.4	66.2	58.1	3266.1
INVENTORY STOCK	12.8	162.1	95.8	108.5	149.8	131.4	371.9	24.0	266.9	300.7	16.3	27.5	376.4
CULTIVATED LAND	74.7	393.3	517.7	61.8	15.8	243.1	196.3	29.7	342.0	310.4	28.1	160.1	164.5
SURPLUS SAVINGS	3.4	-0.9	20.6	33.3	34.1	-8.3	123.6	0.4	-232.2	79.9	2.1	1.2	163.6
INTERNATIONAL TRANSACTIONS													
IMPORTS	9.9	9.2	57.6	69.3	110.9	79.6	179.0	26.4	311.0	45.5	18.7	24.0	606.4
EXPORTS	5.6	10.6	65.7	105.1	130.8	67.1	228.7	17.7	96.8	75.4	13.4	21.0	707.3
PAYMENTS SURPLUS	0.0	-0.3	0.0	-15.7	-83.5	12.0	32.2	-6.8	110.1	15.3	0.0	0.0	-57.7
FOR.INVEST.INFLO	-0.6	-12.5	33.6	-197.0	-1059.4	212.4	362.8	-242.2	2153.5	337.4	-24.5	-4.2	-1539.2
FOR.INC.OUTFLOW	-0.2	-1.0	1.9	-15.8	-85.1	14.4	34.0	-20.3	168.4	27.0	-2.5	-0.8	-118.3
LEVEL OF ABATEMENT ACTIVITIES													
AIR	0.0	0.0	0.0	5.80	6.53	2.61	69.83	0.80	11.48	18.52	0.64	0.0	22.88
PRIMARY WATER	0.0	0.0	0.0	3.52	3.33	0.76	7.89	0.72	3.62	10.50	0.95	0.0	13.44
SECONDARY WATER	0.0	0.0	0.0	0.20	2.13	0.04	0.45	0.00*	0.21	0.60	-0.51	0.0	0.77
TERTIARY WATER	0.0	0.0	0.0	0.04	0.47	0.01	0.10	0.00*	0.05	0.13	-0.11	0.0	0.17
SOLID WASTE	0.0	0.0	0.0	111.59	129.78	332.12	393.49	30.06	147.28	320.62	31.19	37.16	481.07
NET TOTAL EMISSIONS													
PESTICIDES	0.44	0.51	2.01	0.46	1.31	1.45	2.24	0.03	3.97	0.72	0.04	0.50	1.62
PARTICULATES	0.25	3.49	1.34	0.53	0.23	1.38	4.21	0.05	3.70	1.17	0.06	0.39	1.45
BIOLOG. OXYGEN	1.17	8.44	5.54	2.32	1.67	5.74	11.60	0.35	7.28	6.94	0.87	0.53	10.14
NITROGEN (WATER)	0.01	0.08	0.04	0.11	0.07	0.05	0.22	0.01	0.11	0.39	0.04	0.00*	0.53
PHOSPHATES	0.01	0.05	0.02	0.06	0.04	0.03	0.18	0.01	0.08	0.20	0.02	0.00*	0.27
SUSPENDED SOLIDS	0.25	2.85	1.10	1.52	0.95	2.96	6.82	0.18	6.89	3.99	0.21	0.55	4.94
DISSOLVED SOLIDS	4.09	35.35	17.22	14.71	20.34	16.39	51.13	2.37	31.86	52.20	6.35	1.05	73.02
SOLID WASTE	65.52	276.71	295.07	0.0	0.0	53.05	0.0	0.0	0.0	0.0	0.0	37.16	0.0

RESOURCE OUTPUTS

	AAF	ASC	ASL	EEM	JAP	LAT	NAH	OCH	OIL	RUH	SAF	TAF	WEU
COPPER	0.0*	0.0	0.1	0.4	0.3	7.8	4.8	0.5	0.0	2.3	0.1	5.2	0.6
BAUXITE	0.0	0.2	1.3	1.7	0.0	2.3	0.6	17.5	0.3	2.1	0.0	7.1	2.7
NICKEL	1.3	0.0	705.5	0.0	0.0	420.2	349.0	75.8	0.0	535.9	0.0	0.0*	0.0
ZINC	0.0*	0.9	0.4	1.4	3.3	0.6	2.0	0.2	1.5	2.3	0.1	0.0*	4.2
LEAD	0.0*	0.8	0.2	1.1	1.1	0.6	1.6	0.2	1.8	2.2	0.1	0.0*	3.9
IRON	1.4	128.9	101.2	20.1	2.0	205.3	175.0	40.4	24.4	481.1	17.3	72.5	163.6
PETROLEUM	63.9	295.0	75.0	24.1	1.0	768.5	2803.8	11.0	8382.1	2430.6	0.0	0.0	612.0
NATURAL GAS	0.0	0.0	13.0	0.0	0.0	260.2	1685.2	2.0	1260.2	1664.6	0.0	0.0	336.3
COAL	1.7	1098.1	250.3	831.2	142.8	39.8	2459.0	163.9	1.7	1291.6	46.9	29.4	985.7

CUMULATIVE RESOURCE OUTPUT AT END OF PERIOD

	AAF	ASC	ASL	EEM	JAP	LAT	NAH	OCH	OIL	RUH	SAF	TAF	WEU
COPPER	0.*	5.	6.	7.	6.	100.	100.	10.	0.*	48.	3.	100.	13.
BAUXITE	0.	5.	29.	32.	0.	249.	12.	186.	2.	38.	0.	65.	55.
NICKEL	17.	0.	11135.	84.	0.	3859.	12536.	1787.	0.	9921.	182.	145.	209.
ZINC	1.	10.	3.	19.	22.	21.	98.	30.	10.	31.	1.	15.	46.
LEAD	2.	10.	2.	9.	8.	13.	112.	12.	11.	20.	1.	1.	28.
IRON	129.	1865.	1525.	321.	39.	3308.	3628.	1238.	322.	7140.	228.	1289.	3113.
PETROLEUM	1299.	4085.	1126.	722.	30.	17193.	47162.	331.	133155.	36556.	0.	33.	3630.
NATURAL GAS	1.	0.	337.	1125.	0.	3584.	39009.	60.	20648.	27257.	0.	0.*	6017.
COAL	28.	19395.	4730.	16561.	2382.	639.	34828.	3302.	28.	24239.	1437.	469.	19404.

NET EXPORTS OF RESOURCES

	AAF	ASC	ASL	EEM	JAP	LAT	NAH	OCH	OIL	RUH	SAF	TAF	WEU
COPPER	0.0	-0.7	0.0	-0.7	-3.8	6.4	1.4	0.3	-1.1	-1.5	0.0	5.2	-5.6
BAUXITE	-0.0*	-0.5	0.0	0.0	-5.4	1.3	-6.5	16.6	-1.8	-3.3	-0.3	7.0	-7.1
NICKEL	0.0	-23.6	592.6	-48.9	-409.8	319.1	0.0	0.0	-46.7	0.0	-37.5	-1.5	-343.5
ZINC	0.0	0.0	0.0	0.0	0.0	-0.0*	0.0	0.0	0.0	0.0	0.0	-0.0*	0.0
LEAD	-0.0*	0.0	0.0	0.0	0.0	-0.0*	-0.0*	-0.0*	0.0	0.0	0.0	-0.0*	0.0
IRON	0.0	0.0	85.1	-83.4	-245.8	165.3	30.1	10.0	-76.7	140.2	-70.8	70.1	-94.9
PETROLEUM	0.0	0.0	-226.9	-396.5	-1475.7	171.1	0.0	-152.2	4426.3	149.2	0.0	-78.1	-2346.5
NATURAL GAS	-0.8	0.0	-39.6	-230.0	-245.0	-57.1	0.0	-5.6	168.2	168.2	0.0	-0.0*	-3.2
COAL	0.5	17.6	3.5	0.0	-245.9	-21.0	260.6	70.4	-85.7	0.4	0.4	0.2	-0.1
OTHER RESOURCES	0.3	0.2	0.4	-1.3	-2.0	0.7	2.6	-1.4	0.7	0.4	-0.7	-0.7	-2.7
PETROL. REFINING	0.0	0.0*	-2.1	-3.7	-13.8	1.6	0.0*		41.5	1.4			-22.0
PRIMARY METALS	-0.2	-1.3	-0.3	-2.7	-1.1	5.5	1.3	-0.4	-1.8	-0.8	0.1	4.1	-2.4

SCENARIO A2 IN 2000

OUTPUT LEVELS

	AAF	ASC	ASL	EEM	JAP	LAT	NAH	OCH	OIL	RUH	SAF	TAF	WEU
ANIMAL PRODUCTS	6.0	54.5	38.6	21.9	19.6	53.8	66.3	10.5	36.9	50.6	6.3	13.5	87.6
HIGH PROT. CROPS	5.6	38.3	67.3	6.0	4.0	28.6	62.2	0.2	20.7	54.1	2.1	29.4	20.0
GRAINS	59.2	527.5	510.1	104.4	50.9	254.2	424.2	36.0	126.8	337.4	26.5	78.6	271.7
ROOTS	5.1	140.9	104.1	61.4	40.1	85.3	26.8	1.3	92.7	132.2	1.2	100.5	97.0
OTHER AGRICUL.	2.9	55.5	21.7	13.2	19.9	54.6	51.7	5.7	62.5	36.0	6.3	12.0	67.1
OTHER RESOURCES	0.6	3.4	1.8	1.5	3.5	3.1	13.6	0.9	9.2	9.3	0.8	0.5	8.4
FOOD PROCESSING	0.4	10.2	3.1	34.3	50.6	20.3	122.2	10.8	70.9	90.8	2.9	1.3	124.9
PETROL. REFINING	0.3	6.4	0.3	5.3	-0.1	8.3	37.0	4.1	61.0	28.9	0.4	0.0*	11.8
PRIMARY METALS	0.6	15.7	4.5	28.2	41.3	16.8	92.0	4.1	50.0	83.9	2.2	5.1	85.7
TEXT.. APPAREL	2.2	33.3	39.0	24.3	51.9	28.3	79.5	4.8	59.7	39.6	2.8	2.0	94.1
WOOD AND CORK	0.1	4.6	3.9	6.0	9.3	5.4	24.8	1.3	10.7	20.3	0.7	0.7	21.9
FURNITURE. FIXT.	0.4	12.1	4.6	5.2	7.8	15.5	18.4	1.3	48.6	11.5	2.5	2.1	22.0
PAPER	0.2	5.9	1.8	10.1	18.3	4.4	59.7	2.4	5.5	31.6	1.3	0.1	49.8
PRINTING	0.2	3.1	1.5	11.6	21.7	5.2	60.0	3.3	22.8	38.5	1.0	0.2	55.4
RUBBER	0.2	3.2	1.4	12.4	17.7	3.0	35.3	1.9	9.4	26.8	0.6	0.1	38.6
INDUSTRIAL CHEM.	1.0	14.9	6.8	10.2	27.7	9.9	56.3	2.2	24.3	40.4	1.3	0.8	60.9
FERTILIZERS	7.0	44.1	21.7	5.1	14.0	18.6	21.8	1.5	31.4	27.5	3.6	1.0	29.0
OTHER CHEMICALS	0.3	8.1	2.7	12.2	18.1	7.1	49.6	2.8	25.3	33.7	1.2	0.1	61.4
CEMENT	0.3	0.8	0.5	1.2	2.9	6.2	5.0	0.5	5.2	3.8	0.1	0.0*	5.7
GLASS	0.3	6.4	2.3	11.8	23.5	6.2	42.5	2.4	25.9	32.5	1.4	0.3	46.7
MOTOR VEHICLES	0.0*	3.7	0.5	33.5	56.2	3.2	85.1	3.5	10.7	75.1	0.6	0.0*	99.6
SHIPBUILDING	0.4	3.6	0.8	4.2	8.8	2.9	12.8	0.5	22.6	6.1	0.4	0.0*	10.7
AIRCRAFT	0.8	7.3	1.3	9.5	4.8	0.7	45.1	0.4	17.0	50.0	0.2	0.0*	13.5
METAL PRODUCTS	0.9	17.6	6.0	31.7	52.9	14.3	103.7	6.4	70.6	96.4	2.9	0.9	110.5
MACHINERY	0.5	29.2	5.6	53.0	51.9	16.5	109.1	3.5	58.5	98.9	2.2	0.4	120.3
ELECTRICAL MACH.	0.1	13.8	2.7	37.0	57.0	5.2	95.6	3.7	25.1	80.7	1.1	0.1	98.1
INSTRUMENTS	0.4	4.0	0.6	6.3	12.3	2.2	23.0	0.4	14.9	16.1	0.4	0.0*	27.6
OTHER MANUFACT.	0.6	6.8	5.3	5.4	13.0	5.8	22.2	1.3	17.0	17.0	2.1	1.3	21.5
UTILITIES	0.8	8.7	4.0	22.8	34.2	11.7	89.1	5.8	52.4	68.9	1.9	1.5	79.7
CONSTRUCTION	2.6	36.3	17.8	58.2	133.2	50.3	250.2	19.1	313.8	190.5	8.5	6.0	229.2
TRADE	2.3	48.2	21.5	107.7	179.6	69.0	422.1	29.8	257.2	299.9	11.6	9.0	402.9
TRANSPORTATION	1.6	33.3	14.0	27.8	37.9	26.1	122.6	6.6	77.4	86.4	3.5	4.3	125.0
COMMUNICATIONS	0.4	7.0	2.9	13.6	20.7	7.2	55.7	3.4	23.6	41.3	1.2	1.1	48.3
SERVICES	8.0	117.6	60.4	167.9	291.4	133.2	765.9	49.9	423.3	528.8	21.5	22.2	677.3

MILITARY OUTPUT LEVELS

	AAF	ASC	ASL	EEM	JAP	LAT	NAH	OCH	OIL	RUH	SAF	TAF	WEU
AIRCRAFT	0.468	10.614	1.507	14.362	7.523	1.372	48.230	0.971	13.420	64.747	1.351	0.792	22.333
SHIPS	0.085	2.431	0.208	0.252	2.310	0.504	7.065	0.358	1.671	20.843	0.118	0.229	8.050
ELECTRONIC EQUIP	0.322	6.311	1.116	5.763	2.993	0.707	26.353	0.550	6.157	29.034	0.907	0.353	8.762
NEW CONSTRUCTION	0.145	5.263	0.375	2.145	1.010	0.308	5.058	0.188	7.947	10.075	0.210	0.113	3.839
MAINTENANCE	0.106	3.848	0.274	1.569	0.738	0.226	3.698	0.138	5.811	7.367	0.153	0.083	2.807
MISSILES	0.103	1.780	0.193	1.137	0.519	0.136	21.364	0.078	2.402	29.261	0.147	0.066	5.298
AMMUNITION. NEC	0.092	1.842	0.322	1.812	0.872	0.206	7.522	0.160	1.811	8.315	0.264	0.103	2.618
TANKS	0.333	2.473	0.522	10.025	0.801	0.347	3.975	0.115	6.088	11.706	0.281	0.256	5.614
SMALL ARMS	0.006	0.115	0.020	0.112	0.067	0.014	0.505	0.011	0.115	0.551	0.017	0.006	0.193
SM. ARMS AMMUN.	0.015	0.288	0.052	0.268	0.147	0.034	1.191	0.027	0.290	1.294	0.043	0.016	0.416
OTHER ORDNANCE	0.032	0.622	0.111	0.583	0.311	0.072	2.593	0.056	0.618	2.857	0.091	0.035	0.897
TOTAL OUTPUT	1.706	35.586	4.700	38.027	17.290	3.925	127.554	2.653	46.329	186.049	3.582	2.052	60.828

	AAF	ASC	ASL	EEM	JAP	LAT	NAH	OCH	OIL	RUH	SAF	TAF	WEU
FISH													
FISH CATCH	0.6	7.9	9.3	0.8	8.2	14.4	3.8	-0.2	-0.4	6.7	2.2	1.9	9.6
NON-HUMAN USE	0.3	0.1	1.0	0.1	2.0	12.5	1.2	-0.0*	-0.1	0.6	2.0	0.6	1.7
FISH IMPORTS	0.1	0.0	0.3	0.2	0.2	0.1	1.3	-0.0*	0.0*	0.1	0.0*	0.1	1.6
FISH EXPORTS	0.1	0.1	0.3	0.0*	0.5	0.1	0.4	-0.0*	0.1	0.4	0.0*	0.1	2.0
EXPORTS													
LIVESTOCK	0.0*	0.0	0.1	2.2	0.0*	2.4	1.7	3.9	0.0*	0.3	0.1	0.1	9.3
HIGH PROT. CROPS	1.2	0.0	3.7	0.7	0.1	2.7	39.7	0.0*	2.7	1.5	0.3	2.2	5.4
GRAINS	1.5	0.0	9.6	8.0	4.2	20.4	126.3	17.6	0.4	10.5	2.1	0.8	35.9
ROOTS	0.7	0.0	1.4	3.1	0.1	0.8	4.1	2.0	0.4	0.4	0.6	0.6	10.5
OTHER AGRICULT.	1.4	1.0	7.7	2.5	0.0	7.2	5.1	2.0	1.5	1.7	0.6	4.0	12.4
FOOD PROCESSING	0.3	0.4	2.1	1.5	0.5	3.7	4.7	1.8	0.2	0.6	0.3	0.7	10.9
TEXT.. APPAREL	0.8	4.7	23.8	14.7	23.2	3.5	7.0	1.3	4.4	1.3	0.6	0.2	98.5
WOOD AND CORK	0.0*	0.0*	2.4	1.1	1.1	1.1	4.5	0.0*	0.6	4.1	0.0*	0.0*	10.3
FURNITURE, FIXT.	0.0*	0.0*	0.1	1.5	0.1	0.0*	0.1	0.0*	0.6	0.0*	0.0*	0.0*	2.0
PAPER	0.1	0.6	0.5	0.8	2.2	1.3	20.0	0.5	0.2	1.6	1.2	0.0*	37.8
PRINTING	0.1	0.0*	0.4	0.4	0.8	0.5	2.8	0.1	0.0*	0.1	0.1	0.0*	11.7
RUBBER	0.1	0.0*	0.5	0.9	2.6	0.3	1.4	0.1	0.0*	0.6	0.1	0.0*	11.2
INDUSTRIAL CHEM.	0.1	0.7	0.7	1.5	8.5	1.9	9.6	0.7	0.1	1.5	0.8	0.0*	39.5
FERTILIZERS	0.4	1.3	0.3	1.7	1.3	0.7	6.0	0.0*	1.3	3.9	0.0*	0.1	11.6
OTHER CHEMICALS	0.1	0.4	1.4	1.1	2.0	1.4	7.2	0.7	0.5	0.3	0.0	0.1	36.1
CEMENT	0.1	0.1	0.4	0.3	0.5	0.5	3.1	0.0*	0.6	0.1	0.0	0.1	1.6
GLASS	0.0*	0.5	0.4	2.8	3.9	0.5	3.1	0.1	0.1	0.3	0.6	0.1	23.2
MOTOR VEHICLES	0.0*	0.1	1.4	16.0	18.1	1.1	24.0	0.7	0.6	10.5	0.5	0.0*	65.0
SHIPBUILDING	0.0*	0.0	0.1	2.1	3.9	0.0*	2.0	0.0*	0.0*	2.0	0.0*	0.0*	5.4
AIRCRAFT	0.0*	0.0	0.2	0.0*	0.2	0.1	13.4	0.1	0.2	8.6	0.1	0.0*	7.4
METAL PRODUCTS	0.0*	0.1	0.8	0.4	3.1	0.3	3.4	0.2	0.1	2.4	1.1	0.1	13.4
MACHINERY	0.1	0.2	1.7	34.5	14.0	2.0	21.5	0.5	0.3	14.0	0.2	0.0*	84.5
ELECTRICAL MACH.	0.1	0.2	3.4	14.2	25.5	1.1	17.4	0.3	0.2	0.4	0.4	0.0*	66.9
INSTRUMENTS	0.0*	0.0*	0.5	1.6	6.0	0.2	6.6	0.2	0.1	0.8	0.4	0.1	18.0
OTHER MANUFACT.	0.3	0.4	4.2	0.3	3.5	0.3	2.4	0.1	0.1	1.0	1.4	0.5	16.1
SERVICES	0.6	0.0	1.3	0.0	0.4	5.5	9.8	0.4	0.7	0.0	3.4	0.2	32.1
TRANSPORT	0.4	0.0	3.9	0.0	6.7	3.3	16.7	2.3	1.2	0.0	1.0	1.3	64.8
AID INFLOW	4.0	0.0	21.4	0.0	0.8	10.5	9.3	1.6	3.8	0.0	5.7	3.0	36.8
CAPITAL INFLOW	0.1	0.0	6.5	0.0	15.1	13.8	34.3	0.7	8.1	0.0	0.5	0.8	49.5
MILITARY EXPORTS													
AIRCRAFT	0.0	0.1921	0.1921	1.7287	0.0	0.0	7.6832	0.0	0.0	6.1466	0.0	0.0	3.2654
SHIPS	0.0	0.0227	0.0	0.0	0.0	0.0	0.4994	0.0	0.0	0.7264	0.0	0.0	1.0216
ELECTRONIC EQUIP	0.1461	0.0731	0.0731	0.2922	0.0	0.0731	3.0682	0.0	0.0	1.6802	0.0	0.0	1.8993
MISSILES	0.0451	0.0	0.0	0.0861	0.0	0.0	1.8926	0.0	0.0	1.8476	0.0	0.0	0.7210
AMMUNITION, NEC	0.0431	0.0215	0.0215	0.4568	0.0	0.0215	0.9042	0.0	0.0	0.4952	0.0	0.0	0.5598
TANKS	0.0	0.0	0.0	0.0056	0.0	0.0	2.5449	0.0	0.0	1.8924	0.0	0.0	1.6314
SMALL ARMS	0.0028	0.0014	0.0014	0.0137	0.0	0.0014	0.0584	0.0	0.0	0.0320	0.0	0.0	0.0362
SM. ARMS AMMUN.	0.0069	0.0034	0.0034	0.0294	0.0	0.0034	0.1442	0.0	0.0	0.0790	0.0	0.0	0.0893
OTHER ORDNANCE	0.0147	0.0073	0.0073	0.0	0.0	0.0073	0.3086	0.0	0.0	0.1690	0.0	0.0	0.1910
TOTAL EXPORTS	0.2586	0.3215	0.2988	2.6126	0.0	0.1068	17.1038	0.0	0.0	13.0683	0.0	0.0	9.4149
MIL. GRANTS INF.	0.0743	0.1068	0.2192	0.0047	0.0	0.0410	0.0	0.0	0.0	0.0	0.0	0.1599	0.0249

SCENARIO A2 IN 2000

IMPORTS

	AAF	ASC	ASL	EEM	JAP	LAT	NAH	OCH	OIL	RUH	SAF	TAF	WEU
LIVESTOCK	0.1	0.0*	1.2	1.4	1.3	1.3	2.5	0.0*	2.3	0.3	0.2	0.6	8.7
HIGH PROT. CROPS	0.8	0.0*	2.6	3.9	18.2	2.2	2.9	0.3	4.5	0.2	0.1	0.7	23.8
GRAINS	5.4	0.1	35.9	37.7	31.5	26.3	2.6	0.3	15.7	6.0	1.7	9.7	64.3
ROOTS	0.4	0.0*	1.9	3.2	1.9	2.3	0.6	0.1	2.1	0.0	0.0	0.5	9.4
OTHER AGRICULT.	0.2	0.0*	2.6	2.6	3.4	1.8	8.2	0.3	10.1	1.7	0.3	0.5	13.1
FOOD PROCESSING	0.2	0.0*	2.4	1.3	1.1	1.9	3.7	0.1	7.6	0.9	0.2	1.0	7.1
TEXT., APPAREL	1.0	0.1	6.7	7.4	9.6	3.9	22.3	2.8	20.2	11.9	2.2	5.1	90.7
WOOD AND CORK	0.0	0.0	0.2*	0.7	2.1	0.5	2.3	0.3	8.8	0.3	0.3	0.2	9.9
FURNITURE, FIXT.	0.0*	0.0	0.0*	0.3	0.0*	0.2	0.3	0.0*	1.0	0.4	0.0*	0.2	0.9
PAPER	0.2	0.0*	1.1	1.7	2.8	3.2	5.2	0.9	16.9	1.5	1.1	0.6	31.7
PRINTING	0.1	0.0*	0.2	1.2	1.2	1.0	1.1	0.6	4.6	0.0	0.3	0.4	6.6
RUBBER	0.1	0.0*	0.4	0.3	0.1	1.0	1.2	0.2	7.7	0.2	0.2	0.3	6.1
INDUSTRIAL CHEM.	0.4	1.2	3.3	2.6	2.6	4.5	5.9	1.2	9.5	1.9	1.2	0.8	30.7
FERTILIZERS	0.8	1.7	7.5	0.9	1.4	5.3	1.8	0.2	4.2	0.0	0.0*	0.9	4.1
OTHER CHEMICALS	0.2	0.1	2.0	0.7	2.3	2.7	1.8	0.9	21.9	0.7	0.2	1.1	16.7
CEMENT	0.0*	0.0*	0.2	0.0	0.0*	0.1	0.1	0.0*	2.6	0.2	0.0	0.1	0.5
GLASS	0.1	0.0*	0.4	1.3	0.7	1.2	1.8	0.5	14.1	0.4	0.4	0.5	14.3
MOTOR VEHICLES	0.2	0.4	1.9	5.4	0.9	6.8	37.6	3.4	27.4	1.6	1.8	0.4	50.3
SHIPBUILDING	0.1	0.1	0.5	0.7	0.2	0.6	0.4	0.9	0.6	3.8	0.0*	0.4	6.0
AIRCRAFT	0.2	0.0*	0.6	0.0	2.8	1.9	5.8	0.9	2.3	0.0	0.6	0.3	15.0
METAL PRODUCTS	0.1	0.1	0.7	0.2	0.2	1.6	2.1	0.4	10.1	0.5	0.2	0.9	7.3
MACHINERY	0.7	0.7	6.3	11.1	3.8	13.5	17.5	2.7	47.2	8.5	2.7	3.0	56.8
ELECTRICAL MACH.	0.4	0.1	4.9	3.3	3.0	7.6	15.0	1.6	42.2	2.0	1.4	1.1	47.3
INSTRUMENTS	0.1	0.2	1.0	0.7	1.4	1.8	4.2	0.7	8.3	0.9	0.6	0.4	14.2
OTHER MANUFACT.	0.3	0.2	2.1	0.3	1.5	1.0	8.2	0.5	2.5	1.0	0.7	0.3	12.8
SERVICES	0.0	0.0	0.1	0.0	2.7	4.5	13.5	1.1	5.2	0.0	0.2	0.1	26.6
TRANSPORT	0.8	0.0	4.8	0.0	13.5	7.1	10.6	3.0	13.6	0.0	1.6	2.0	44.6
AID OUTFLOW	0.5	0.4	2.5	0.0	3.8	4.3	19.1	1.7	30.8	2.3	0.8	1.8	29.0
CAPITAL OUTFLOW	0.1	0.0	3.0	0.0	6.6	16.0	10.3	5.1	59.7	0.0	2.6	1.1	24.9

MILITARY IMPORTS

	AAF	ASC	ASL	EEM	JAP	LAT	NAH	OCH	OIL	RUH	SAF	TAF	WEU
AIRCRAFT	1.3330	0.3184	1.4468	2.5276	0.7448	0.7381	0.4871	0.1447	7.2198	1.2949	0.2378	0.4262	2.2887
SHIPS	0.1719	0.0243	0.1705	0.0630	0.0462	0.3087	0.0714	0.0111	1.0242	0.2932	0.0790	0.1403	0.1597
ELECTRONIC EQUIP	0.6531	0.1262	0.5758	1.0143	0.2604	0.2886	0.2662	0.0545	2.5119	0.0	0.1007	0.1440	1.0163
MISSILES	0.2658	0.0943	0.2662	1.3870	0.2790	0.0729	0.2158	0.0418	1.2924	0.0840	0.0219	0.0353	0.5339
AMMUNITION. NEC	0.1870	0.0368	0.1660	0.3189	0.0759	0.0841	0.0760	0.0158	0.7387	0.1182	0.0293	0.0419	0.2985
TANKS	0.6175	0.1286	0.4444	0.5313	0.2131	0.1635	0.0402	0.0424	2.8675	0.0056	0.0935	0.1207	1.1447
SMALL ARMS	0.0112	0.0023	0.0101	0.0197	0.0058	0.0057	0.0051	0.0011	0.0468	0.0131	0.0019	0.0025	0.0212
SM. ARMS AMMUN.	0.0311	0.0058	0.0271	0.0471	0.0128	0.0139	0.0120	0.0026	0.1182	0.0289	0.0047	0.0067	0.0483
OTHER ORDNANCE	0.0652	0.0124	0.0572	0.1026	0.0271	0.0293	0.0262	0.0056	0.2522		0.0100	0.0144	0.1036
TOTAL IMPORTS	3.3357	0.7492	3.1641	6.0116	1.6650	1.7047	1.1999	0.3196	16.0716	1.8379	0.5788	0.9321	5.6149
MIL. GRANTS OUTF	0.0	0.1717	0.0	0.0	0.0	0.0	0.1370	0.0	0.0	0.2672	0.0	0.0	0.0550